Invitation
to
Struggle

Invitation
to
Struggle

Congress, the President and Foreign Policy

Second Edition

Cecil V. Crabb, Jr.
Louisiana State University

Pat M. Holt
Former Staff Director
Senate Foreign Relations Committee

A division of Congressional Quarterly Inc.
1414 22nd Street N.W., Washington, D.C. 20037

JK
573
.C 61
1984

Library of Congress Cataloging in Publication Data

Crabb, Cecil Van Meter, 1924-
    Invitation to struggle.

    Bibliography: p.
    Includes index.
    1. Presidents—United States. 2. United States.
Congress. 3. United States—Foreign relations—
1945- ,c61 . I. Holt, Pat M.   II. Title.
JK573 1984   327.73   84-5904
ISBN 0-87187-308-7

The Constitution ... is an invitation to struggle for the privilege of directing American foreign policy.

—Edward S. Corwin
The President: Office and Powers

Preface

On the eve of World War II, one of America's most eminent constitutional authorities made the observation quoted above. Indeed, he continued, the Constitution made the struggle between the president and Congress all but inevitable. Corwin's widely quoted statement—made while the United States was still devoted to an isolationist foreign policy—has lost none of its cogency in the intervening years. At the end of the eighteenth century, President George Washington complained adamantly about Senate opposition to the proposed Jay Treaty with England, and many legislators no doubt believed that "His Majesty" (as President Washington was sometimes called) was trying to exclude them from foreign policy decisionmaking. More than a century later, President Woodrow Wilson and the Senate clashed over the provisions of the Treaty of Versailles following World War I.

During the 1970s Presidents Nixon, Ford, and Carter repeatedly complained about congressionally imposed restrictions upon their diplomatic freedom of action. During the early 1980s the diplomacy of the Reagan administration toward the Middle East, Latin America, arms control, and other areas and issues was momentously affected by congressional viewpoints and decisions. As had other recent chief executives, Reagan deplored efforts by Congress to limit his diplomatic prerogatives and in some cases to determine the foreign policy of the United States.

The American foreign policy process continues to be characterized by an invitation to struggle between executive and legislative officials, and all indications are that this struggle will remain a prominent and influential feature of the American approach to foreign relations for the indefinite future. And if the past is a reliable guide to the future, it may also be anticipated that this struggle will take new, and often highly influential, forms in the years ahead. In some instances, its outcome could be decisive in determining the role of the United States in international affairs.

v

Invitation to Struggle, second edition, was written primarily with two groups of students and general readers in mind. For those chiefly interested in recent American diplomacy, the study provides insight into important issues of contemporary foreign policy, particularly those arising since the Vietnam War. For those concerned more with the process of American policymaking, three issues should be of special interest.

First, the role of the president in foreign policy is examined. The increasingly difficult problem of achieving unified, coherent, and effective policymaking among a widening circle of executive agencies—and of assuring the president's control over the activities of the executive branch—is a theme that appears in every chapter.

Second, our study focuses upon the place of Congress in external policymaking and upon the significant developments on Capitol Hill that affect the legislative role in the foreign policy process. How have recent changes in legislative rules and procedures affected Congress's ability to exert its influence successfully in the sphere of foreign relations? How well organized and equipped are the House and Senate to function as partners with the chief executive in foreign affairs? What can be identified as the major and continuing impediments to a constructive foreign policy role by the legislative branch? These and other fundamental questions are considered in depth.

A third perennial and vital issue of interest to the student of American policymaking is the nature and influence of public opinion in the formulation and administration of national policy. The role of interest groups in both domestic and foreign policymaking has become increasingly influential and must be taken into account more fully than ever before by students of American foreign policy.

Particularly in the study of foreign policy, examples are necessary to illuminate the roles of officials and institutions in the American governmental process. Therefore, this book contains three general chapters and five case studies of particular events or policy areas. For this second edition, all of the key studies have been brought up to date, and a special effort has been made to draw upon the diplomatic experiences of the Carter and Reagan administrations.

Case studies are most useful as learning devices when they are examined within the context of general political principles. The first two chapters (Part I) of *Invitation to Struggle*, second edition, supply that perspective. In Chapter 1 the reader will find an overall discussion of the constitutional and historical powers of the president and of the role of executive agencies in the diplomatic field. Recent trends affecting the president's position of diplomatic leadership—such as the progressively acute problem of uncoordinated activities by executive agencies and the decline of the State Department's preeminent role in foreign affairs—are identified and evaluated.

Chapter 2 focuses upon the constitutional and historical powers of Congress in foreign relations. The impulse supporting congressional militancy in external affairs can be fully understood only against this background. The forces and conditions that have induced Congress to play a more assertive and independent foreign policy role since the Vietnam War are also identified.

Five case studies (Part II) provide the basic data for our inquiry into executive-legislative relations in the post-Vietnam War period. Each deals with a noteworthy development or issue in recent American diplomacy and illustrates one or more important aspects of presidential and congressional authority in external affairs. For example, how have developments during and after the Vietnam War affected the ability of the United States to enter into long-term agreements with other countries? That crucial question is examined in our discussion in Chapter 3 of the Panama Canal treaties. What are the prerogatives and influence of the president and Congress in relying upon military aid as a crucial instrument of American diplomacy? What is the impact of domestic and foreign lobbying activity upon the American foreign policy process? These questions are evaluated in Chapter 4, which deals with the Arab-Israeli conflict and the sale of AWACS aircraft to Saudi Arabia. Or, what was the impact of the Vietnam experience upon traditional executive and legislative control over the armed forces—as illustrated by issues such as the stationing of American forces in the NATO area or the Reagan administration's reliance upon armed force to achieve diplomatic goals in Lebanon, the Caribbean, and Central America? Chapter 5 provides a detailed analysis of this question. Chapter 6 presents an up-to-date discussion of the complex problem of conducting intelligence operations within the framework of traditional American democratic values and ethical principles. Another continuing challenge—efforts by the United States to preserve and strengthen human rights beyond its own borders—is the subject of Chapter 7. This chapter forcefully illustrates both Congress's keen interest in the problem and the positive and negative consequences for American diplomacy of legislative efforts to produce solutions for it.

In the concluding chapter, the post-Vietnam War era of struggle between the White House and Congress for control over the foreign policy machinery is placed in a more theoretical perspective. On the basis of experience thus far, what are some of the major consequences of this struggle for the ability of the United States to meet its responsibilities as a superpower in the international system? How durable are the causes of Congress's diplomatic activism? Conversely, what are the prospects for a revival of forceful executive leadership in diplomatic affairs in the years ahead? What kind of new balance may emerge between executive and legislative prerogatives in foreign relations? These and other fundamental questions are addressed in Chapter 8 (Part III).

The second edition of *Invitation to Struggle* is a complete revision of the earlier work. Chapters 1, 2, 4, and 8 were written by Cecil V. Crabb, Jr., and Chapters 3, 5, 6, and 7 were written by Pat M. Holt. The authors are indebted to many individuals who have contributed directly and indirectly to this study, and their assistance is most gratefully acknowledged. The comments, suggestions, and criticisms received by the authors from students, faculty members, and other readers of the first edition have been invaluable, and these have been reflected in this new edition. In particular, the authors wish to express their genuine appreciation to two members of CQ Press. Joanne Daniels provided encouragement and advice at every stage; her assistance was indispensable. Nola Healy Lynch supplied capable and essential editorial guidance in the production stage. Harriet F. Crabb read several chapters of the manuscript and made numerous suggestions for its improvement. Members of the LSU Library staff—most especially the head of the Documents Department, Jimmie H. Hoover, and Robert A. Scull—as always were skillful and ingenious in assisting with problems of research and bibliography. Josephine Scurria and Lell Annison typed successive portions of the manuscript, and their contribution is recognized with sincere thanks.

While acknowledging the essential contributions of others, the authors accept sole responsibility for any errors of fact or judgment that may be found in these pages.

Cecil V. Crabb, Jr.
Pat M. Holt

Contents

Invitation
to
Struggle

PART I

The Process of
Foreign Policymaking

A unique feature of the American governmental system is that its powers are exercised by separate executive, legislative, and judicial branches. From the perspective of constitutional theory, these are often described as equal and coordinate branches of the government. In practice, however, their powers and influences are not equal, especially in the foreign policy sphere. The purpose of Part I (Chapters 1 and 2) of our study is to provide an overall context within which congressional efforts to play a more influential role in foreign affairs can be understood.

Throughout American history the judiciary has largely been content to play a passive role in the foreign policy process. When the Supreme Court has concerned itself with foreign policy questions (which it does rarely), it has nearly always taken one of two positions. Either the Court has declared foreign policy issues to be political questions that are not susceptible of resolution by the judicial system[1] or it has forcefully upheld the exercise of executive power in foreign relations. Over the years a series of Supreme Court decisions has thus reinforced the claims of successive presidents that in foreign affairs the chief executive is the dominant organ of government. Insofar as fears about the emergence of an "imperial presidency"[2] have resulted from vigorous and unrestrained presidential leadership in foreign affairs, that phenomenon has received strong impetus from the constitutional interpretations of the Supreme Court.[3]

Both the diplomatic experience of the United States and certain provisions of the U.S. Constitution dictate that we begin our inquiry by focusing upon the role of the executive branch in the conduct of foreign affairs. Although recent years have witnessed a new congressional militancy in foreign relations, the fact remains that the president is still in charge of American foreign policy. For the most part, Congress's powers are limited to telling the White House what it cannot do beyond America's borders. The power to decide what the United States will undertake in its relations with other countries and to carry out specific programs, such as arms control or foreign aid or mediation in the Arab-Israeli dispute, resides with the chief executive. As we shall see in Chapter 1, every incumbent president has at his disposal a variety of instruments that give him an unequaled position for influencing the diplomatic destiny of the United States. More than at any other time in American history perhaps, the nation's influence abroad depends upon presidential decisions—including, of course, decisions to work collaboratively with Congress in the foreign policy process.

Congress is also assigned, in the American constitutional system, a number of responsibilities that impinge directly and indirectly upon foreign affairs. In whatever degree legislators have felt in recent years that their views have been ignored by the White House, the U.S. Congress has more power to influence foreign affairs than its counterpart in any other country. Along with its constitutional prerogatives, Congress has also acquired over the course of 200 years extraconstitutional powers and informal techniques for affecting the course of foreign relations. One tendency since World War II—the erosion of any sharp distinction between domestic and foreign affairs—has significantly enhanced the influence of Congress. Chapter 2 provides an overall discussion of the formal and informal prerogatives of Congress in the foreign policy field. In addition, the forces that have produced a new congressional militancy in external affairs are identified and analyzed. Chapters 3 through 7 examine detailed case studies of congressional behavior with regard to selected foreign policy issues.

Notes

1. Referring to the interpretation of a treaty, in 1855 a federal judge ruled that this was a "political question" and was not among the powers which were "confided by the people to the judiciary ... but to the executive and the legislative departments of our government." See *Taylor v. Morton*, 23 F. Cas. 784 (C.C.D. Mass. 1855) (No. 13,799), and an earlier case, *Foster v. Neilson*, 2 Pet. 253 (1829).
2. Two landmark decisions affirming the president's prerogatives in foreign relations were the *Prize Cases*, 67 U.S. (2 Black) 635 (1863), and *United States v. Curtiss-Wright Export Corp.*, 299 U.S. 304 (1936).

   The concept of the imperial presidency, which has come into wide currency since the Vietnam War and Watergate crises, is merely a variation on a very old theme in American history: pervasive apprehension about the possible or actual abuse of executive power in the American system of government. This fear strongly colored the attitudes of the Founding Fathers and those who drafted the early state constitutions, in which the powers of the office of governor were severely limited. Based upon the Vietnam and Watergate experiences, the idea of the imperial presidency suggests a chief executive who routinely infringes upon the constitutional authority of the legislative and judicial branches; who believes himself to be above the law, particularly in the conduct of foreign relations; who manipulates and deceives Congress and the American people in order to accomplish his domestic and foreign policy objectives; and who surrounds the operations of the executive branch with a wall of secrecy designed to conceal the activities of himself and his subordinates. As a leading student of the presidential office has asserted, this conception of the presidential office implies a "radical transformation" in the American system of government, which is founded upon the doctrine of separation of powers. See Arthur M. Schlesinger, Jr., *The Imperial Presidency* (Boston: Houghton Mifflin Co., 1973), p. viii. This study provides a detailed analysis of the emergence of the imperial presidency over 200 years of American history. Yet is must also be emphasized that—especially since the New Deal of President Franklin D. Roosevelt—the American people have also fundamentally accepted the idea of a strong or forceful president who takes the lead in meeting internal and external challenges energetically and successfully. Perhaps even more today than in the 1930s, citizens look to the White House, rather than to Congress or the courts, for the dynamic leadership required to solve urgent national problems. Insofar as it is constitutionally and ethically objectionable, therefore, the imperial presidency has two primary connotations: it suggests behavior by the chief executive and his subordinates that is patently *illegal* or of questionable constitutional validity; and it suggests a chief executive who is *unsuccessful* in achieving their major policy goals. It is, for example, interesting to speculate about whether President Johnson would have been viewed as epitomizing the imperial presidency if the United States had *won* the Vietnam War, since many of Johnson's acts during that conflict were comparable to those of President Roosevelt during World War II and to those of President Abraham Lincoln during the Civil War.

3. During the late 1970s and early 1980s the federal courts disposed of several important cases involving the control of foreign relations in the United States. In *Edwards v. Carter,* 580 F.2d 1055 (D.C. Cir. 1978), cert. den. 436 U.S. 907 (1978), the judiciary upheld the right of the president and Senate to dispose through the treaty process of property belonging to the United States, as provided for in the new Panama Canal treaties negotiated by the Carter administration. In another case, which grew out of the Iranian hostage crisis in 1979-1980, the Supreme Court upheld the right of the president to dispose of several billion dollars in Iranian assets, which had been frozen after the hostages were seized. In *Dames and Moore v. Regan,* 453 U.S. 654 (1981), the Court stated that in the foreign policy field Congress had accorded the chief executive more freedom to settle claims with foreign countries than was the case in domestic affairs. In *Agee v. Vance,* 483 F. Supp. 729 (1980), affirmed in *Agee v. Muskie,* 629 F.2d 80 (1980), reversed in *Agee v. Haig,* 453 U.S. 280 (1981), the Supreme Court upheld the right of the executive branch to deny a passport to a former CIA employee whose writings were viewed as endangering the lives of current CIA agents and as detrimental to national security. For more detailed summaries and commentary on these cases, see Warren Christopher, "Ceasefire between the Branches: A Compact in Foreign Affairs," *Foreign Affairs* 60 (Summer 1982): 990-995.

The Executive Branch and Foreign Affairs: Locus of Decisionmaking

1

During the late 1960s, at the height of the Vietnam War, one of America's most experienced political commentators said, "I cannot think of a single major foreign-policy move any President wanted to make since the Second World War that he was unable to carry through because of the opposition of the press or of Congress." [1]

The diplomatic experiences of the Nixon, Ford, Carter, and Reagan administrations provided considerable evidence that the once largely unrivaled position of the president in the foreign policy field was undergoing serious challenge. Indeed, by the early 1980s many informed students of the American foreign policy process believed that the era of the imperial presidency had been superceded by almost uncontrolled congressional activism and dynamism in the foreign policy field. By the Reagan administration this change posed a serious and continuing question about the internal cohesion and constancy of America's relations with other countries.

Yet any understanding of the foreign policy process in the United States must begin with recognition of a transcendent reality. The motive force, the locus of decisionmaking, in foreign relations is the executive branch, headed by the president. The American chief executive is not only a national leader; more than any other head of state in modern history, he has also become a *world* leader. Policy decisions made in the White House can determine whether there is global peace or war; whether the United States has a favorable image in black Africa; whether regional stability exists in the Middle East; and whether the nations of the Third World have access to the foreign assistance required for their development.

As later chapters will show, Congress plays an increasingly assertive role in the foreign policy realm, and some legislators believe it should become an equal partner with the executive in external decisionmaking.

The quest is likely to be long and arduous. After two centuries of American diplomatic experience, the president has emerged as the "ultimate decider" or the "decision maker of last resort." [2] Despite challenges to this leadership position on Capitol Hill, the chief executive possesses constitutional powers and other techniques for exerting his influence over foreign affairs that are unequaled.

Basic Definitions

Before we examine the constitutional and historical bases of presidential leadership in foreign affairs, we must present a few definitions. By *foreign policy*, we mean those external American goals for which the nation is prepared to commit its resources. This definition enables us to distinguish between the nation's foreign policy and a variety of hopes, visions, and dreams (such as universal democracy and perpetual peace) often espoused by individuals and groups within the American society. Unless the objective—such as deterring the Soviet Union, protecting the security of the North Atlantic Treaty Organization (NATO), assisting in the economic development of India, or preserving the stability of the Middle East—involves some application of the economic, military, intellectual, or other resources of the nation, it cannot be seriously viewed as forming part of its foreign policy.

A closely related term is *foreign policy process*. This denotes a complex and often time-consuming series of steps by which officials in the executive and legislative branches formulate the nation's diplomatic goals and decide upon the most appropriate means for reaching them. To cite an important case from the nation's postwar diplomatic record, in a speech before a joint session of Congress early in 1947, President Harry S Truman promulgated the Truman Doctrine. The goal, formulated over the preceding months by executive and legislative policymakers, was the containment of Soviet expansionism into vulnerable areas, such as the Mediterranean and the Middle East. Initially, the means employed was the Greek-Turkish Aid Program of 1947, which provided economic and military assistance to these countries. In time, other means (such as the Marshall Plan for European recovery and the NATO defense system) were also used in implementing the containment strategy. The meaning and usefulness of the containment principle, as of all long-term diplomatic strategies, were periodically reexamined after 1947.

Another concept, which has come to the fore since World War II, is *national security policy*. It includes those activities in the foreign policy field, as well as in domestic affairs, designed to protect the independence and integrity of the United States. At its most basic level, national security policy is concerned with the defense of the nation against actual and potential enemies. Construed more broadly, it involves preventing threats to national security, collecting and digesting information about the behavior of potential enemies, creating and maintaining necessary military alliance systems, supplying friendly countries with arms aid, and taking other steps aimed at enhancing the security position of the United States under widely varying conditions abroad.

While the Department of Defense plays perhaps the most central role in national security policy, in the postwar period the Department of State—along with a growing number of other federal agencies—is also intimately involved. At least implicitly, American officials have become aware of Clausewitz's dictum, "War is the continuation of politics by other means." * One of the implications of this principle is the idea— highlighted by the concept of cold war between the United States and the Soviet Union—that political and military relations among nations are opposite sides of the same coin. For example, political (or diplomatic) decisions sometimes lead to armed conflicts among nations; in turn, the results of war—and one nation's perception of another's military strength—crucially affect what diplomats are able to achieve at the conference table.

Awareness of these realities led to the creation in 1947 of the National Security Council (NSC), the highest presidential advisory agency for national security policy. The NSC is headed by the president. Its other members are the vice president, the secretary of state, and the secretary of defense. Other civilian and military officials may be, and frequently are, invited to participate in the deliberations of the NSC and the formulation of policy recommendations. As we shall see more fully later in this chapter, by the 1970s the NSC—particularly under the forceful direction of Henry Kissinger during the Nixon and Ford administrations—had evolved into a kind of rival State Department. During some periods the influence of the president's national security adviser eclipsed that of the secretary of state. This reality, for example, was a major factor leading to the early resignation of Secretary of State Alexander Haig during the Reagan administration.

The National Security Council was created to blend diplomatic, military, and other relevant policy considerations into a unified national security policy for the United States. It is important to note that the NSC is solely an *advisory* organ to the president. Chief executives may and do utilize the NSC very differently. (For example, President Ronald Reagan encouraged full and frank discussion among his principal advisers, while he listened to the viewpoints being expounded on particular issues.) Whatever his individual operating style, the president ultimately decides upon the policy of the United States government, after considering the views of his White House aides, cabinet officers, and other advisers. The membership of the NSC was deliberately constituted by Congress to

---

*Carl Maria von Clausewitz was a Prussian general in the Napoleonic period. After the defeat of Napoleon, he wrote the celebrated treatise *On War*, containing his reflections upon the relationship between armed conflict and the political process. For an illuminating condensation of his thought, see Roger A. Leonard, ed., *Clausewitz On War* (New York: Capricorn Books, 1968).

preserve and underscore another fundamental principle of the American constitutional system: civilian control over the military establishment. All members of the NSC are civilians, and, although military officers may be invited to NSC sessions, the military point of view is normally conveyed to the president through the secretary of defense.

Another term that requires brief explanation is *diplomacy.* The concept is perhaps inherently and inescapably ambiguous and often causes widespread public confusion. At the risk of oversimplification, we may say that it has two primary connotations. Diplomacy can refer to the entire range of a nation's external relationships—from routine diplomatic communications between governments, to heads-of-state summit conferences, to the recognition of one government by another, to cultural and scientific exchange programs. Alternatively, diplomacy can and often does have a more limited connotation: the resolution of disputes and conflicts among nations *by peaceful methods.* In this sense, diplomacy is a substitute for war and violence; or it is an effort to prevent the resolution of international controversies by reliance upon armed force.[3]

Traditionally, Americans have been suspicious of diplomacy and of officials engaged in it. In the public mind diplomacy is associated with Old World political values and machinations held to be at variance with the democratic ethos of the New World. One argument invoked to justify the old isolationist approach to foreign affairs was that Americans lacked skill and training in diplomacy; hence in any encounter with experienced diplomats of the Old World, the United States would almost certainly lose! (This point of view was reinforced by the results of several diplomatic conferences during World War II, such as the meetings at Yalta and Potsdam in 1945, which many Americans interpreted as diplomatic victories for the Soviet Union.) No doubt this historical frame of mind contributes to the poor image that the State Department usually has with the American public and with Congress.[4]

The President's Constitutional Authority

The preeminent position of the chief executive in the American foreign policy process stems from two broad sources of power: those conferred by the Constitution (including those implied from key constitutional provisions); and those that are an outgrowth of tradition, precedent, and in some instances, historical necessity. Let us examine each of these categories in detail.

Almost since the beginning of the Republic, constitutional authorities have debated whether the Founding Fathers intended to make the conduct of foreign policy largely an executive responsibility, whether they meant for Congress to be the dominant organ, or whether they desired some kind of approximate balance of power between the two branches in the foreign policy field. Arguments are still heard on this issue, and the question will no doubt be debated in the years ahead.[5] Yet two facts seem beyond contention. The original intention of the founders of the Republic proved to be a less crucial consideration in determining the outcome than numerous other influences, such as the impact of forceful personalities upon the presidential office, the crises confronting the nation at home and abroad, and the decisions of the Supreme Court bearing upon the problem. Irrespective of what the founders desired, as a result of 200 years of American history the tendency has been toward executive pre-eminence in nearly every aspect of the foreign policy process.

In the Constitution, the position of the president in foreign affairs rests upon several important provisions. Article II vests the executive power of the government in the president. The presidential oath of office (Article II, Section 1) requires the chief executive to "preserve, protect and defend the Constitution of the United States." This oath confers upon the president a constitutional responsibility for the preservation of national security.

Commander in Chief

The Constitution (Article II, Section 2) also designates the president as "Commander in Chief of the Army and Navy of the United States," which today includes, of course, the U.S. Air Force. In common with other constitutional provisions, this one has engendered controversy throughout American history concerning its precise meaning. Did the Founding Fathers intend that the president should merely function symbolically or ceremonially as commander in chief (much like the British monarch in modern history), leaving the determination of military strategy and the deployment of the armed forces to others, possibly Congress? (The case study in Chapter 5 focuses upon congressional prerogatives and claims regarding the use of the armed forces for foreign policy ends.) Or did they (like President Franklin D. Roosevelt during World War II and President Lyndon B. Johnson during the Vietnam War) contemplate that chief executives would actually determine military strategy and tactics, sometimes with momentous implications for the future military and diplomatic fortunes of the United States? [6]

American diplomatic experience has left no doubt about the answer. Successive presidents—following the precedent of Abraham Lincoln perhaps—have interpreted their authority in this realm broadly and dynamically, and their position as commander in chief of the armed forces is clearly one of their most influential powers in the foreign policy field. The list of specific steps or actions taken by the White House under this constitutional provision is almost endless. Here we can do no more than cite a few outstanding examples.

As commander in chief, presidents since George Washington have time and again ordered the armed forces to carry out missions in distant parts of the world. Throughout its history the United States has been involved in approximately 125 "undeclared" wars and other instances of violent conflict abroad conducted under presidential authority. For example, in 1846 President James K. Polk unquestionably (and almost certainly intentionally) provoked Mexico into war when he ordered the army to occupy disputed territory along the Rio Grande. In the face of strong congressional opposition, President Theodore Roosevelt sent the American navy on a cruise around the world. (The president's real objective was to impress Japan with the nation's naval power.) On his own authority, President Franklin D. Roosevelt ordered the navy to shoot on sight German submarines that entered the hemispheric security zone. And President Harry S Truman personally made the decision to use two atomic bombs against Japan in 1945. In 1950 Truman also ordered American armed forces in the Pacific to resist North Korea's aggressive thrust into South Korea, thereby involving the United States in one of the most prolonged and expensive undeclared wars in its history.

Early in his administration President Dwight D. Eisenhower threatened Communist China and North Korea with the possible use of American nuclear weapons, if they resumed hostilities in the Korean conflict. Beginning with Eisenhower, a succession of chief executives expanded America's military commitments to the government of South Vietnam, thereby in time virtually guaranteeing massive American involvement in the conflict between North and South Vietnam. In what was perhaps the most dangerous cold war encounter after World War II, President John F. Kennedy in 1962 presented the Kremlin with an ultimatum demanding the removal of Soviet offensive missiles from Cuba. In this context, Kennedy placed the air force on worldwide alert, and he interposed the American navy between Cuba and the Soviet ships that were apparently bringing new missiles to the island. Little doubt exists that Kennedy was prepared to *use* whatever degree of force was required to eliminate this Soviet threat.[7]

During the closing months of his administration, President Jimmy Carter relied upon his authority as commander in chief of the armed forces in employing military power for foreign policy goals. After the Soviet invasion of Afghanistan late in 1979, for example, Carter issued the Carter Doctrine, pledging the United States to defend the security of the oil-rich Persian Gulf area.[8] This pledge was reiterated and strengthened by President Ronald Reagan, so that in effect a new Carter-Reagan doctrine placed the Persian Gulf area under the military protection of the United States. A few weeks later, President Carter ordered the Pentagon to undertake a mission designed to rescue American hostages in Iran. Congress and the American people were informed of this mission after it had been launched and had failed to achieve its objective.

Relying upon his constitutional powers as commander in chief, the president can take other steps affecting America's relations with other countries. It is the president's prerogative, for example, to terminate military hostilities with belligerents and to enter into truce negotiations with them. At a later stage the White House also normally initiates diplomatic negotiations designed to produce a peace treaty. A presidential decision *not* to employ the armed forces (as in President Carter's reluctance to have the United States become embroiled in several conflicts in black Africa) can have a significant impact upon America's influence regionally and globally.

With the concurrence of the Senate, the president can appoint and promote high-ranking military officials; and on his own authority—as in Truman's widely publicized dismissal of General Douglas MacArthur during the Korean War—he can also relieve military commanders. While ultimate authority to determine the size and nature of the American military establishment resides with Congress, the president can and does play a crucial role in that decision. His annual budget message to Congress—along with countless other communications to the legislative branch and the testimony provided by executive officials before congressional committees—usually has a decisive impact upon legislative attitudes and behavior.

To the minds of many Americans by the mid-1960s, White House reliance upon the armed forces to achieve diplomatic objectives, often with little or no consultation with Congress, symbolized the imperial presidency. Limiting this presidential prerogative has been a major goal of those legislators who advocate a more influential role in foreign affairs. A noteworthy step in this direction was the passage of the War Powers Resolution in 1973. (We shall examine this resolution more fully in Chapter 5.) A decade later Congress (especially the Democratic-controlled House) sought, with no very notable success, to place strict limits upon President Reagan's freedom to use the armed forces against rebel groups active in Central America.

Treaty-Making Power

Article II, Section 2 of the Constitution states that the president has the power "by and with the Advice and Consent of the Senate, to make treaties, provided two thirds of the Senators present concur." The ability of the chief executive to enter into formal agreements with other countries in the form of treaties—and less formal accords and understandings by means of executive agreements—is another influential tool of presidential leadership.

Controversy has always surrounded the meaning and requirements of this constitutional provision. For example, precisely what did the founders intend by giving the president the power to "make" treaties? Did they mean that the process of *negotiating* treaties was an exclusively executive function? Or does "the advice and consent of the Senate" extend to the negotiation of treaties, as well as to senatorial consideration of them? Again, whatever the constitutional arguments pro and con, American diplomatic experience since the Washington administration has answered the question. Successive presidents have taken the view that the executive branch makes (or negotiates) treaties and then submits them to the Senate for its acceptance or rejection. In the post-World War II period, senators (and occasionally representatives) are invited by the

White House to participate in the negotiation of treaties. This practice reached its zenith under the Truman administration, when Republicans and Democrats alike sought to achieve a bipartisan foreign policy. President Carter employed this device in the negotiations on the new Panama Canal treaties. Nevertheless, the negotiation of treaties—and more broadly, all official negotiations with foreign governments—remains an executive responsibility. Chapter 3 is devoted to a case study of the negotiation and ratification of the Panama Canal treaties by the Carter administration. Consequently, here we shall attempt to gain only a brief, overall understanding of the president's use of this power to manage foreign relations.

The process of treaty ratification is sometimes misunderstood and needs to be reviewed before we proceed. First, the president's agents (the secretary of state or other high-ranking diplomatic officials) conduct negotiations with other governments, leading to an agreement that is formally embodied in a treaty. Only the White House can initiate such negotiations, and it has the power to terminate them when the diplomatic interests of the United States dictate this course.

Second, after the treaty has been negotiated and signed by the parties to it, the document is submitted to the Senate for its consideration. At this stage, the Senate has several choices. After deliberation and debate, the Senate can *approve* the treaty by the required two-thirds majority. (Throughout American diplomatic history the vast majority of treaties has received senatorial approval.) Conversely, the Senate can *reject* the treaty, by failing to give it a two-thirds majority. Alternatively, the Senate can take two other possible actions. It can attach amendments to it, as the Senate did to the Treaty of Versailles after World War I. It can also append reservations and understandings to it, clarifying or interpreting the treaty's provisions.*

Then, after the Senate has completed its deliberations, the treaty must be *proclaimed* by (meaning that it must be acceptable to) the president. This is the third and last stage of the ratification process. It is thus incorrect to say that the Senate ratifies treaties. The Senate plays a key role in the ratification process, but in the end the treaty becomes the law of the land only when it is signed and proclaimed by the president. Throughout the entire process of treaty making, the chief executive retains the initiative. The chief executive decides to undertake negotia-

---

*An *amendment* to a treaty changes its language and provisions, thereby probably requiring its renegotiation with the other parties to it. *Reservations* and *understandings* specify the American interpretation of its provisions. For example, in several international agreements, the United States has specified that the accord does not supersede the Monroe Doctrine, under which Washington has historically protected the defense of the Western Hemisphere. In Senate deliberations on the SALT II arms limitation agreement with the Soviet Union in 1979, several senators insisted upon an understanding that the Soviet Union would adhere to pledges (given orally) not to expand certain components of its military strength. As we shall see in Chapter 3, in consenting to the new Panama Canal treaties, the Senate appended certain conditions to its approval of them. In reality, with the passage of time the differences among these various categories of changes have become increasingly indistinct.

tions leading to an agreement, agrees to the provisions of the treaty, submits it to the Senate for its concurrence, and signs the treaty, thereby completing the ratification process. At any stage the president may in effect withdraw the treaty from active Senate deliberation by requesting that body not to proceed with consideration of it. President Carter made such a request of the Senate regarding the SALT II arms limitation agreement in 1980. Alternatively, the president may ask the Senate to return the treaty to the White House, a request with which the Senate nearly always complies. In the SALT II case, President Carter and his advisers realized that prospects for favorable Senate action on SALT II were rapidly declining; officials in the executive and legislative branches alike viewed Soviet behavior in Afghanistan and other settings as increasingly at variance with the concept of détente. As in the case of President Woodrow Wilson after World War I, a chief executive may also refuse to sign a treaty acceptable to the Senate, if he believes it contains provisions detrimental to the national interest.

Can a president also terminate an existing treaty? This question was posed by the action of the Carter administration in December 1978 when it established full diplomatic relations with the People's Republic of China and concurrently notified the Republic of China (Taiwan) that the security pact with that government would be allowed to lapse. Predictably, Carter's action precipitated considerable public and congressional opposition. Since the security treaty with Taiwan had been approved by the Senate, some legislators were convinced it could be terminated only with the concurrence of the Senate or of Congress as a whole. Initially this viewpoint was supported by a U.S. district court, which held that legislative concurrence was needed to terminate the security pact with Taiwan. But on December 13, 1979, by a vote of 7-2, the Supreme Court disagreed with this interpretation, holding that the president had the constitutional authority to terminate the defense pact with Taiwan on January 1, 1980. Four members of the Court held that the controversy was a political question that was not subject to judicial determination and that had to be resolved between the president and Congress.[9]

Executive Agreements

In lieu of formal treaty accords with other countries, incumbent presidents in the modern period have increasingly made use of executive agreements.* Since World War II such agreements have accounted for

---

*Under the Constitution a distinction can be made between a treaty and an agreement (or compact) with other countries, although the differences are not always legally and practically clear. An *executive agreement* is an understanding between heads of state or made under their authority; it may be either written or oral; and many agreements ultimately require congressional approval (as in providing funds for their implementation) before they can become effective. Many executive agreements (for example, those related to the sale of surplus agricultural commodities abroad) are negotiated pursuant to authority delegated by Congress. These are sometimes described as *statutory agreements.*

almost 95 percent of the understandings reached between the United States and foreign countries. While executive agreements are not mentioned in the Constitution, they have a venerable tradition going back to the earliest days of the Republic. During the past half-century such agreements have been made frequently, and in the following cases they have had a momentous effect upon the course of American foreign relations: President Roosevelt's destroyer base deal with Great Britain in 1940; several agreements arrived at with Soviet Russia and other countries by the Roosevelt administration during World War II (notably at the Yalta, Potsdam, and other wartime conferences); a series of understandings during the 1950s and 1960s between Washington and Saigon, promising American support for the government of South Vietnam; another series of agreements (beginning with the Truman administration) according to which the United States assumed a de facto commitment for the security of Israel; a widely publicized oral pledge by the Nixon administration to Hanoi, calling for massive American assistance to Southeast Asia in the post-Vietnam War period; understandings arrived at by President Carter and Chinese Deputy Premier Deng Xiaoping, providing for cultural and scientific exchanges between the two countries.

Another such agreement in recent diplomatic experience is the detailed understanding finally worked out between the Carter administration and the revolutionary government of Iran, providing for the release of American hostages. As noted earlier, among its numerous provisions this accord called for the return of several billion dollars in Iranian assets in the United States (an understanding the federal courts subsequently declared to be a constitutional exercise of presidential authority, despite the existence of private claims against these assets). In its efforts to create and maintain a stable peace in the Middle East, the Reagan administration also engaged in a number of formal and informal understandings with the governments of Israel and Lebanon concerning America's future involvement in implementing the terms of agreements reached and in conducting negotiations with other countries.

According to one estimate (and estimates vary widely), between 1946 and 1976 the United States signed 7,201 agreements with foreign countries (excluding over 60 secret agreements that the State Department reported to Congress between 1972 and 1977).[10] Perhaps no presidential prerogative in foreign affairs has generated such concern on Capitol Hill in recent years as the White House tendency to engage in agreements (or "national commitments") with other countries without legislative knowledge, scrutiny, or concurrence. As Sen. J. William Fulbright, chairman of the Senate Foreign Relations Committee, lamented:

> The Senate is asked to convene solemnly to approve by a two-thirds vote a treaty to preserve cultural artifacts in a friendly neighboring country. At the same time, the chief executive is moving military men and materiel around the globe like so many pawns in a chess game.[11]

In 1972 Congress passed the Case Act, which requires that *all* executive agreements be reported to Congress for its information. If Congress objects to an agreement, it may then take such action as seems indicated. Some agreements require separate congressional approval.[12]

Appointment Power

Article II, Section 2 of the Constitution also provides that the president shall "nominate, and by and with the Advice and Consent of the Senate, shall appoint Ambassadors, other public Ministers, and Consuls." Subject to senatorial confirmation, the president chooses the nation's highest-ranking diplomatic officials. Traditionally, an ambassador serves as the alter ego of the head of state (or the president); foreign diplomats are accredited to the president. It is, of course, expected that an incumbent president will appoint officials who share his conception of the nation's role in foreign affairs.

As they have with the treaty power, resourceful chief executives throughout American diplomatic history have discovered methods for circumventing limitations upon their appointment power. One such device is for the president to make an interim appointment; the individual so appointed may hold office and perform important duties while the Senate is not in session. After the Senate reconvenes, the president has three choices: he may submit the name of the interim appointee for Senate confirmation; the interim appointee's period of service will come to an end, and the president will nominate another individual (more acceptable to the Senate) for the position; or the president may decide not to fill the position at all.

The chief executive may also, and frequently does, use cabinet officers to undertake diplomatic assignments. In 1979 President Carter relied upon Secretary of the Treasury Michael Blumenthal to arrive at certain understandings with the People's Republic of China before the United States opened an embassy in that country.[13] In the same period Secretary of Defense Harold Brown assured the government of Saudi Arabia and other Persian Gulf states that, in the light of the revolutionary upheaval in Iran, their security would be protected by the United States.[14]

The appointment of personal representatives is another device presidents have used to bypass senatorial confirmation of diplomatic officials. During World War II President Roosevelt relied heavily upon his personal aide, Harry Hopkins, to conduct negotiations both with Great Britain and with the Soviet Union. The distinguished public servant W. Averell Harriman served as the personal representative of several presidents during and after World War II. During the Iranian hostage crisis in 1979-1980, President Carter relied upon White House aide Hamilton Jordan, who conducted secret negotiations with intermediaries who had contacts with the revolutionary regime in Tehran. The agreement that finally secured the release of the hostages was in large part the work of a high-ranking State Department official, Warren Christopher (who relied heavily upon the government of Algeria to gain the consent of Iran). Under the Reagan administration, presidential envoy Philip C. Habib spent several months in his efforts to gain a peace agreement for strife-torn Lebanon. Following the precedent of some of his predecessors, Habib insisted upon the right to report on his activities directly to the president.[15] In recent years chief executives have also used the vice president—and sometimes even the first lady—as diplomatic envoys.

Recognition of Foreign Governments

Article II, Section 3 of the Constitution confers upon the president another influential prerogative in the foreign policy field. It provides that the president "shall receive Ambassadors and other public Ministers" from foreign countries. The power of the president to recognize other governments is derived from this constitutional provision.

In normal diplomatic relations between two nations, each formally recognizes the legitimacy of the other's government. The act is symbolized by the exchange of ambassadors (or ministers) between them and the establishment of an embassy within the other country. Foreign diplomats, it must be reiterated, are accredited to the president of the United States. Therefore, the decision as to whether to receive diplomatic representatives from other countries—and, hence, whether to accord formal recognition to their governments—belongs solely to the president. In 1933 President Roosevelt decided (after the Communist regime had existed for more than 15 years) to accord formal diplomatic recognition to the Soviet Union. In 1972 President Nixon made the same decision regarding the People's Republic of China, thereby ending the 23-year period of nonrecognition of its Marxist regime. Both decisions aroused widespread public and congressional controversy.

For many years two theories have existed about the criteria that ought to be employed when the president recognizes another government. What might be called the classic international law conception holds that such recognition depends primarily upon whether the government in question is stable, has established its authority throughout the country, and is fulfilling its international obligations. If so, it should be recognized, irrespective of the nature of its government or ideological system. Applying this traditional standard, most governments throughout the world (not including the United States) recognized the People's Republic of China soon after the end of the Chinese civil war in 1949.

The other theory, the Wilsonian or distinctively American approach, holds that recognition is dependent upon the nature and character of the government in question. Specifically, it relies upon such criteria as whether the government enjoys popular support, whether it respects the rights of its citizens, and whether its conduct accords with international law. In 1913 President Wilson invoked such principles when he refused to recognize the new government of Mexico, headed by Victoriano Huerta (a regime Wilson called "a government of butchers"). Basically the same reasons dictated America's refusal for many years to recognize the Communist regime in Russia and Mao Tse-tung's regime in China.

Nonrecognition of Foreign Governments

If the president can recognize foreign governments, the president can also withdraw or withhold such recognition. In extreme cases the president can dramatically sever diplomatic relations with another country, as Woodrow Wilson did with imperial Germany before America entered World War I. Another presidential option is to withhold American recognition for an indefinite period, until a country achieves internal political stability or perhaps modifies its behavior. The president can provide a warning to another country by calling the American ambassador home "for consultation," as President Carter did on January 2, 1980, when he recalled the U.S. ambassador to Moscow, Thomas J. Watson, in response to the Soviet Union's invasion of Afghanistan. And the president can require foreign diplomats in the United States to leave the country if their behavior becomes unacceptable to the White House.

Informal Techniques of Leadership

In addition to these constitutional powers, the chief executive possesses certain informal and extraconstitutional techniques for the management of foreign affairs. Five of these are especially important.

First, the president has unequaled access to the information sources required for effective decisionmaking. This information is available to the White House from many origins, including departments and agencies within the executive branch, American embassies and other overseas posts, the intelligence community, and foreign governments. The scope and nature of information available to the White House about events and tendencies abroad remain one of the president's most influential resources for affecting the course of American diplomacy. As we shall see more fully in Chapter 2, however, it is also a resource that the legislative branch has increasingly acquired in order not to remain dependent upon information supplied largely by executive officials. Moreover, despite the tendency of some recent chief executives and their subordinates to abuse the principle, the confidentiality of this information is often protected by the principle of executive privilege.

Second, one of the most noteworthy trends in the evolution of the presidency has been the chief executive's influential role as a legislative leader. Article II, Section 3 of the Constitution requires the president periodically to provide Congress with information on "the State of the Union." His annual State of the Union address, however, is merely one among literally hundreds of messages and recommendations sent from the White House to Capitol Hill. Even more important may be the president's Budget Message, normally a document of several hundred pages, containing detailed budget recommendations in all spheres of domestic and foreign governmental activity. As a rule, Congress uses the budgetary recommendations submitted by the White House as a guide to its own deliberations. Although it may depart from presidential recommendations in certain respects, congressional action is massively influenced at all stages by the wishes of the president. After Congress has approved the budget, the president still possesses discretion in the administration of the funds available to the executive branch. For example, after encountering considerable opposition to his request for expanded economic and military aid to El Salvador in 1983, President Reagan and his advisers stated that by "reprogramming" budgetary allocations and shifting funds from one program to another they would manage to acquire the funds the White House needed to achieve the administration's goals in Central America.[16] Such budgetary discretion, it must be emphasized, might serve as an expedient in the short run, but it is dependent on congressional tolerance. In the long run the administration's diplomacy in Central America was contingent upon congressional willingness to provide the financial resources needed to fund it. Some recent presidents have also impounded (or refused to spend) funds appropriated by Congress for diplomatic purposes not approved by the White House. The frequent use of this power by President Nixon led Congress to pass the Congressional Budget and Impoundment Control Act of 1974, which limited the chief executive's discretion in this realm.

Modern presidents interpret their legislative role actively and dynamically. To the electorate, the ability of a chief executive to manage Congress—and, in the process, to maintain at least minimally collaborative relations with it—has become a leading criterion by which the success of an incumbent president is measured. Among his other deficiencies as a national leader, for example, by even his own admission Jimmy Carter neglected his legislative responsibilities; both his domestic and his foreign policy programs suffered from that neglect. By contrast, during his presidential campaign Ronald Reagan repeatedly emphasized the importance of cooperative executive-legislative relations in the foreign policy sphere; and his administration accorded that aspect of the president's duties high priority. In some measure, Reagan's reputation as the Great Communicator stemmed from his ability to persuade an often reluctant Congress to support his policies.[17]

A third instrument—and, in many respects, perhaps the most effective technique—available to the president for managing foreign relations is the ability to influence public opinion. Even before the era of modern communications media, chief executives understood the potency of this instrument. President Theodore Roosevelt once observed:

> People used to say to me that I was an astonishingly good politician and divined what the people are going to think.... I did not "divine" how the people were going to think; I simply made up my mind what they ought to think, and then did my best to get them to think it.[18]

As a molder of public opinion at home and abroad, the president of the United States is in a uniquely favorable position vis-à-vis Congress and other rivals (most likely only a president could be nicknamed the Great Communicator). Routinely, the activities of the chief executive are given extensive coverage by the news media. The president's actions and statements dominate the news outlets (attempts by political opponents or rival political parties to respond to major presidential addresses, for example, often attract only a fraction of the audience available to the president). When the White House believes it desirable, the president can obtain national TV and radio time to acquaint the people with a crisis or significant development in foreign affairs and inform them of the steps he proposes to take in response to it. According to an informed student of American public opinion, once a president has made a foreign affairs decision that becomes known to the public, he automatically receives the support of at least 50 percent of the American people, irrespective of the nature of the decision. Despite recent fears of the imperial presidency, the American people continue to believe—and most people implicitly approve of the fact—that the president is in charge of foreign policy. Conversely, as the political demise of the Carter administration demonstrated, the American people are not enamored of a chief executive who appears to be indecisive and to have lost control of events abroad.[19]

At one time or another every incumbent president since the 1930s has been accused of managing the news to achieve his foreign policy objectives.[20] President Franklin D. Roosevelt was a master of radio communications; he used his "fireside chats" to the American people with unchallenged effectiveness to rally public opinion behind his policies. During the Cuban missile crisis of 1962, President Kennedy made a dramatic national TV presentation informing the nation about the construction of Soviet missile sites in Cuba and presenting his strategy for responding to that danger. During the early 1980s President Reagan relied upon his highly developed talents in communication to rally public support behind his program for substantial military expansion, including such projects as the MX missile system and a larger navy. President Reagan also largely dispelled the idea (widely circulated by his critics) that he opposed arms control agreements with the Soviet Union and that he had fundamentally altered America's longstanding ties of friendship with Israel.

In the fourth place, one of the oldest techniques of presidential leadership and an important instrument in the foreign policy field is the president's role as a political leader. Normally, an incumbent president is automatically the acknowledged leader of his political party. Congressional, state, and local candidates usually value the endorsement of the president in their political campaigns. While the number of patronage appointments available to the White House has declined over the past 50 years, the president still can make a limited number of appointments to federal office. Moreover, White House influence and entrée can be useful to legislators and citizens in dealing with the federal bureaucracy. Most crucial perhaps, leaders and members of the president's own party are constantly aware that the results of the next presidential election will depend substantially upon the president's record in dealing with major internal and external issues. An outstanding and popular record can be a decisive force in achieving victory at the polls; a weak and unpopular record poses an obstacle to political victory that will be extremely difficult for the president's party to overcome.

Finally, one of the most decisive instruments of presidential leadership in foreign affairs was illustrated by President Theodore Roosevelt's diplomacy in building the Panama Canal. The first Roosevelt was committed to a policy of "making the dirt fly" in Panama—that is, he was determined to build the canal, despite the opposition of legislators and other critics. Toward that end, he authorized the construction of the canal even before the Senate had approved the Hay-Bunau-Varilla Treaty (1904). Several years later President Roosevelt observed:

> If I had followed traditional, conservative methods I would have submitted a dignified State paper ... to Congress and the debates on it would have been going on yet; but I took the Canal Zone and let Congress debate; and while the debate goes on the Canal does also.[21]

Nearly half a century later, during the Greek crisis of 1947, President Truman committed the United States to a policy of "containment" toward expansive communism. Speaking to his colleagues in the Senate, Sen. Arthur H. Vandenberg asserted:

> The overriding fact is that the President has made a long-delayed statement regarding Communism on-the-march which must be supported [by Congress] if there is any hope of ever impressing Moscow with the necessity of paying any sort of peaceful attention to us.[22]

Senator Vandenberg was alluding to the president's power to commit the nation to a position or course of action in foreign affairs. Once the chief executive had done so publicly, it was extremely difficult for Congress or public opinion to repudiate the president's policy. President Reagan understood and used this technique of presidential leadership when, in the spring and summer of 1983, he called upon Congress and the American people to support the administration's policies toward Central America. Many members of Congress, for example, were clearly in a dilemma concerning the Reagan White House's Latin American diplomacy. On the one hand, public and legislative sentiment were apprehensive about possible involvement in "another Vietnam" in the Western Hemisphere; and the administration's policies in dealing with political upheaval in Central America elicited vigorous criticism at home and abroad. On the other hand, after President Reagan had publicly identified a Communist threat to the security of Central America—and after he had pointedly informed Democrats in Congress that they would bear a significant part of the responsibility for Communist gains in the region—even critics of the administration's policies were reluctant to deny the White House the resources it needed to counter Communist machinations in the region. As the party that had been accused of having lost China to communism in the early post-World War II period, Democrats were sensitive to the accusation that they were again indifferent to the consequences of Communist gains abroad.

Towering above constitutional grants of authority to the president and various informal modes of executive leadership is this reality: the president of the United States is the head of state and acknowledged leader of the most powerful nation perhaps in the history of the world. The American people look to the White House for effective leadership in responding to internal and external crises and in protecting American interests abroad. When White House leadership in foreign affairs was characterized as indecisive and irresolute—as occurred in the Carter administration—the president's popularity was likely to drop sharply. When the chief executive provided clear and forceful direction to the nation's diplomacy, experience indicated that his actions would usually receive overwhelming public approval.[23]

The Foreign Policy Bureaucracy

The Role of the State Department

In the American system of government, the executive agency most directly concerned with foreign affairs is the Department of State, headed by the secretary of state, the highest-ranking cabinet officer. The first incumbent in the office under the Reagan administration, Secretary of State Alexander Haig, envisioned himself as the vicar of American foreign policy—a claim which, as Haig discovered painfully, was not without contestants in the executive hierarchy.

The State Department is America's foreign office; under the authority of the president it supervises relations with over 150 independent nations around the world, with organizations such as the United Nations, and with regional bodies such as the Organization of American States (OAS). Yet from the perspective of its annual operating budget (about $2 billion for 1984) and its size (under 24,000 employees), the State Department ranks as one of the smallest executive departments. (The Department of the Interior, for example, has some three times as many employees.)

Traditionally, the State Department's primary concern has been political relations with foreign countries. Its five regional bureaus serve as the nucleus for communicating policy decisions to American embassies abroad and for receiving communications from them. Since World War II there has also been a significant expansion in the department's functional bureaus, such as economic and business relations, international organization affairs, public affairs, and (one of the newest concerns) oceans and international environmental and scientific affairs.

Still another postwar development has been the department's recognition of a growing congressional role in foreign relations. An assistant secretary of state for congressional relations is assigned specific responsibility for maintaining constructive relations with Congress, and this function has become an increasingly important and time-consuming dimension of State Department activities. The Office of Congressional Relations collects and analyzes information on legislative attitudes toward foreign policy issues; it provides services requested by members of Congress, such as foreign travel arrangements; and, when required, it plays a prominent role in White House lobbying on Capitol Hill for the president's foreign policy program. State Department services to Congress sometimes take interesting forms. Former secretary of state Dean Acheson recounted that legislators often felt compelled for domestic political reasons to oppose certain external programs (like foreign aid). In one case, the State Department helped a legislator resolve that dilemma "by the promise of a powerful speech against the foreign aid bill when it came up for final vote in the House. We [the State Department] duly wrote it and all parties profited!" [24]

Under the Carter administration the promotion of international human rights became a conspicuous American diplomatic goal. During the Ford administration Congress had provided for a Coordinator of Human Rights to be appointed by the president and subject to Senate confirmation. Now it created the new Bureau of Human Rights and Humanitarian Affairs, headed by an assistant secretary of state. One of its missions was certifying that specified countries were making satisfactory progress in safeguarding human rights as a condition for the continuation of American aid. In some cases (and under the Reagan administration El Salvador was a prominent example) such certifications became highly controversial issues on Capitol Hill and in the news media. During the Reagan administration, which considerably deemphasized the human rights dimension of American diplomacy, the influence of this bureau within the State Department declined significantly.

Also under the direct supervision of the State Department is the Agency for International Development (AID). Established in 1961, this agency was given responsibility for administering American economic and technical assistance programs to other countries. An indication of America's declining involvement in foreign aid is provided by the reduction in AID's employees: from more than 15,000 in 1965 to just over 5,000 in 1983.

Routinely, newly elected presidents announce that they regard the secretary of state as their chief foreign policy adviser and expect this official to provide overall direction to governmental activities in foreign affairs. Yet in practice, the decline of the State Department's preeminence in the foreign policy field since World War II has been evident to all qualified observers. The department's image with the White House, with other executive agencies, with Congress, and often with other governments, has been chronically poor. To the minds of some presidents, the State Department has epitomized bureaucratic inertia, devotion to traditionalism, and lack of imaginative leadership.[25] Ever since the administration of President Franklin D. Roosevelt, presidents have been prone to bypass the State Department; using one device or another, they have ignored it and made crucial decisions without consulting it.[26]

On June 25, 1982—less than 18 months after he took office—Secretary of State Alexander Haig resigned his position, after a series of internal conflicts and controversies that impaired the foreign policy cohesion of the Reagan administration. Haig's tribulations as the head of the State Department were merely a particularly graphic example of a phenomenon that appears to have become endemic in the American foreign policy process since World War II. With rare exceptions, every secretary of state since the New Deal has left office under a cloud of congressional and public criticism. Some (like John Foster Dulles and Henry Kissinger) were repeatedly accused of making decisions unilaterally and of ignoring their State Department subordinates. Others (like Dean Rusk and William Rogers) faced the complaint that they were weak and not forceful enough in presenting State Department viewpoints to the president and to their colleagues in the cabinet. Since the early 1950s more than 60 major studies have been undertaken of the State Department's organization and operations; many of these have been followed by reorganizations of the department in the hope of restoring its once largely unchallenged role in the foreign policy process. Haig's dramatic resignation indicated, however, that the quest has remained elusive.[27]

The erosion of the State Department's position can be explained by many factors and developments, some within the department and others extrinsic to it. Critics of the department have complained that it has been slow to adapt its procedures and ideas to a rapidly changing world, leaving the White House no choice but to look elsewhere for creative and imaginative policy recommendations. Another trend—the growing involvement of a host of other executive agencies in foreign relations—has diluted the State Department's authority and responsibility. Among all the departments and agencies of the national government, the State Department suffers from certain unique disabilities. As has often been said, the department has no domestic constituency to support its activities. Unlike the programs of the Departments of Labor and Agriculture, those of the State Department are not usually supported by powerful domestic lobbies and citizens' groups. As often as not, the State Department has what might be called negative constituents: those individuals and groups who vocally oppose American foreign policy toward Greece, or Cuba, or Central America. (One of these—the pro-Israeli lobby in the United States—is discussed in Chapter 4.)

On Capitol Hill, the State Department is likely to be regarded as a troublemaker for legislators; it advocates costly foreign economic and military aid programs, which are frequently unpopular with the American people and are political liabilities for members of Congress. Alternatively, the State Department is often envisioned as the "Department of Bad

News." Each year since World War II the State Department has had to report to Congress and the American people on some actual or potential crisis in the Middle East, some ominous Soviet threat to American security, or discouraging information about the economic deterioration of countries throughout the Third World. Somehow, many Americans believe, if "the department operated more effectively," the United States would confront more favorable conditions abroad.[28] The frustration felt by members of Congress and their constituents on foreign policy issues is directed at the State Department—and this fact in turn adversely affects the department's morale and performance.

The Intelligence Community

Two other categories of executive agencies involved in the foreign policy process require brief examination. One of these is called the *intelligence community* and consists of the agencies and governmental bureaus that exercise intelligence functions within the American government. As specified by Executive Order 12333, issued by President Ronald Reagan on December 4, 1981, the following agencies comprised the intelligence community:

Central Intelligence Agency
National Security Agency
Defense Intelligence Agency
"The offices within the Department of Defense for the collection of specialized national foreign intelligence through reconnaissance programs"
Bureau of Intelligence and Research of the Department of State
Army Intelligence
Navy Intelligence
Air Force Intelligence
Marine Corps Intelligence
Federal Bureau of Investigation
Department of the Treasury
Department of Energy
Staff elements of the Director of Central Intelligence

Intelligence is a minor part of the overall activities of some of these agencies in terms of money spent or people employed. Nonetheless, it is important in terms of national security and the total flow of information to the United States government. The function that makes the FBI part of the intelligence community is *counterintelligence*, that is, identifying covert foreign agents in the United States and frustrating foreign efforts at espionage and subversion. The role of the State Department's Bureau of Intelligence and Research is primarily analysis. The main contribution of the Treasury Department is to provide economic, financial, and monetary information. The function of the Department of Energy is to collect intelligence on energy matters generally.[29]

As every reader of the daily headlines is aware, in recent years public controversy has surrounded the activities of the CIA and other members of the intelligence community. Charges have been made that intelligence agencies have sought to assassinate political leaders abroad, that they have sponsored attempts to overthrow foreign governments, or that they have infringed upon the rights of American citizens; such accusations have become commonplace in the news media. By contrast, the CIA and other agencies involved in the intelligence process have also encountered criticisms (heard particularly after the Iranian revolution in 1979) that they were failing to provide policymakers with objective and up-to-date estimates enabling them to predict major developments abroad and to respond effectively to them.

Two general observations about intelligence activities within the American democratic system are worth making here. First, today, as in the past, the intelligence function continues to be recognized by officials in both the executive and the legislative branches and by a majority of citizens, as an essential contribution to the preservation of national security and to the achievement of American diplomatic objectives. In 1947 the Central Intelligence Agency was established in large part because of vivid recollections by the American people and their leaders of the military disaster at Pearl Harbor (rightly or wrongly viewed as an intelligence failure by the American government). No less than in the past, today most informed Americans are aware of the adverse consequences of a crippled or inadequate intelligence service. Three events in 1979—the belated discovery of a large Soviet military force in Cuba, the collapse of the Iranian monarchy, and the Soviet invasion of Afghanistan—called attention to the fact that intelligence operations by the United States government still left policymakers unprepared for crucial global developments. Then, in 1983, a successful terrorist attack against U.S. Marines in Lebanon again called graphic attention to the dangers implicit in inadequate intelligence operations.

Second, the dilemma created by the establishment of the CIA in the postwar era, and by the subsequent expansion of the intelligence community, largely remains unresolved today. It arises out of the conflict between two antithetical ideas. One of these is the realization that failure to conduct effective intelligence operations can lead to serious diplomatic reversals, as in the Japanese attack against Pearl Harbor or America's lack of preparedness for the collapse of the Iranian monarchy. The other is that open diplomacy, freedom of the press, public disclosure of information, and other concepts in the American tradition must also govern the foreign policy process. The tension in a democracy between these two ideas is real, continuing, and perhaps inescapable. If, as Chapter 6 suggests, congressional efforts to monitor and regulate intelligence operations have been less than completely satisfactory, the reason may be that the dilemma admits no simple or easy solution.

Propaganda and Informational Programs

The other executive agency that plays a key role in foreign affairs is the United States Information Agency (USIA), formerly called the International Communication Agency (ICA). Although it is a separate administrative agency, USIA takes its policy guidance from the State Department. The agency's mission is to conduct propaganda and informational activities abroad in behalf of the American government. Perhaps its best-known activity is the Voice of America, the nation's worldwide radio network. In addition, the USIA engages in a variety of other activities and programs, such as the production and distribution of films; the preparation of press releases; the sponsorship of cultural, scientific, and other kinds of exhibits and lectures; and the operation of American cultural centers and libraries overseas.

Ever since its creation in the early postwar period, controversy has surrounded the mission of America's propaganda establishment. The USIA has had a stormy existence; during some periods, frequent turnover has occurred among officials engaged in propaganda activities. In large part, this phenomenon can be explained by the conflict between two conceptions of the agency's proper mission. One view holds that it was intended to be primarily a propaganda instrument of the American government. As such, its dominant function ought to be portraying the internal and external policies of the United States in the most favorable light possible to foreign societies. The other conception is that USIA's principal mission is to engage in a Campaign of Truth, as America's propaganda and informational program was designated by the Truman administration. This view would require the agency to be factual and objective in its depiction of the American society, with no attempt to gloss over its shortcomings and failures. (The underlying assumption of this approach is that objectivity is "the best propaganda" for a democratic nation.) The conflict between these two schools of thought has impeded the effectiveness of American propaganda and informational campaigns in the past and will likely continue to do so in the future.[30]

The Military Establishment and Foreign Affairs

Among national policymakers and informed citizens, World War II produced a realization that was not always present in earlier eras of American diplomacy: the military establishment plays a vital role in the foreign policy process. As late as that global conflict, both civilian and military officials tended to separate political and military questions sharply, as illustrated by President Franklin D. Roosevelt's view that the resolution of political questions arising during the war ought to await the outcome of military hostilities.[31] By the end of the war—after a new political-military conflict known as the cold war had erupted among the Allies—American officials recognized the indissoluble link between these two aspects of national policy.

Following a prolonged study, the Department of Defense was created in 1947 and other reforms of the American military establishment were undertaken. While the traditional American pattern of separate military services was preserved, they were brought under the jurisdiction of a single department, headed by a civilian secretary of defense. The Joint Chiefs of Staff (consisting of the commanders of each of the military branches and a chairman) was created to formulate unified military strategy.

By the mid-1980s the Department of Defense had more than 914,000 civilian employees; the armed forces consisted of 2.1 million personnel; and President Ronald Reagan's defense budget for fiscal year 1984 was $280.5 billion. According to projections, military spending was scheduled to reach $465 billion annually by the end of the 1980s because of substantial expansion of army divisions, navy carrier groups, transport aircraft, and several other components of the armed forces. Even more than in the past, defense spending on this scale inevitably created public and congressional apprehension about undue military influence in making foreign policy decisions and about the power available to the president in his role as commander in chief of the armed forces. But in fact a significant buildup in the American defense establishment had been initiated by President Carter, who was responding to a pervasive perception of American military weakness during the late 1970s. Ronald Reagan had been elected to the presidency in no small measure to remedy this deficiency and to restore America's diplomatic credibility.

If the decline in American military strength had become a matter of national concern during the Carter presidency, under Ronald Reagan a different problem existed. This was whether the president and his advisers were too likely to conceive of external challenges confronting the United States in military terms and to prefer military solutions for complex diplomatic issues. To express the problem differently, in the light of the traumatic Vietnam War experience, how were officials of the Reagan administration prepared to *use* the nation's growing armed strength for diplomatic ends?

Even during the Korean and Vietnam wars, however, American experience since World War II has remained reassuring on one basic constitutional principle. A civilian—the president—is the commander in chief of the armed forces; the members of the National Security Council are civilian officials; and the foreign policy process remains controlled by the elected civilian officials of the United States government. No convincing evidence exists that the fundamental constitutional precept of civilian control over the armed forces is in jeopardy.

Other Executive Agencies and Foreign Affairs

A striking and highly significant development since World War II has been the increased interest and involvement in foreign relations by departments and agencies within the executive branch. The list of agency involvement is almost endless, and it becomes longer every year. The Departments of Agriculture, Commerce, Defense, Treasury, Transportation, Interior, and Labor all have responsibility for problems with a foreign policy dimension. For example, the Agriculture Department has played a pivotal role for many years in the Food for Peace program, which ships American food products to needy countries; it is also keenly interested in promoting agricultural exports to countries such as Japan and other customers; and it has sent hundreds of experts abroad to assist less developed societies in raising their agricultural output. As has always been the case, the Commerce Department seeks to expand American business, investment, and trade opportunities abroad. The Treasury Department is actively concerned with fiscal and monetary issues, such as the soundness of the American dollar overseas. The Transportation Department seeks to formulate a national transportation policy, integrating both domestic and foreign resources. Even the Interior Department has responsibilities that impinge upon foreign affairs (such as water reclamation projects involving the United States and Mexico).[32]

A growing number of smaller and lesser-known federal agencies have acquired responsibilities giving them a role in foreign relations. The National Aeronautics and Space Administration (NASA) sponsors space programs that directly affect the global balance of military power and America's ability to monitor the military progress of other countries. The Arms Control and Disarmament Agency is responsible for preparing reports and recommendations to the president on arms limitation proposals (such as SALT II). The Department of Energy is concerned about the proliferation of nuclear weapons abroad and about the safe disposal of nuclear waste products by all nations.

This proliferation of executive agencies involved in foreign affairs has had a parallel tendency within Congress, as we shall see more fully in Chapter 2. Today there is hardly a legislative committee or subcommittee whose activities do not relate in some way to foreign affairs. The resulting *linkage* (the connections often established between an expanding number of executive agencies and the corresponding committees of Congress) poses an increasingly difficult problem for the creation and maintenance of unified governmental efforts abroad.

Coordinating Executive Efforts Abroad

Threats to the unity of American foreign policy can arise from several sources, two of which are directly pertinent to our study: divisions and conflicts within the executive branch and disunity between the White House and Congress on foreign policy questions. At this stage, our interest is confined to the former problem. As Senator Vandenberg once bluntly informed the Truman administration: members of the Republican party wanted to cooperate with the White House in behalf of a "bipartisan foreign policy," but they could only do so with one secretary of state at a time! The problem to which Vandenberg alluded has become more acute since the early postwar period. The Carter administration's response to the collapse of the Iranian monarchy in 1979, for example, became, in the words of one report,

> the subject of fierce internal debate [within the executive branch], with many officials asserting that interagency disputes and bureaucratic compromises have hampered the efforts of Mr. Carter and his top advisers to fashion and carry out an overall strategy.[33]

The Carter administration's diplomatic efforts were impeded by "the creation of large, unwieldy committees," which—although designed to unify executive efforts in foreign affairs—had compounded the problem of "defining coherent policy goals and seeing them through." Another commentator found that by the end of the 1970s the foreign policy process in the United States was characterized by "fragmentation" and involved "a number of conflicting actors and centrifugal forces." [34]

Despite significant changes in the tone and direction of American foreign policy by the Reagan administration, such complaints did not come to an end under Republican management of foreign affairs. Early in the Reagan presidency, complaints were heard that Secretary of Defense Caspar Weinberger was functioning as the de facto secretary of state; that the foreign policy of the Reagan administration lacked "predictability and coherence"; that statements by Secretary of State Alexander Haig did not really represent the viewpoints of the president; and that "open political combat" had erupted among the president's advisers on relations with the Soviet Union and other major foreign policy questions. Even after Secretary of State Haig's resignation, and his replacement by George Shultz, disunity continued to prevail among officials in the executive branch on several key foreign policy issues. In its efforts to stabilize the Middle East, for example, the Reagan administration's viewpoints were confused by the somewhat contradictory statements of Secretary Shultz and Defense Secretary Caspar Weinberger concerning the role of American armed forces in enforcing any peace agreement reached. Similar confusion about the nature of the challenge and America's proper response to it marked the administration's approach to revolutionary turmoil in Latin America. A public opinion poll taken early in 1983 showed that only 35 percent of those responding believed that President Reagan was "in control" of the executive branch.[35]

As successive executive departments and agencies have been drawn into the foreign policy process, incumbent presidents have relied upon various administrative devices to unify their activities. As we have already seen, the National Security Council was established early in the postwar period to provide such coordination on issues directly affecting national security. Interdepartmental committees function at all levels of the national government with regard to specific foreign policy issues involving more than one agency. Some chief executives, such as President Johnson, have relied upon special groups of advisers (called, in Johnson's case, the Tuesday group) to arrive at unified policy decisions. President

Reagan sought advice from a small group of aides (known as the executive cabinet) on foreign policy issues. Under President Kennedy the concept of the *country team* was introduced: in an effort to unify American governmental activities in foreign countries, all officials within a given country perform their duties under the supervision of the American ambassador (who, of course, receives his instructions from the State Department, and ultimately from the president). Several presidents have also designated the secretary of state as their principal foreign policy adviser and directed that he assume responsibility for assuring unified executive efforts in foreign affairs.

Undoubtedly most of these techniques have been useful. Their value, however, has often depended heavily upon the personality and operating style of the incumbent president. On some occasions, the executive branch has displayed extraordinary unity in dealing with a particular foreign policy issue (as in the Kennedy administration's handling of the Cuban missile crisis in 1962).[36] Yet the problem of fragmented and divided efforts within the executive branch continues to serve as an impediment to effective diplomacy by the United States.

To a significant degree, the problem reflects several facts about America's role in international relations. The United States is a superpower, with major and minor commitments in every region of a world gripped by rapid, and often revolutionary, change. As often as not, these commitments have been assumed as the result of insistent urging by other countries, which both elicit American assistance in solving their problems and are resistant to American dictation or guidance in doing so. By the 1980s the dilemma—the necessity to employ American power abroad without overtly intervening in the political affairs of other nations, and often in the process triggering an anti-American reaction—continued to confront American policymakers.

To cite merely one example, the Reagan administration sought (not altogether successfully) to resolve the dilemma in responding to the challenge of revolutionary upheaval and violence in Central America. As in the Central American context, the actions and policies of the United States government increasingly affect the lives of citizens and groups at home and abroad. Efforts to "stabilize" governments in Latin America, for example, require some combination of effective reform programs within the country concerned, American economic and military assistance, external investment and economic modernization, programs designed to check rapid population growth, and other measures; and these steps nearly always involve several governmental agencies in Washington. To express the idea differently, in Latin America and other settings the successful achievement of *political* goals abroad (the traditional province of the State Department), has become a function of cultural, educational, informational, economic, military, demographic, commercial, scientific, and many other dimensions of governmental activity in the contemporary world.

The tendency toward fragmented and uncoordinated executive activities in the foreign policy field reflects a fundamental change in the nature of the international system within the past two decades or so. What is sometimes called the *international agenda* (those global and regional issues of dominant concern in Washington and other capitals) has changed significantly since the early postwar period. As Secretary of State Henry Kissinger said in 1975, "The problems of energy resources, environment, population, the uses of space and the seas, now rank with questions of military security, ideology, and territorial rivalry which have traditionally made up the diplomatic agenda." [37]

If executive agencies involved in the foreign policy process sometimes seem confused and disunified in their activities, the reason may be essentially that they *are* confused and uncertain about how the United States can effectively use its power to respond to a variety of novel and difficult problems that demand solution during the second half of the twentieth century. In turn, the disunity sometimes evident within the executive branch has greatly compounded the problem of achieving cooperative executive-legislative relations on major foreign policy issues.

Notes

1. James B. Reston, "The Press, the President and Foreign Policy," *Foreign Affairs* 44 (July 1966): 560.
2. Roger Hilsman, *The Politics of Policy Making in Defense and Foreign Affairs* (New York: Harper and Row, 1971), p. 18.
3. For more detailed discussion of the meaning and connotations of diplomacy, see Elmer Plischke, "The New Diplomacy: A Changing Process," *Virginia Quarterly Review* 49 (Summer 1973): 321-345.
4. For fuller elaboration of this point, see the discussion on the "different worlds" that the State Department and Congress occupy, in Smith Simpson, *Anatomy of the State Department* (Boston: Houghton Mifflin Co., 1967), pp. 152-183.
5. For a succinct discussion of the intentions of the founders regarding the powers of the president and Congress in foreign affairs, see the report prepared by the Library of Congress for the House Foreign Affairs Committee, *Background Information on the Use of the United States Armed Forces in Foreign Countries,* 91st Cong., 2d sess., 1970. A more detailed treatment of individual constitutional provisions is provided in *The Constitution of the United States of America: Analysis and Interpretation* (Washington, D.C.: Library of Congress, 1973).
6. A useful compendium of conflicting interpretations of the president's prerogatives over the armed forces is provided in the Senate Foreign Relations Committee, *Hearings on the War Powers Legislation,* 92d Cong., 1st sess., 1971.
7. An informative discussion of the president's use of the armed forces to

achieve diplomatic goals since World War II is Herbert K. Tillema, *Appeal to Force: American Military Intervention in the Era of Containment* (New York: Thomas Y. Crowell Co., 1973).

8. The context, meaning, and implications of the Carter Doctrine are explained more fully in Cecil V. Crabb, Jr., *The Doctrines of American Foreign Policy: Their Meaning, Role, and Future* (Baton Rouge: Louisiana State University Press, 1982), pp. 325-371. The ill-fated rescue mission in Iran is discussed in greater detail in Jimmy Carter, *Keeping Faith: Memoirs of a President* (New York: Bantam Books, 1982), pp. 459-513.

9. See the *New York Times,* December 20, 1979, dispatch by James Reston; and the editorial, "Unmaking a Treaty," on January 20, 1979. For summaries of the Supreme Court's decision in the case, see the *Washington Post,* December 14, 1979; and the *Congressional Quarterly Weekly Report,* December 15, 1979, p. 2850.

10. Loch Johnson and James M. McCormick, "Foreign Policy by Executive Fiat," *Foreign Policy* 28 (Fall 1977): 117. This article provides a comprehensive and illuminating discussion of White House reliance upon executive agreements since World War II and of Congress's response to that tendency.

11. Ibid., p. 118.

12. Ibid., pp. 118-124.

13. *New York Times,* March 2, 1979.

14. *New York Times,* February 13, 1979.

15. See W. Averell Harriman and Elie Abel, *Special Envoy to Churchill and Stalin: 1941-1946* (New York: Random House, 1975). Hamilton Jordan's role as a presidential envoy during the Iranian crisis is the theme of his book, *Crisis: The Last Year of the Carter Presidency* (New York: G. P. Putnam's Sons, 1982). Philip Habib's assignment as a special representative of the president to the Middle East is discussed in the *New York Times,* July 23 and November 2, 1982.

16. President Reagan's budgetary flexibility in responding to revolutionary upheaval and violence in Central America is discussed in the *New York Times,* March 1, 1983, dispatch by Tom Wicker.

17. For more detailed discussion of lobbying by governmental agencies, see *The Washington Lobby,* 4th ed. (Washington, D.C.: Congressional Quarterly, 1982).

18. Quoted in Sidney Warren, *The President as World Leader* (New York: McGraw-Hill Book Co., 1964), p. 23.

19. See Daniel Yankelovich, "Farewell to 'President Knows Best,'" *Foreign Affairs* 57 (1978): 670. Despite the fact that this observer believed that "automatic" public approval of presidential leadership in foreign affairs was declining, Ronald Reagan utilized his skills as a communicator very effectively in convincing the American people that he could and would reverse the decline of American power abroad. See, for example, the analysis of Reagan's media skills in John Herbers, "The President and the Press Corps," *New York Times Magazine,* May 9, 1982.

20. See, for example, the complaints expressed by several national news reporters about White House news "management," in David E. Haight and Larry D. Johnston, *The President: Roles and Powers* (Skokie, Ill.: Rand McNally, 1965), pp. 275-281.

21. Quoted in Thomas A. Bailey, *A Diplomatic History of the American People,* 8th ed. (New York: Appleton-Century-Crofts, 1969), p. 497.

22. Arthur H. Vandenberg, Jr., ed., *The Private Papers of Senator Vandenberg* (Boston: Houghton Mifflin Co., 1952), p. 344.

23. See the discussion of congressional perceptions of President Carter's diplomatic leadership in the *New York Times*, February 17, 1979.

24. Dean Acheson, *Present at the Creation: My Years in the State Department* (New York: W. W. Norton and Co., 1969), p. 93.

25. Perhaps no modern president has been more prone to bypass the State Department than President Kennedy. For a discussion of Kennedy's views toward the department, see Theodore C. Sorensen, *Kennedy* (New York: Harper and Row, 1965), pp. 287-290. On one occasion, Soviet Premier Nikita Khrushchev complained to Kennedy about his own diplomatic officials, who "specialized in why something had not worked forty years ago," and he urged Kennedy to formulate his own views. See Sorensen, *Kennedy,* pp. 554-555.

26. A recent example was provided by the Carter administration's diplomacy during the Iranian crisis of 1979. According to one report the president sent a high-ranking American military officer attached to NATO to confer directly with Iranian military leaders; this official "was told by the White House to bypass the United States Embassy" in Tehran. Similarly, discussion between members of the White House staff and Iranian diplomatic officials left the American ambassador to Iran in ignorance about these communications. See the *New York Times*, January 12, 1979, dispatch by Richard Burt.

27. For a more detailed analysis of the State Department's postwar decline, see Robert Pringle, "Creeping Irrelevance at Foggy Bottom," *Foreign Policy* 29 (Winter 1977-1978): 128-140.

28. Robert A. Dahl, "Congress and Foreign Policy," in Sidney Wise and Richard F. Schier, eds., *Studies on Congress* (New York: Thomas Y. Crowell Co., 1969), pp. 207-208.

29. The evolution of the American intelligence system during and after World War II is discussed in Allen Dulles, *The Craft of Intelligence* (New York: New American Library, 1965). More detailed information on the agencies comprising the intelligence community may be found in Lyman B. Kirkpatrick, Jr., *The U.S. Intelligence Community: Foreign Policy and Domestic Activities* (New York: Hill and Wang, 1973); and in David Wise and Thomas B. Ross, *The Invisible Government: The CIA and U.S. Intelligence* (New York: Random House, 1974). See also the text of President Ronald Reagan's Executive Order 12333, December 4, 1981, which specifies the composition and duties of the agencies comprising the intelligence community, in *Weekly Compilation of Presidential Documents*, vol. 17, no. 49, pp. 1336-1348.

30. Background on the evolution of American propaganda and informational programs since World War II is provided in John W. Henderson, *The United States Information Agency* (New York: Praeger Publishers, 1969) and Terry L. Deibel and Walter R. Roberts, *Culture and Information: Two Foreign Policy Functions* (Beverly Hills, Calif.: Sage Publications, 1976). More extended discussion of the role of propaganda and informational programs under the Reagan administration may be found in "International Communications and Information Objectives," Department of State, Current Policy no. 377 (March 4, 1982), pp. 1-4; and in the *New York Times,* July 20, 1982, dispatch by Bernard Weinraub, and July 24, 1982, dispatch by Edward W. Barrett.

31. For a typical expression of this view during World War II by a high-ranking American military leader, see Gen. Omar N. Bradley, *A Soldier's Story* (New

York: Holt, Rinehart and Winston, 1951), p. 536. And for the Roosevelt administration's approach to political issues during the war, see Gaddis Smith, *American Diplomacy during the Second World War* (New York: John Wiley and Sons, 1966), pp. 12-16.

32. A noteworthy tendency since World War II has been the active role taken by the labor movement in the United States with regard to foreign policy issues. For background on this development, see Ronald Radosch, *American Labor and United States Foreign Policy* (New York: Random House, 1969). American labor's more recent foreign policy activities and interests are discussed in Lane Kirkland et al., "Labor's International Role," *Foreign Policy* 26 (Spring 1977): 204-248. Another agency whose activities have increasingly drawn it into the foreign policy process is the Treasury Department. For a recent analysis of its international role, see Karin Lissakers, "Money and Manipulation," *Foreign Policy* 44 (Fall 1981): 107-127.

33. *New York Times,* January 12, 1979, dispatch by Richard Burt.

34. Stanley Hoffmann, "A View from at Home: The Perils of Incoherence," *Foreign Affairs* 57 (Winter 1978-1979): 463.

35. The problem of intra-executive rivalries and conflicts over foreign policy under the Reagan administration is analyzed more fully in Thomas L. Hughes, "Up from Reaganism," *Foreign Policy* 44 (Fall 1981): 3-24; Zeer Schiff, "Green Light, Lebanon," *Foreign Policy* 50 (Spring 1983): 73-86; Andrew Knight, "Ronald Reagan's Watershed Year," *Foreign Affairs* (Special Issue 1983): 511-541; *U.S. News and World Report,* May 23, 1983, pp. 20-22; *New York Times,* May 18, 1983, dispatch by James Reston; and the data from the *New York Times*/CBS News Poll in the *New York Times,* January 25, 1983.

36. For an interesting and informative discussion of successful executive efforts to coordinate foreign policy decisionmaking, see Robert F. Kennedy, *Thirteen Days: A Memoir of the Cuban Missile Crisis* (New York: New American Library, 1969).

37. Secretary Kissinger's views are quoted in Joseph S. Nye, Jr., "Independence and Interdependence," *Foreign Policy* 22 (Spring 1976): 135.

Congress and Foreign Affairs: Traditional and Contemporary Roles

2

When the 96th Congress convened early in 1979, Sen. Frank Church, D-Idaho, became the new chairman of the Senate Foreign Relations Committee. Senator Church announced that under his direction the committee proposed to play an active and influential role in the foreign policy process. He was determined that the committee would achieve a role of "prominence in foreign affairs" and he promised to provide "the kind of leadership that will give it a common purpose and direction." When the viewpoints of the committee differed from those of the White House on important diplomatic questions, the committee "should become the main forum for opposing the White House and opening up public debate." [1]

Senator Church's conception of the role of the Senate Foreign Relations Committee reflected in microcosm the new assertiveness witnessed in recent years on Capitol Hill with regard to foreign affairs. In 1973 Sen. Sam J. Ervin, D-N.C., called upon his legislative colleagues to challenge the prevailing idea that "American foreign relations are within the [exclusive] domain of the President"; Congress should reassert its "primary responsibility for the determination of substantive foreign policy." [2] After he entered the Oval Office in 1981, President Ronald Reagan discovered that the impulse toward congressional activism in foreign affairs had lost little momentum. On two issues in particular—legislative demands that the White House renew the quest for an arms control agreement with the Soviet Union, and congressional restrictions imposed upon the administration's diplomacy in Central America and Lebanon—the House and Senate were apparently determined to exert their influence in the foreign policy field. If they had not been inclined to do so earlier, in the period after the Vietnam War incumbent presidents were compelled to admit that Congress had become a potent force in the American foreign policy process. [3]

Congressional Assertiveness:
The Challenge and the Problems

All informed students of recent American foreign relations are aware that in the early post-World War II period the great milestones in the nation's diplomacy—establishment of the United Nations (1945), the Greek-Turkish Aid Program (1947), the Marshall Plan for European recovery (1948), NATO (1949), and President Truman's Point IV program of aid to the developing countries (1949)—emerged as the result of collaboration between executive and legislative policymakers. Over the next 20 years, however, congressional influence in foreign relations declined, reaching its nadir at the time of the Vietnam War; the chairman of the Senate Foreign Relations Committee, Sen. J. William Fulbright, D-Ark., among others in the Congress, lamented this decline.[4] By the mid-1970s, however, Presidents Nixon and Ford—joined sometimes even by their supporters on Capitol Hill—complained about the "restraints" that legislators had imposed upon the executive branch's ability to respond to foreign crises. In the early 1980s President Reagan similarly deplored legislative efforts to limit his freedom of action in Central America and the Middle East.

According to an informed commentator on the legislative process in the United States, Congress has "always been uncertain about its role in the field of foreign affairs."[5] Can Congress become a dynamic and effective force in foreign relations? Can it, as some proponents of a more influential legislative role advocate, emerge as a partner with the president in the foreign policy realm? A revitalization of legislative influence in external affairs faces numerous major and minor obstacles, most of which we shall discuss later.

At the outset we need to be cognizant of the existence and consequences of a problem that has impeded effective legislative participation in the foreign policy process for more than two centuries and may be a more formidable obstacle today than at any other stage in American history. In 1777 the Continental Congress established the five-member Committee for Foreign Affairs to conduct external relations. Yet, as one study found, "partisanship and personalities, frequent changes in personnel and the use of special committees, impaired the efficient functioning of the committee and made a coherent policy impossible." Congressional management of foreign relations was characterized by "fluctuation,... delay and indecision"; and this was a primary reason why, despite their suspicion of executive power, the Founding Fathers strengthened the powers of the executive branch in the Constitution. As much as any other single factor, it was the mismanagement of foreign affairs by Congress under the Articles of Confederation that led to the calling of the Constitutional Convention in 1787.[6]

Contemporary evidence indicates that the same conditions—the continuing diffusion of power and responsibility in the Congress and an inability to coordinate its activities in foreign affairs—are no less present today than in the late eighteenth century.[7] To illustrate the problem, let us examine the organization of the 98th Congress (1983), with particular reference to the Senate. The Senate had a total of 19 standing and select committees. Three of these—Foreign Relations, Armed Services, and Intelligence—were directly and extensively involved in the foreign policy process. Yet nearly every Senate committee exercised jurisdiction over some aspect of foreign affairs. For example, the Committee on Agriculture, Nutrition and Forestry had a subcommittee on Foreign Agricultural Policy;[8] the Banking, Housing and Urban Affairs Committee had a subcommittee on International Finance and Monetary Policy; and the Judiciary Committee had a subcommittee on Immigration and Refugee Policy. The Foreign Relations Committee had subcommittees in seven areas: Africa; arms control, oceans, and the environment; East Asia and the Pacific; Europe; the Near East and South Asia; the Western Hemisphere; and international economic policy.

A similar pattern can be found in the House of Representatives, where the network of overlapping committee jurisdictions is even more complex and confusing. In 1983, for example, the House had 26 standing and select committees, almost all of which had one or more subcommittees active in the foreign policy field.

A few examples from recent American diplomatic experience will highlight the problems created by this diffusion of responsibility in formulating and carrying out a unified national policy abroad. In 1962, in the face of outspoken White House opposition, the House Ways and Means Committee voted to deny trade concessions to Yugoslavia and Poland. Although this action was ultimately rejected by Congress, it threatened to reverse the policy of "building bridges" to Eastern Europe, a policy to which the United States government was committed.[9] Periodically since the early 1960s, members of the House and Senate have called for a reduction in the size of the American troop commitment to the NATO area. From Kennedy to Reagan, incumbent presidents have confronted legislative demands that America's contribution to Western defense be reduced significantly, in the expectation (not shared by the White House) that the European allies will expand their defense efforts proportionately. Another source of European disaffection toward the United States, stringent American control over nuclear weapons stationed in the NATO area, has its origins largely in congressionally imposed restrictions on the dissemination of nuclear technology.[10]

During the late 1960s the Senate Foreign Relations Committee was investigating the Johnson administration's conduct of the Vietnam War. After witnessing the factionalism present within the committee, one member said, "There are 19 men on it, and they represent 21-1/2 viewpoints." A pervasive feeling existed on Capitol Hill that the Senate Foreign Relations Committee was "rudderless and floundering" and that it was rapidly losing its influence as the Senate's voice on foreign policy issues.[11]

In 1977 President Carter encountered pervasive congressional opposition to his policies toward South Korea, Southeast Asia, and southern Africa. More than at any other time in recent memory, political leaders in the House and Senate were hard pressed to rally support on Capitol Hill for the president's foreign policy proposals.[12] Yet Congress was experiencing very little success in arriving at unified foreign policy positions of its own. On national security policy, for example, right-wing groups on Capitol Hill opposed further arms limitation (as in the SALT II accords with Moscow) and called for increased American defense spending; left-wing and liberal groups opposed increases in the national defense budget; and a third group demanded across-the-board reductions in all government spending.[13] By the late 1970s the House of Representatives sought to acquire greater influence in foreign policy decisionmaking. Yet the House was perhaps internally more fragmented—and thus less able to exert its influence effectively—than at any other stage in recent American history.[14] Under the Carter administration the Senate finally approved, and the president signed, the new Panama Canal treaties. The House Merchant Marine and Fisheries Committee was sharply critical of the agreements; several of its members were determined to prevent the treaties from taking effect. Meanwhile, four other committees of the House were considering legislation needed to implement the new Panama treaties.[15]

Executive-legislative differences in the foreign policy field also marked the Reagan administration's diplomatic efforts. Three issues in particular evoked strong legislative initiatives in foreign affairs. First, debate continued over the size of the administration's military budget, especially over the proposed expenditures for new weapons such as the MX missile system. Owing to congressional opposition, the Reagan White House was compelled to restudy the questions of whether to build the missile and its basing mode. Second, congressional voices were outspoken in urging President Reagan and his advisers to demonstrate progress in arriving at an acceptable arms limitation accord with the Soviet Union. Organizations that favored a nuclear freeze between the superpowers had considerable support on Capitol Hill (especially in the House of Representatives). Third, fearing another Vietnam, many legislators were plainly apprehensive about the Reagan administration's efforts to destabilize the Sandinista regime of Nicaragua, to provide large-scale military aid to the government of El Salvador, and to take other steps that might lead to a massive American military commitment in Central America. This fear provoked renewed congressional activity on another front (discussed more fully in Chapter 6): legislative restraints upon the operations of American intelligence agencies in Latin America and other regions.

The Reagan administration's diplomatic efforts were noteworthy for another reason: the president's call for a revival of bipartisanship as the foundation stone of American foreign policy. The heyday of bipartisan cooperation in foreign affairs after World War II occurred during the Truman and Eisenhower administrations, when executive and legislative officials collaborated to produce such diplomatic landmarks as the Greek-Turkish Aid Program (1947), the European Recovery Program (1948), and the North Atlantic Treaty Organization (1949). In 1983 President Reagan called for a return to constructive bipartisan cooperation in foreign relations, a goal also endorsed by a number of legislators.[16] The new emphasis upon bipartisanship indicated awareness in both the executive and the legislative branches that each had an essential role to play in the foreign policy process. Increasingly, for example, congressional relations had become one of the most important and time-consuming responsibilities of the secretary of state. (Lack of finesse in this dimension of his job was one factor that lead President Reagan to accept the resignation of Secretary of State Alexander Haig.) [17]

These developments illustrate the interplay between the two contrary forces that provide the principal theme of this chapter: the determination of Congress to play a more dynamic role in foreign affairs and, at the same time, the existence within the legislative branch of serious problems that impede its ability to do so effectively.

Congress's Constitutional Prerogatives

Like the executive branch, Congress has both formal constitutional and extraconstitutional prerogatives in foreign relations. Before analyzing them in detail, we need to make several general observations to set these powers in perspective.

For the Founding Fathers, Congress was unquestionably viewed as the dynamic organ of the American system of government, as the voice of the people, and as the depository of American democratic ideals. For a number of reasons—not least, their colonial experience—the founders of the Republic were profoundly suspicious of executive power. Americans and their representatives at the Constitutional Convention believed that the abuse of power by executive officials, such as King George III, the British prime minister, and the colonial governors, was largely responsible for the American Revolution. While the prerogatives of the president of the United States were less circumscribed than those of the state governors, it is noteworthy that the powers and responsibilities of Congress are listed first in the Constitution; further, they are specified in much greater detail than those of the chief executive or the judiciary.

Did the Founding Fathers expect Congress to play the leading role in foreign affairs as well as in domestic affairs? Or, as the Supreme Court decided in 1936, did they understand that under the Constitution these were different realms?[18] For 200 years constitutional authorities have debated this question, and even today the answer is unclear.* Convinced

---

*Many commentators on American diplomacy draw a distinction in roles between the executive and the legislative branches in making and conducting foreign policy. Yet this traditional distinction is becoming increasingly difficult to draw and maintain in practice. The *conduct* of foreign policy—involving such questions as how foreign aid is actually

as they were that Congress uniquely embodied and reflected the people's will, the founders were also cognizant that throughout history the conduct of foreign affairs was an *executive* function.

As Secretary of State Thomas Jefferson said, "The transaction of business with foreign nations is executive altogether." [19] From their immediate experience, when the Continental Congress attempted to conduct the revolutionary war, they were also aware of innumerable practical problems that could arise if the foreign affairs of the new republic were entrusted to 26 senators and 65 representatives. The Washington administration's frustrating experience in trying to arrive at a unified position within the national government on the question of the Jay Treaty with England in 1794 was an early case study in intragovernmental conflict on a major diplomatic issue. According to one historian, the treaty was only ratified after "stormy sessions" in both houses of Congress.[20]

Whatever their precise intentions regarding the role of Congress in foreign affairs, the founders gave the legislative branch important constitutional prerogatives in the foreign policy field. Of the 18 powers given to Congress in Article I, Section 8 of the Constitution, 7 affect foreign policy directly. But Congress has four constitutional prerogatives that are preeminent. Two prerogatives belong to the Senate alone, giving it a unique role in the foreign policy process: advice and consent to treaties and the confirmation of executive appointments. The Senate and the House of Representatives share two other powers specified in the Constitution: the power to appropriate funds and the power to declare war.

Advice and Consent Prerogative

Article II, Section 2 states that the president may make treaties "by and with the Advice and Consent of the Senate . . . provided two thirds of the Senators present concur."

Why did the framers of the Constitution require that agreements with other countries be approved by an extraordinary (two-thirds) majority of the Senate? The answer appears to be clear: as much as any other major constitutional provision, this one reflected the isolationist sentiments of the Founding Fathers and their determination that American involvement in international politics remain extremely limited. The provision reflected the American "congenital distrust of Europe." [21] And why was congressional participation in treaty making limited to the Senate alone? From their experience under the Articles of Confederation, the drafters of the Constitution were painfully familiar with the consequences of foreign policy mismanagement by the entire Congress. The

---

administered or whether the president should use armed force to achieve a particular foreign policy objective—is not a matter that Congress today is willing to leave solely to the executive branch. In other words, how the White House *conducts* foreign policy will affect legislative attitudes and behavior in the *making* of foreign policy.

smaller, indirectly elected (until 1913), and more mature Senate—capable of withstanding the whims of public opinion—was expected to serve as a kind of council of state to advise the president in foreign relations.

As we noted in Chapter 1, the ratification of international agreements by the United States involves a multistage process, in which the Senate plays a decisive role: it acts upon treaties submitted to it by the president. As we have pointed out, the Senate does not ratify treaties. It may give (or withhold) its "advice and consent" to them; but a treaty is ratified only when it has been approved by the Senate and signed by the president, who promulgates it as part of the "law of the land" (as treaties are designated in Article III, Section 2 of the Constitution).

Throughout the course of American diplomatic history, the vast majority of treaties has been approved by the Senate, with a few celebrated exceptions—as when, after World War I, the Senate so emasculated the Treaty of Versailles with amendments and reservations that it was unacceptable to President Woodrow Wilson.[22] Occasionally the threat of an adverse Senate vote on an unpopular treaty can induce a president to withdraw it from further Senate consideration, as occurred when President Carter withdrew the SALT II arms control agreement with the Soviet Union in 1980.

In the postwar period it has become common practice for the White House to invite senators to participate in the negotiations leading to major international agreements. This practice has come to be viewed as a method cf imparting bipartisanship to foreign affairs and of enhancing the prospects for favorable senatorial action on a treaty.[23] Indeed, today the Senate probably expects to be included in important treaty negotiations. Legislators have even undertaken diplomatic negotiations on their own, sometimes in the face of expressed presidential opposition to their actions, as we shall see more fully in Chapter 8.

Since 1789 the Senate's unique prerogative in the treaty-making process has given the upper chamber a distinctive and prestigious position vis-à-vis the House of Representatives in foreign affairs. Until World War II the voice of Congress on diplomatic issues was usually expressed through the Senate. It was Senate opposition that rejected American membership in the League of Nations after World War I; and during the interwar period powerful voices in the Senate expressed the isolationist sentiment that actuated American foreign policy. During and after the war influential senators—such as Arthur H. Vandenberg, R-Mich., and Tom Connally, D-Texas—cooperated with the Roosevelt and Truman administrations to lay the foundation for the active internationalist role that the United States assumed after 1945.[24] In the 1960s the Senate (more specifically, the Senate Foreign Relations Committee) again took the lead as it spearheaded congressional opposition to America's role in the Vietnam War.

The House of Representatives was for the most part content to play a subordinate role in the foreign policy process; membership on the House Foreign Affairs Committee (for several years called the International Relations Committee) was largely viewed as a symbolic assignment that few legislators coveted. As late as 1970 the chairman of the Foreign Affairs Committee regarded it as a junior partner in foreign policy decisionmaking; in his opinion the committee should normally support the executive branch's foreign policy positions.[25]

A noteworthy trend within Congress in recent years has been the extent to which the House of Representatives has sought to reverse its traditionally subordinate role in the foreign policy realm. If the House is assigned no formal constitutional responsibility in treaty making, it can—and recent experience has shown that it will—use other prerogatives (such as its predominant position in the appropriations process) to exert its influence in foreign relations. This viewpoint was illustrated by the remarks of one legislator early in 1979 in connection with the Panama Canal treaties:

> We in the House are tired of you people in the State Department going to your tea-sipping friends in the Senate. Now you good folks come up here and say you need legislation [to implement the Panama Canal treaties] after you ignored the House. If you expect me to vote for this travesty, you're sorely in error.[26]

Yet the Senate zealously preserves its prerogatives in the treaty-making process. Regarding House efforts to intrude upon its domain, the chairman of the Senate Foreign Relations Committee said, "Their nibbles end up being big bites, and we [are] being bitten to death." [27]

Confirmation Prerogative

The other (and much less influential) senatorial prerogative is the power to confirm executive appointments. To the minds of the Founding Fathers, these two unique senatorial powers—to approve treaties and to confirm diplomatic appointments—were interrelated. That is, the Senate should play a key role in the appointment of the officials who would engage in treaty negotiations; by doing so, the Senate would have a voice in framing the instructions given to these officials.[28] Within a relatively short time, however, this linkage broke down. Throughout American history the Senate has customarily approved the president's diplomatic appointees. But, as with other legislative prerogatives, since the Vietnam War the Senate has relied upon this one to express its viewpoints on particular aspects of foreign relations. President Reagan's first diplomatic defeat occurred some six months after he entered the White House, when the Senate Foreign Relations Committee voted to reject his nomination of Ernest W. Lefever as assistant secretary of state for human rights and humanitarian affairs. A number of senators (joined by members of the House) not only questioned Lefever's qualifications for the position; their opposition was also directed at the declining emphasis upon human rights in the Reagan administration's diplomacy. More typically, early in 1983 anti-Reagan forces in the Senate ultimately failed to block his appointment of Kenneth L. Adelman as head of the Arms Control and

Disarmament Agency. Yet even the failure conveyed the Senate's keen interest in progress toward arms control by the superpowers.[29]

At the beginning of the Eisenhower administration, the Senate balked at, but nonetheless confirmed, the nomination of Charles E. Bohlen as ambassador to the Soviet Union (Bohlen was identified with what his critics considered to be the pro-Soviet policies of the Roosevelt administration).[30] Similarly, at the end of the 1970s President Carter's nomination of Leonard Woodcock as the first American ambassador to the People's Republic of China also encountered vocal Senate opposition before being confirmed.[31] In both instances, Senate discontent was directed perhaps more at the substance of American diplomacy than at the qualifications of the nominees. In neither case, however, did Senate opposition produce any significant change in the foreign policy of the incumbent administration.

Power of the Purse

The remaining two powers to influence foreign relations conferred upon Congress by the Constitution are shared by the Senate and the House of Representatives. One of these—the prerogative relied upon most decisively by the British Parliament to establish its primacy over the monarchy—has historically been called the *power of the purse*. In reality, this is two interrelated powers: congressional control over the sources of revenue available to the national government (such as taxation, tariff revenues, and loans); and legislative approval for all expenditures by the government, in accordance with the constitutional requirement (Article II, Section 9) that "no money shall be drawn from the Treasury, but in Consequences of Appropriations made by Law."

Since all expenditures must be approved by Congress, it may increase funds for particular programs above White House recommendations; it may also refuse to grant funds for programs and policies in the foreign policy field; it may terminate programs already in existence; it may provide the required funds with the proviso that certain conditions be met abroad; and it may exercise legislative oversight of the administration of external programs, investigating such questions as whether they are achieving their objectives or whether their continuation is in the national interest.

A few brief examples from the year 1982 will illustrate the scope and importance of legislative reliance upon the power of the purse to influence external policy. During that year, for example, Congress reduced the Reagan administration's proposed defense budget by $17.6 billion—the largest cut in the White House's recommended defense spending in recent memory. Congress refused to accept President Reagan's request for funds to produce the Pershing II and MX missile systems; this was the first time in the postwar era that Congress had turned down a president's recommendation for new strategic weapons. By only one vote, the House of Representatives narrowly defeated a recommendation calling upon the executive branch to negotiate a nuclear freeze agreement with the Soviet Union. Congress also placed a ceiling (315,000 troops) on the number of American forces that could be stationed in Western Europe; in a related move, it reduced moderately America's financial contribution for funding the NATO defense program—thereby unmistakably signaling the existence of pervasive dissatisfaction on Capitol Hill with the level of support for this program contributed by the NATO allies.

During 1982, also, President Reagan's widely publicized development program for the Caribbean area—called the Caribbean Basin Initiative—encountered considerable opposition in the House and Senate and from several segments of American public opinion. Congress was unwilling to grant the Caribbean nations the kind of tax and trade preferences contemplated by this program. Conversely, over White House objections, Congress increased American military aid to Israel by some $200 million over the Reagan administration's budget request. The House and Senate, however, refused to provide the White House with a substantial increase in military and economic assistance for El Salvador. At the same time, Congress rejected demands by the administration's critics that American assistance to rightist groups opposing the Marxist government of Nicaragua should be terminated, although it did specify that such American aid should not be utilized to overthrow the Sandinista regime in Nicaragua or to provoke a war between Nicaragua and Honduras.

By its inaction on the White House budget request, Congress failed to provide funds for an American contribution to the African Development Bank (forcing the Reagan administration to default on its commitment to that program). In making available $514 million for America's contribution to the United Nations and other international organizations, Congress specified that no funds could be expended to benefit the Palestine Liberation Organization (PLO); and Congress expressed its opposition to many of the activities of the United Nations Educational, Scientific and Cultural Organization (UNESCO), because of their overtly anti-American cast. In providing funds for assistance to Morocco, Congress stipulated that its government should endeavor to resolve the conflict with Polisario rebel groups in the Western Sahara by peaceful means; Congress specified that future American aid to Pakistan would be conditioned upon that country's progress in respecting human rights; and as a general principle, Congress affirmed the idea that American economic assistance should be utilized primarily to relieve global poverty.[32]

In earlier years Congress had relied upon the power of the purse to achieve such diverse diplomatic goals as prohibiting American economic and military aid to certain African countries; endeavoring to prevent the proliferation of nuclear weapons throughout the international system; preventing the White House from extending American aid to North Vietnam and other Southeast Asian states; blocking the White House from reducing American military forces in South Korea without the concurrence of the House and Senate; and demanding that the president preserve the vital interests of the United States in any future agreements with the government of Panama.[33]

Authorization and Appropriations Process. Foreign policy programs that require expenditures for their implementation must be approved by Congress in two stages. As an example, take the annual foreign aid budget proposed by the White House. Initially Congress must authorize the foreign aid program. The first major step in this process is for foreign assistance to be considered by the Senate Foreign Relations Committee and the House Foreign Affairs Committee. Theoretically, in the authorization phase these committees are concerned with such questions as: Does foreign assistance promote the diplomatic interests of the United States? Can particular foreign aid projects (to Bolivia, or to Morocco, or to India) be justified? Is there a strong likelihood that the objectives of the foreign aid program can be achieved? Assuming that both committees eventually approve the foreign aid program, it must then be approved by the House and by the Senate; both houses must ultimately agree upon a common authorization measure before this stage is completed.

Next the foreign aid bill must go through the appropriations stage.[34] After the program has received legislative authorization, funds must be provided for its implementation. This is the province of the House and Senate appropriations committees. Custom has established that the House of Representatives—through its Appropriations Committee—plays the dominant role in the appropriations process.[35] In the postwar period the House Appropriations Committee has had a decisive voice in influencing certain aspects of American foreign policy.

Theoretically, neither the House Appropriations Committee nor that of the Senate is concerned with the merits of the foreign aid program already authorized by Congress. The two appropriations committees are supposed to concentrate upon such matters as whether federal revenues are available to finance foreign aid (along with all other expenditures previously authorized). In practice, however, the lines between the two appropriations committees and the jurisdictions and interests of the authorizing committees have become indistinct and are seldom observed rigidly. From 1955 to 1965, for example, the foreign aid program encountered its most formidable opposition on Capitol Hill from the Foreign Operations Subcommittee of the House Appropriations Committee. Headed by Rep. Otto Passman, D-La.—an outspoken and determined opponent of foreign aid—the subcommittee subjected the foreign aid allocation to "Passmanization," in the course of which massive cuts were made in the program. Passman accused executive policymakers of attempting to "grab the check," thus forcing American taxpayers to pay for every social and economic need throughout the world.[36]

According to longstanding custom, the Senate Appropriations Committee functions as a "court of review" for the actions taken by its counterpart in the House. As a rule, some—occasionally most—of the cuts made by the House in foreign aid (and other programs) are restored by the Senate Appropriations Committee, leaving the final amounts to be set in a compromise between the two chambers.

Problems of Budgetary Procedures. For many years, students of the national legislative process, together with many members of the House and Senate, have recognized and deplored the fact that Congress's treatment of the budget is fragmentary, highly decentralized, and lacking in any real sense of priority among literally hundreds of budgetary categories. In an effort to remedy these longstanding defects Congress enacted the Budget and Impoundment Control Act in 1974. The act created separate budget committees in the House and in the Senate, whose responsibility it would be to prepare a tentative, and later a final, budget for each chamber. This budget would presumably reflect each chamber's sense of spending priorities and would balance total budgetary outlays against anticipated governmental revenue. Without entering into a detailed analysis of recent budgetary procedures in Congress, our purpose is served by noting that this attempt at centralized budgetary control on Capitol Hill has not achieved its objectives thus far. Some students of congressional procedure in fact believe that these changes have made foreign policy measures, such as the foreign aid program, uniquely vulnerable on Capitol Hill. The process of budgetary accommodation now required in the House and Senate, in the view of one commentator, "has the greatest impact on the weakest programs," making foreign aid "a prime target" (especially in a national election year). Among its other consequences, existing congressional budgetary procedure has "institutionalized the weakness of American economic policy toward the third world" by placing a premium upon legislative reductions in overseas spending instead of domestic programs.[37]

By many criteria, the power of the purse has been and remains the most potent weapon available to Congress for determining public policy. Yet even in the post-Vietnam era of congressional activism, it remains an underutilized instrument of legislative influence in foreign affairs. As we observed in Chapter 1, by using emergency funds at their disposal, by reprogramming budgeted funds, and by other devices, resourceful presidents can usually get access to funds needed in the short run for their diplomatic undertakings. Ultimately the threat of major reductions in funds by Congress can of course restrain the president or compel changes in diplomatic undertakings advocated by the executive branch. Yet, as was evident when Congress dealt with the Reagan administration's policies toward Central America, legislators have often been inhibited from entirely cutting off funds for particular projects (such as the administration's aid to anti-Communist groups within the region) by a powerful deterrent: fear that (as national elections approached) Congress would be held responsible by the president and the American people for the loss of one or more Central American nations to communism. This prospect unquestionably restrained many of the Reagan administration's critics on

Capitol Hill from terminating funds requested by the White House for El Salvador and anti-Communist forces in the area.[38] As we also noted in Chapter 1, congressional efforts to provide more funds for particular foreign policy programs than requested by the White House risk the impoundment of such funds by the chief executive. In recent years, however, Congress has placed new restrictions upon the president's right *not* to spend money that has been legally appropriated.[39]

War Powers Prerogative

Constitutional Powers. Four consecutive provisions of Article I, Section 8 collectively comprise the war powers of Congress. These confer upon Congress the power to "declare war," to "raise and support Armies," to "provide and maintain a Navy," and to make rules for the regulation of the armed forces. These provisions have served as the basis for forceful assertions of legislative influence in external policy in recent years. The Truman administration was widely criticized on Capitol Hill for ignoring legislative viewpoints and prerogatives when it involved the United States in the Korean War during the early 1950s. In time, the Johnson and Nixon administrations faced even more outspoken congressional disapproval of their escalation of the Vietnam War and of the invasion of Cambodia without the explicit approval of Congress. More recently, two examples of legislative initiative in the foreign policy process—passage of the 1973 War Powers Resolution and efforts to limit the kinds of national commitments undertaken by the executive branch—indicate Congress's determination to influence the course of foreign relations by exerting its powers over the military establishment.

Declarations of War. Although the Constitution grants to Congress the power to declare war, several developments in modern international relations have combined to render this legislative prerogative largely a formality. In contrast to international practice for several centuries before the Constitution was drafted, in modern history nations have seldom declared war before engaging in hostilities. When Congress does issue a declaration of war (which has become rare), the declaration itself asserts that a condition of warfare actually exists; it is not an occasion for Congress to debate whether hostilities ought to exist.

More than a century ago the Supreme Court held in a landmark case that the existence of a state of war depended upon prevailing conditions; the president was not required to await a declaration of war from Congress before responding to external threats.[40] Since the Vietnam conflict chief executives have repeatedly referred to "functional equivalents" of a declaration of war, such as congressional approval of the national defense budget during the Vietnam War; Congress's enactment of the draft; and the passage of measures like the 1964 Gulf of Tonkin Resolution, which approved the president's use of armed force in responding to threats to American security interests.[41]

Force and Diplomacy.   Only 5 (out of some 125) wars and violent encounters in which the United States has been engaged have been declared by Congress; most of these incidents of armed conflict have involved major and minor episodes in which the president or a local U.S. official employed the armed forces for foreign policy ends. Neither of the two prolonged and costly post-World War II military engagements—the Korean War (called a police action by the Truman administration) and the Vietnam War—was formally declared by Congress, primarily because the incumbent president did not request Congress to do so.

The creation of a worldwide network of military alliances since World War II has also eroded the power of Congress to declare war. Article 5 of the NATO agreement, for example, provides that the parties shall regard an attack upon one signatory as an attack against them all— a provision which, according to many commentators, is tantamount to the threat of "automatic war" by the United States against an aggressor. Despite laments on Capitol Hill about the tendency of modern presidents to bypass Congress in decisions to employ the armed forces abroad, some legislators have said that a declaration of war in each case involving military hostilities abroad would be inadvisable since it might turn a limited war into a global nuclear conflict. (This danger was inherent in the Vietnam conflict.) [42]

Separation of Powers.   At the Constitutional Convention an early draft of the document gave Congress the right to "make war"; this language was later changed, granting Congress the power to "declare war." Suspicious as they were of executive authority, the founders recognized that the successful prosecution of a war requires *both* executive and legislative participation; one branch cannot conduct war alone. No one was more mindful of this than George Washington, who had endured many frustrating experiences trying to get coordinated policy and effective support from the Continental Congress during the revolutionary war. Accordingly, the chief executive is also given important war powers; the president is designated commander in chief of the military establishment. As with other constitutional issues, the precise balance or allocation of war powers between the two ends of Pennsylvania Avenue has been determined more by experience, precedents, and circumstances than by the intentions of the founders or by contending legal theories. On this front, the overall tendency has been for legislative prerogatives to be eclipsed by forceful assertions of executive initiative and leadership.

Included in the legislative war powers is the requirement that Congress "raise and support Armies" and that it "provide and maintain a Navy." Reflecting the American people's aversion to a standing army, the Constitution prohibits Congress from making appropriations for the army for longer than two years. (No such limitation exists with regard to naval appropriations.) This requirement assured that the questions of whether the nation needed a large military establishment and of what kinds of armed forces it required would be subject to frequent legislative review.

Throughout modern history, however, Congress has seldom used its power over the military establishment to its fullest potential for the purpose of influencing the course of American diplomacy. From the end of World War II until the termination of the Vietnam War the tendency was for Congress to provide the kind of armed forces requested by the White House. After the Vietnam conflict, until the end of the 1970s, defense spending was deemphasized in favor of expanded domestic programs. Even before President Carter left the White House, however, a significant expansion occurred in the national defense budget as a result of the revolution in Iran and the Soviet invasion of Afghanistan. Determined to restore American military strength vis-à-vis the Soviet Union, President Reagan called for a new intercontinental missile system (the MX), a significantly expanded navy, the new stealth bomber, and other measures needed to achieve the goal. By 1983 the Pentagon's budget was about $246 billion; and by 1986, according to the Reagan administration's projections, this total would rise to $365 billion. Expenditures of this magnitude provided ample scope for congressional influence in determining the size and nature of the American military establishment. Yet as in the past, even some legislators who opposed the kind of military expansion recommended by the Reagan administration were reluctant to oppose the White House overtly on an issue directly affecting the national security of the United States. For example, several legislators who were skeptical about the proposed MX missile system ultimately voted to support research and development funds for the missile, in part because failure to do so might in time crucially impair the strategic deterrent power of the United States.[43]

The War Powers Resolution. Mounting legislative dissatisfaction with the president's use of the armed forces for foreign policy ends was forcefully demonstrated when the House and Senate passed the War Powers Resolution over President Nixon's veto in 1973.[44] As much as any other step taken by Congress in recent years, this measure symbolized legislative disenchantment with the imperial presidency and a determination to become an equal partner with the executive in the foreign policy process. The main provisions and significance of the War Powers Resolution* are more appropriately discussed in the case study dealing with the deployment of the armed forces (Chapter 5). At this stage, it suffices to make a few general observations about it.

In the language of the resolution, its purpose was to ensure that the "collective judgment of both the Congress and the President will apply to

---

*One provision of the resolution was nullified by the Supreme Court's 1983 decision, in an unrelated case, regarding the legislative veto. *Legislative veto* is the name given to the procedure whereby Congress *permits* executive officials to engage in certain specified activities (such as the president's commitment of the armed forces abroad), unless and until Congress revokes his authority to do so. Normally, Congress's "veto" of executive actions is the introduction of United States Armed Forces into hostilities," or into situations in which hostilities are believed to be imminent, abroad. By this measure Congress insisted that its consent be obtained for the prolonged use of American troops in foreign conflicts; otherwise, the president would be required to withdraw American forces from actual or potential combat zones.

In the relatively brief time that has elapsed since Congress passed the War Powers Resolution, it is difficult to assess its long-term impact upon the American foreign policy process. Since 1973 advocates of a more influential congressional voice in foreign policy decisionmaking have in general applauded the resolution, believing that it was a significant step toward that goal. Other commentators and informed citizens (including a growing number of legislators) have been considerably less sanguine. Some have questioned whether, in a context of foreign crisis, the resolution would really inhibit the president's reliance upon armed force to promote national security and diplomatic objectives; by the early 1980s experience had tended to confirm these doubts. Other students of the American constitutional system have believed that the resolution in fact *strengthened* the position of the president as commander in chief of the armed forces, by according him wide latitude to deploy them with little effective hindrance by Congress.

Chief executives have given ambivalent answers regarding their authority over the armed forces. On the one hand, several postwar presidents (such as Johnson, Nixon, and Reagan) have taken the position that their authority over the armed forces was derived from the Constitution and could not, therefore, be limited by statutes or congressional resolutions. On the other hand, after passage of the War Powers Resolution other presidents (namely, Ford and Carter) vocally complained about congressional restrictions upon their powers in foreign affairs (for specific instances of their responses to the resolution see Chapter 5). Early in his administration President Reagan carried out a show of force in the Gulf of Sidra against the government of Libya; several months later he ordered a detachment of 1,200 U.S. Marines to engage in peace-keeping operations in Lebanon.[45] As is explained more fully in Chapter 5, in the case of Lebanon, Congress explicitly sanctioned the president's action by approving the marines' continued presence for 18 months, pursuant to the War Powers Resolution.

Events since 1973 had demonstrated convincingly that formidable difficulties confront any attempt to constrain the president's reliance upon the armed forces abroad by statutory means. Diplomatic and national security aspects of the problem often militated heavily against such

---

cast on a case-by-case basis, as was contemplated by the provisions of the War Powers Resolution. The Court held that the legislative veto was an unconstitutional exercise of legislative power, since the Constitution specifically provided for the procedures that must be followed (that is, passage by both houses of Congress and the signature of the president) for the enactment of legislation. The decision affected numerous pieces of legislation. (See *Immigration and Naturalization Service v. Chadha*, 51 U.S.L.W. 4907, 1983.)

attempts and gave to the chief executive advantages that his congressional critics were hard pressed to match. The Reagan administration's reliance upon the armed forces to achieve its diplomatic goals in Latin America and the Middle East illustrated the problems and dilemmas often encountered by the president's critics. In September 1982, for example, after the Reagan administration determined that a large contingent of marines was required to preserve peace and stability in Lebanon—and even after the position of American forces became increasingly vulnerable and precarious—it proved extremely difficult for Reagan's critics to compel their withdrawal from the country. President Reagan, the Great Communicator, skillfully exploited the prerogatives available to him to silence or outmaneuver his critics. Reagan and his advisers, for example, contended that the precipitous withdrawal of American forces from Lebanon would raise serious questions about the nation's diplomatic credibility and staying power under adverse conditions. As the Reagan foreign policy team assessed the matter, America's "retreat under fire" could produce a dangerous threat to global peace and national security in the months ahead. (As it happened, when the security of U.S. troops in Lebanon became more precarious early in 1984, the president on his own volition withdrew them.) In addition, the president repeatedly informed his detractors that if the White House were compelled to withdraw American troops from Lebanon, Central America, and other unstable regions, the responsibility for new Communist gains in these areas would rest squarely with his critics!

Under these circumstances, the president's critics found themselves in a dilemma from which there was no easy escape. On the one hand, against their own convictions and in the interest of national unity, President Reagan's critics could support or acquiesce in his diplomatic moves. Or they could overtly oppose his use of armed force for diplomatic ends—and in the process assume the responsibility for a possible diplomatic failure abroad for which they would be widely blamed. Faced with this quandary, the president's detractors were severely challenged to produce diplomatic alternatives capable of commanding wide public support and of promoting the diplomatic interests of the United States.

The problem that the War Powers Resolution addressed was in many respects analagous to the situation confronting the United States during the 1930s, when Congress sought to keep the nation out of World War II by passing the neutrality legislation. In the end, that effort failed, primarily because legal efforts to keep America out of hostilities were inadequate to protect the security of the United States in an increasingly dangerous external environment. Supported by public opinion, President Franklin D. Roosevelt frequently circumvented and, in some instances, ignored legal constraints upon his diplomatic freedom of action—and in the process placed the blame upon Congress for the nation's lack of preparedness after the Japanese attack upon Pearl Harbor in 1941! As in the pre-World War II period, perhaps the only effective constraints upon the president's reliance upon the armed forces for national security and diplomatic ends is the creation of external conditions that make such reliance unnecessary. As postwar experience has shown, that is a time-consuming, frustrating, and continuing challenge for which there is likely to be no early solution.

Economic Powers

The Constitution also confers upon Congress certain general responsibilities that we may classify as comprising its economic powers, several of which have become increasingly important in the conduct of foreign relations. These include the power to levy and collect taxes, to impose tariffs upon imports, to borrow money, to regulate interstate and foreign commerce, and to coin money and regulate its value. Collectively, the economic powers of Congress are vast, affecting almost every sphere of national life.

Legislative assertiveness in the foreign policy field within recent years may be an inevitable result of the steady growth in the federal budget (over $906 billion for 1984). Each year Congress is called upon to authorize and appropriate funds for literally hundreds of government programs, many of which impinge upon foreign relations. Congressional activities in the energy field, for example, directly affect American foreign policy toward the Middle East. Legislative measures to control inflation at home are a major influence in determining the value of the dollar overseas; these measures will also influence intangible but crucial developments such as the degree of confidence that foreign governments have in American leadership. The priority that Congress establishes between domestic and foreign spending is a major factor in determining the Soviet-American strategic balance, Washington's ability to fight limited wars, or the capacity of the United States to respond to the economic needs of the Third World.

Throughout most of the 1970s legislative attitudes reflected an opinion that appeared to enjoy wide public support: domestic needs should be given highest priority by national policymakers. According to some critics of American interventionism, the United States should set its own house in order before it attempted to solve the world's problems.[46] This viewpoint (part of what was sometimes called the post-Vietnam War syndrome), however, was largely abandoned by the end of the decade, as a result of Soviet expansionism in Afghanistan, Moscow's overt interventionism in Poland, ongoing revolutionary ferment in Latin America, continuing conflict in the Middle East, and other developments. After pledging in his campaign to "make America great again," President Ronald Reagan called for a substantial expansion in the national defense budget, even at the expense of certain domestic and entitlement programs. The Reagan administration's approach to external policy was that the United States could afford whatever measures were necessary to maintain its strength and credibility as the leader of the non-Communist world.

Few of the economic powers of Congress have more significant implications for foreign policy than its power to regulate commerce. The trade wars among the American states under the Articles of Confederation led to conditions of economic turmoil and instability—a primary reason the Constitutional Convention was assembled. Congress, therefore, was given the exclusive power to regulate trade both among the states and between the United States and foreign countries.

Beginning with the Reciprocal Trade Program inaugurated by the Roosevelt administration, the United States has sought to maximize its foreign trade on the basis of reciprocal tariff concessions with other countries. Congress grants the president considerable discretion to negotiate trade agreements with other nations, and Congress periodically engages in major revisions of the trade laws—often at the instigation of domestic industries threatened by rising imports (as in the case of automobiles from Japan, textiles from Hong Kong, and fruit and vegetables from Mexico). In dealing with trade questions, Congress is continually subjected to pressure from domestic industries, business groups, labor unions, farmers, and others seeking to improve their competitive positions. On several occasions in recent years, for example, the House and Senate have forcefully conveyed to Japan the American society's concern about the rising volume of Japanese imports and, conversely, about Tokyo's resistance to expanded American sales in the Japanese market.[47] Such congressional warnings are sometimes welcomed by the president and his advisers, who are trying to win new trade concessions from other countries.

Incident to its power to regulate commerce, from time to time Congress investigates the behavior of American business firms overseas. In recent years it has inquired into allegations that American corporations bribed officials in other countries to obtain preferential consideration. Political intervention in the affairs of Chile by the International Telephone and Telegraph Company has also been the subject of intensive legislative investigation.[48]

Today hardly any foreign policy activities lack an economic dimension. For example, in four out of the five case studies that follow—beginning with Senate consideration of the new Panama Canal treaties, through legislative efforts to promote the cause of human rights abroad—economic considerations in some measure shaped congressional attitudes and behavior. By the 1980s, America's relations with Japan were heavily conditioned by the outcome of trade and tariff negotiations between the two countries. Even with regard to ideological and ethical issues at the forefront of congressional concern—such as promoting human rights in the Soviet Union or achieving racial equality in southern Africa—Congress has used economic instruments, such as trade concessions and boycotts, to influence events abroad.[49] This may be merely one indication of a larger phenomenon in modern international relations: definition of a nation's power in *economic terms,* rather than according to purely military criteria.

The Oversight Function

Since the mid-nineteenth century many students of the legislative process have agreed that "control of the government—the oversight function—is probably the most important task the legislature performs." As a
result, "the bureaucracy lives under the heavy frown of congressional
supervision all the time." [50] Although it is not specifically mentioned in
the Constitution, the congressional power of investigation is a basic and
influential legislative function, one that Congress has relied upon repeatedly in the modern period to influence foreign affairs. During the 1930s,
for example, the investigation carried out by the Nye Committee into
America's participation in World War I had a momentous impact upon
public opinion, strongly reinforcing the existing isolationist mentality.[51]
Conversely, during World War II the Truman Committee (the Special
Senate Committee Investigating the National Defense Program, headed
by Sen. Harry S Truman, D-Mo.) investigated problems related to the
war effort. This committee was widely cited as a model of constructive
investigation by Congress.[52]

In the early postwar period committees of the House and Senate
examined political, social, and economic conditions in Europe; their
reports played key roles in formulating the Greek-Turkish Aid Program
(1947), the Marshall Plan (1948), and NATO (1949). Later congressional
investigations focused upon why the United States "lost" China to communism. These inquiries yielded few positive results—and in the process,
they impaired morale in the State Department and other executive
agencies for many years to come.[53]

One of the most influential investigations in recent diplomatic experience was conducted during the late 1960s by the Senate Foreign
Relations Committee on American participation in the Vietnam War.
This exhaustive and well-publicized inquiry served as a focus for the
emerging internal opposition to the war and was a major factor in the
Nixon administration's decision to terminate it. During the Reagan administration, committees of the House and Senate investigated foreign
policy activities carried out by executive officials in Central America,
such as economic and military aid to the government of El Salvador and
intelligence operations directed against the Marxist government of Nicaragua. Despite the Reagan administration's disclaimers, many legislators
believe that American intelligence agencies were seeking to overthrow the
Sandinista regime of Nicaragua. In some instances, relying upon the
information disclosed, Congress has unquestionably effected changes in
both the tone and the substance of American diplomacy toward the
region. Even some congressional critics of Reagan's diplomacy, however,
were obviously reluctant to run the risk of losing Central America to
communism. At a minimum, such investigations directed the attention of
the news media and public opinion to this dimension of American foreign
policy, and they compelled the White House to seek a bipartisan consensus for its Latin American policies.[54]

Informal Methods of Legislative Influence

In addition to its constitutional prerogatives, Congress has evolved certain informal, and sometimes extremely effective, methods for influencing the course of foreign relations. One of these is the ability of the House and Senate (or both) to pass resolutions expressing the opinions of legislators on diplomatic issues.* Such resolutions are not legally binding upon the executive branch, although expressions of congressional sentiment are not ignored by the president and his advisers. A noteworthy example of this legislative technique was provided in 1983 by the efforts on Capitol Hill to persuade the Reagan administration to accept a nuclear freeze. On May 4, for example, the House of Representatives adopted a nuclear freeze resolution, which endorsed the idea but also provided that the freeze would be suspended if progress in achieving arms control between the superpowers was not made within a specified period of time. It was perhaps a commentary upon such resolutions that both the pro- and the anti-nuclear freeze forces viewed the resolution as a victory! Its advocates believed that the resolution compelled the Reagan administration to intensify the quest for arms control; its critics believed that the resolution had no legal effect and that its provisions did little to solve substantive problems in Soviet-American arms control negotiations. Some legislators also expressed the view that the resolution was an attempt by Congress to intrude into the president's constitutional jurisdiction in foreign affairs.[55]

As Congress prepared for Memorial Day holidays in 1983, according to one report a number of legislators "were enjoying springtime in Paris—and Rome and Berlin and Athens and Budapest and Brussels and Prague and Geneva." Especially attractive for legislators was the Paris Air Show, attended by several members of the House Science and Technology Committee. Altogether during this period, 59 members of the House and 7 senators were traveling to some 16 different countries (plus Puerto Rico). Legislators were on such diverse missions as studying the prospects for peace in the Middle East, examining Soviet advances in aircraft and technology (at the Paris Air Show), and discussing the possibility of negotiations among rival political factions in Central America.[56]

Foreign junkets by legislators have become a routine part of congressional procedure since World War II. In most instances, such trips are planned as a normal and legitimate aspect of lawmaking or of legislative investigations. Sometimes also, legislators may be encouraged to travel abroad by the executive branch; and foreign governments may and do

---

*Resolutions expressing the opinions of one or both houses of Congress may take various forms. A *concurrent resolution* conveys the opinion of both houses on a particular question. However, it is not law and thus does not require the president's signature. Similarly, a *sense of the House* or a *sense of the Senate* resolution may express the viewpoint of one chamber on a question. While executive policymakers are interested in congressional sentiment, they are not bound by such resolutions.

frequently extend invitations for visits by legislators. Occasionally, legislators travel abroad for the avowed purpose of engaging in diplomatic negotiations and discussions with foreign governments.[57]

To the minds of most legislators, such foreign trips have become indispensable, providing Congress with firsthand evidence of conditions abroad and lessening its dependence upon data supplied by the executive branch. They also serve to counteract provincialism and undue immersion in constituency business, which limit legislative perspectives on international issues.

Although the era of oratory on Capitol Hill (and elsewhere) may have ended, even today speeches by individual legislators can have a significant impact upon American foreign relations. Both within Congress and outside it, addresses and statements by senators, especially on foreign policy issues, are newsworthy and influence the attitudes of executive policymakers. In the late 1940s, for example, Sen. Arthur H. Vandenberg, R-Mich., was a symbol of bipartisanship in American foreign policy and the most authoritative Republican voice on Capitol Hill on diplomatic questions.[58] During the Vietnam War, Sen. J. William Fulbright, D-Ark., served as an influential critic of the Johnson administration's diplomacy in Southeast Asia, Latin America, and other regions.[59] By the time of the Reagan administration, Sen. John Tower, R-Texas, had emerged as an outspoken supporter of a stronger military establishment, while Sen. Sam Nunn, D-Ga., was acknowledged to be a well-informed critic of prevailing defense doctrines.[60] Because of their experience and expertise, such individuals often exercise considerable influence in shaping the attitudes of their legislative colleagues.

Congress and Postwar Diplomacy

Since the late 1960s Congress has exhibited a new dynamism and militancy in exerting its prerogatives in external affairs. For the first two decades after World War II Congress was largely content to leave the management of foreign relations to the executive branch—thereby providing impetus for the emergence of the imperial presidency; when it did play a significant role in foreign relations, Congress normally supported the diplomatic policies and programs advocated by the White House. Recalling the decisive impact upon American diplomacy Congress had in earlier periods of American history and concerned about the steady accretion of executive power, many members of the House and Senate have advocated a return to a more influential role in the realm of external policy.

Congress's dynamic involvement in the foreign policy process must be viewed from the perspective of the diplomatic experience of the twentieth century. The post-Vietnam War era of legislative assertiveness in foreign relations, for example, may be regarded as another stage in the "democratization" of American diplomacy that began under President

Wilson. Although he was not always consistent with his own principle, Wilson believed in "open covenants, openly arrived at," in involving public opinion decisively in the foreign policy process, and in other measures designed to make the conduct of diplomacy consonant with America's democratic values. As the branch of government most representative of the people (as many legislators believe), Congress can justify its diplomatic assertiveness by reference to such Wilsonian principles.[61] The perspective of history also reminds us that there have been many earlier periods of congressional activism in foreign relations—such as the era of the Spanish-American War and the decade of the 1930s. In the latter period, not even President Franklin D. Roosevelt—one of the nation's most skilled political leaders—was able to impose his will upon a Congress strongly attached to isolationism.

The Expanding Role of Government

The expanding role of government in all spheres of life, both at home and abroad, is another factor that has contributed to a growing congressional involvement in foreign affairs since the New Deal. In 1946, for example, total annual expenditures by the United States government were some $62 billion; by 1983 this total had increased approximately 1500 percent. In one budget category—national defense spending—expenditures by the late 1970s exceeded by about 50 percent the *total* federal spending of 30 years earlier. Nearly every important foreign (or closely related domestic) policy of the United States in the postwar period—containing Soviet expansionism, meeting the economic needs of societies throughout the Third World, stabilizing world price levels for major commodities, dealing with global environmental problems—provides an opportunity and an incentive for Congress to leave its imprint upon America's diplomatic record.

The emergence of the United States as a superpower after World War II and its adoption of an internationalist foreign policy were also crucial developments enhancing the role of Congress in foreign relations. Before the war—isolationism had been the American rule of foreign policy for over 150 years—congressional interest and participation in diplomatic issues was often minimal. During the isolationist period the United States really had no foreign policy, as the term was defined in Chapter 1. America was not then willing to commit its national resources to external goals.

After World War II, however, even leading proponents of that approach acknowledged that the isolationist era had ended.[62] Its demise was symbolized by President Harry S Truman's historic address to Congress on March 12, 1947, inaugurating America's containment policy against expansive communism. In proposing the Greek-Turkish Aid Program, Truman put the choice squarely before Congress: either it would support whatever measures were required to preserve peace and security abroad or it would risk widespread global instability and the possible outbreak of

World War III.[63] Painful as the choice was for many legislators, Congress faced the realities of the postwar era and supported the measures dictated by America's emergence as a superpower.

Domestic Implications of Foreign Policy

The growing interrelationship between domestic and foreign affairs since World War II also provided momentum for congressional assertiveness in external policy. This phenomenon is illustrated by the Food for Peace program, whereby American agricultural products are sold or donated to needy societies overseas. One study has called the program "a popular form of foreign aid on Capitol Hill because it benefits the donor economy more than the recipient." With considerable encouragement from Congress, the Department of Agriculture seeks to dispose of agricultural surpluses abroad, as a crucial step in maintaining the prosperity of American farmers.[64] Other examples of this interrelationship—such as the dependence of American prosperity upon access to, and the price of, Middle East oil—could be cited. A State Department official has said that nowadays "no member of Congress can ignore foreign policy decisions and expect to be re-elected." Legislators can no longer say, "That's up to the president and Congress can't do anything about it." [65]

The Impact of the Vietnam War

A number of other factors have also combined to inject Congress forcefully into the foreign policy process since the period of the Vietnam War. More than any other single development, that traumatic and divisive conflict convinced many legislators that presidential dominance in the foreign policy field must end. Rightly or wrongly, many Americans blamed the emergence of the imperial presidency for the nation's ill-fated involvement in Southeast Asia. To critics of the war, the Johnson and Nixon administrations had "manipulated" and deceived Congress concerning the nature and extent of America's participation in the war and had misled the nation about the prospects for victory in it.[66] For Americans—who, as President Johnson repeatedly stated, were not accustomed to losing wars—the Vietnam experience perhaps inevitably produced a new era in executive-legislative relations and evoked demands on Capitol Hill for more effective restraints upon presidential power. For many years thereafter (as during the Reagan administration's diplomacy in Central America and the Middle East a decade later), congressional and public apprehensions about "another Vietnam" strongly colored legislative viewpoints and actions on foreign policy issues.

Implicit in the impulse toward congressional activism in foreign affairs has been the idea that the exertion of a more independent and forceful role *by Congress* in dealing with diplomatic questions enhances the prospects for international peace, stability, and a more constructive use of American power abroad. Consequently, since the Vietnam conflict legislators have echoed the demand that Senator Vandenberg directed at the Truman administration: legislators want to be in on the "take-offs" as well as the "crash landings" in foreign affairs.[67] At a minimum—as in congressional insistence that the Reagan administration rethink the production and deployment of the MX missile system—such legislative assertiveness can require executive policymakers to create a basic consensus *before* they undertake costly and far-reaching commitments by the United States.

Changes within Congress

Internal changes within Congress itself—and within the broader context of American public opinion and the political system—have also encouraged and sustained its activism in foreign affairs. Three such tendencies within the legislative branch have been noteworthy. One of these is the fact that Congress is getting younger: the average age of legislators has declined, and the viewpoints of many of its members today tend to reflect this change (which in turn to some extent mirrors the skepticism displayed by American youth toward the political establishment). Newly elected members of the House and Senate, for example, are no longer content to serve the expected apprenticeship before they express their viewpoints forcefully on public policy questions. (As we shall see in Chapter 3, one of the most crucial battles in the Senate over the new Panama Canal treaties was fought over an amendment offered by freshman Sen. Dennis DeConcini.)

The second and related change within Congress has been the demand for procedural reforms. Traditional concepts—such as the seniority principle governing the selection of committee chairmen, and the often vast powers exercised by the chairmen of committees and subcommittees—have come under repeated attack. This trend toward democratization within the House and Senate has given individual legislators a more influential role in congressional deliberations and has accorded them new opportunities to express their ideas on major policy questions.[68]

The third significant change within Congress has been the rapid and dramatic growth in the legislative staff. In recent years the congressional staff has grown more rapidly than the executive bureaucracy. By the early 1980s the combined staff of the House and Senate totaled 23,000 people! This rapid growth sometimes provided a powerful impetus for congressional activism in foreign affairs. In recent years, I. M. Destler has observed, legislative staffs "grew in size and in foreign policy expertise. . . . Committed, activist staff aides were the driving force behind many [congressional] initiatives" in foreign relations, especially in the Senate. In some cases, the influence of staff assistants serving congressional committees appeared to be more decisive than that of the committee members themselves in determining the outcome of legislation.[69] Yet this proliferation in the congressional staff has compounded a problem we shall examine more fully in Chapter 8: the challenge of achieving unified and coordinated congressional actions in the foreign policy field.

Changes in Public Opinion

Two significant forces in American public opinion have also encouraged Congress to exert its influence in foreign relations. One is the noteworthy increase in lobbying activities directed at Congress (and the executive branch). The case study in Chapter 4 on the Arab-Israeli conflict illustrates this phenomenon. Pressure group activity has always been a conspicuous feature of the American political system. But most students of the American government would agree that both the intensity and the skill of lobbying campaigns have increased significantly since World War II. A novel development in recent years has been the extent to which foreign governments, often in alliance with interest groups within the United States, have undertaken lobbying campaigns designed to influence the course of American foreign policy (see Chapters 3 and 4).[70]

The other salient characteristic of American public opinion that has provided Congress both an opportunity and an incentive to assert its prerogatives in foreign affairs is the evident lack of a public consensus on the nation's goals in international relations and on the best means for achieving them. This lack of consensus was perhaps an inevitable outcome of the Vietnam War and of certain other diplomatic setbacks experienced by the United States in the years that followed.[71]

At the risk of some oversimplification, we may divide the postwar history of American diplomacy into three stages. First there was the period from the early postwar era to the late 1960s, in which a durable national consensus existed in behalf of two ideas: that Communist expansionism threatened the security of the United States and other independent nations and that it had to be resisted by the strategy of containment. Next there followed the period through the late 1970s, characterized by disillusionment with American involvement in the Vietnam conflict and by the diplomatic retrenchment that followed the end of that conflict. In this period a significant number of Americans and their leaders sometimes doubted America's ability to achieve *any* worthwhile foreign policy objective, and they were extremely cautious about the commitment of the nation's power overseas.[72]

Then by the late 1970s a new era in congressional and public attitudes toward foreign affairs had emerged as a result of a number of diplomatic reverses—such as the collapse of the Iranian monarchy, the ensuing American hostage crisis, and the Soviet incursion into Afghanistan—and a pervasive feeling at home and abroad that the diplomatic credibility of the United States was being steadily eroded. To a significant degree, Jimmy Carter was defeated in 1980 because of a public perception that he was an indecisive chief executive who had allowed American power and influence abroad to deteriorate; by contrast, Ronald Reagan entered the Oval Office determined to "make America great again."

Yet as had many presidents in the past—especially when the nation was experiencing economic adversity—President Reagan also found it extremely difficult to create and maintain a consensus in behalf of his foreign policy goals. The popular and congressional apprehensions that had led to Jimmy Carter's political defeat did not necessarily translate into a set of clear and consistent diplomatic objectives having broad support among the American people and their representatives on Capitol Hill. Public opinion polls, for example, indicated that Americans remained apprehensive about growing Soviet military strength and about Moscow's diplomatic intentions; but they were also concerned about another Vietnam if the United States intervened in foreign crises. The people appeared to support President Reagan's diplomatic moves; but they also wanted to reduce the defense budget and the foreign aid program. They favored closer cooperation with the NATO allies; but there was no overwhelming public sentiment in favor of giving the allies a more decisive voice in shaping American diplomatic and military strategy. In brief, by the early 1980s public and congressional attitudes on foreign policy issues were more than ordinarily characterized by the presence of anomalies, contradictions, and mutually exclusive objectives.[73]

In the light of the Vietnam War and of the events of the 1970s, what kind of balance should the United States endeavor to maintain between indiscriminate interventionism and isolationism in foreign affairs? How useful was the slogan "No more Vietnams" as a guide for American diplomacy toward Latin America, sub-Saharan Africa, the Middle East, and other regions in which the nation had major diplomatic commitments? How would the expanded and modernized military establishment proposed by President Reagan, and supported by a majority in the House and Senate, be *used* to achieve foreign policy goals? Such questions were likely to serve as primary issues in a national foreign policy debate for many years in the future. In the search for answers, Congress will almost certainly express its viewpoints on them vigorously and play a leading role in trying to forge a new bipartisan consensus as a foundation for the nation's diplomatic activities.

Notes

1. For a detailed presentation of Senator Church's views, see the *New York Times*, November 24, 1978, dispatch by James Reston.
2. See Senator Ervin's views, as quoted in the *New York Times*, October 12, 1973, dispatch by Linda Charleton.
3. Douglas J. Bennet, Jr., "Congress: Its Role in Foreign Policymaking," *Department of State Bulletin* 78 (June 1978): 35-36.
4. See Senator Fulbright's views on the decline of the influence of the Senate Foreign Relations Committee in the *New York Times*, January 30, 1972, dispatch by John W. Finney.

5. Holbert N. Carroll, *The House of Representatives and Foreign Affairs* (Pittsburgh: University of Pittsburgh Press, 1958), p. 3.

6. See Paul A. Varg's discussion titled "Foreign Affairs and the Articles of Confederation," in his book *Foreign Policies of the Founding Fathers* (East Lansing: Michigan State University Press, 1963), pp. 46-66; and Albert C. V. Westphal, *The House Committee on Foreign Affairs* (New York: Columbia University Press, 1942), pp. 14-15.

7. For detailed examinations of the problems impeding Congress's role as an effective legislative body, see Richard Bolling, *House out of Order* (New York: E. P. Dutton, 1965); the two studies by Joseph Clark, ed., *Congress: The Sapless Branch* (New York: Harper and Row, 1964) and *Congressional Reform: Problems and Prospects* (New York: Thomas Y. Crowell Co., 1965); Roger H. Davidson et al., *Congress in Crisis: Politics and Congressional Reform* (Belmont, Calif.: Wadsworth Publishing Co., 1966).

8. For a more detailed discussion of the agricultural dimensions of postwar American foreign policy, see "The Question of Changing U.S. Food Export Policy," *Congressional Digest* 53 (December 1954): 289-314; and Donald F. McHenry and Kai Bird, "Food Bungle in Bangladesh," *Foreign Policy* 27 (Summer 1977): 72-89.

9. *New York Times,* June 17, 1962.

10. *New York Times,* November 16, 1965, dispatch by John W. Finney; and *New York Times,* February 26, 1967, dispatch by John W. Finney.

11. See Marvin Kalb, "Doves, Hawks and Flutters in the Foreign Relations Committee," *New York Times Magazine,* November 19, 1967.

12. *New York Times,* June 22, 1977, dispatch by Graham Hovey.

13. *Congressional Quarterly Almanac 1977* (Washington, D.C.: Congressional Quarterly, 1977), p. 319.

14. *New York Times,* July 3, 1977, dispatch by Adam Clymer.

15. "House Opponents of Panama Canal Turnover Opposing Implementing Legislation," *Congressional Quarterly Weekly Report,* February 17, 1979, p. 306; and *New York Times,* February 19, 1979.

16. *New York Times,* April 29, 1983, dispatch by Hedrick Smith; and *New York Times,* May 10, 1983, dispatch by John F. Burns. See also the discussion of the importance of renewed bipartisanship in American foreign policy by Sen. Charles H. Percy, R-Ill., chairman of the Senate Foreign Relations Committee, in "The Partisan Gap," *Foreign Policy* 45 (Winter 1981-1982): 3-15.

17. See Lee H. Hamilton and Michael H. Van Dusen, "Making the Separation of Powers Work," *Foreign Affairs* 57 (Fall 1978): 17-40; *New York Times,* June 30, 1982, dispatches by James Reston and by Richard Holbrooke; and *New York Times,* August 19, 1982, dispatch by Bernard Gwertzman.

18. In *United States v. Curtiss-Wright Export Corp.,* 299 U.S. 304 (1936), the Supreme Court recognized a fundamental distinction between the powers of the national government in domestic and foreign affairs. In that case, the prerogatives of the chief executive to manage foreign relations were forcefully affirmed.

19. Jefferson's views on the role of the president in foreign affairs are quoted in Francis O. Wilcox, *Congress, the Executive, and Foreign Policy* (New York: Harper and Row, 1971), p. 146.

20. Julius W. Pratt, *A History of United States Foreign Policy* (Englewood Cliffs, N.J.: Prentice-Hall, 1955), pp. 79-80.

21. Dexter Perkins, *The American Approach to Foreign Policy* (New York: Atheneum, 1968), p. 191.

22. For historical background on the Senate's actions with regard to treaties, see W. Stull Holt, *Treaties Defeated by the Senate* (Baltimore: Johns Hopkins University Press, 1933).

23. Cecil V. Crabb, Jr., *Bipartisan Foreign Policy: Myth or Reality?* (New York: Harper and Row, 1957), pp. 168-170.

24. The senatorial contribution during this period is highlighted in Arthur H. Vandenberg, Jr., ed., *The Private Papers of Senator Vandenberg* (Boston: Houghton Mifflin and Co., 1952).

25. See the views of Rep. Thomas E. Morgan, chairman of the House Foreign Affairs Committee, as cited in Wilcox, *Congress, the Executive, and Foreign Policy*, p. 6.

26. See the views of Rep. John D. Dingell in *U.S. News & World Report*, March 19, 1979, p. 46. For detailed discussion of efforts by the House of Representatives to compel the Reagan White House to undertake negotiations with rebel groups in Central America, for example, see the *New York Times*, May 12 and May 13, 1983, dispatches by Martin Tolchin.

27. See the views of Sen. Frank Church, as quoted in Loch Johnson and James M. McCormick, "Foreign Policy by Executive Fiat," *Foreign Policy* 28 (Fall 1977): 133.

28. See the study prepared by the Library of Congress for the Senate Foreign Relations Committee, *The Senate Role in Foreign Affairs Appointments*, 92d Cong., 1st sess., 1971, pp. 3-10.

29. Ibid., p. 11. More detailed discussion of President Reagan's disagreement with the Senate over the appointments of Ernest W. Lefever and Kenneth L. Adelman may be found in *Reagan's First Year* (Washington, D.C.: Congressional Quarterly, 1982), pp. 42-43; *New York Times*, May 22, 1981, dispatch by David Shipley; *New York Times*, February 26, 1983, dispatch by Francis X. Clines; and *New York Times*, February 27, 1983, dispatch by Hedrick Smith.

30. See Dwight D. Eisenhower, *Mandate for Change: 1953-1956* (Garden City, N.Y.: Doubleday and Co., 1963), pp. 212-213.

31. See the views expressed at Senate hearings on the confirmation of Leonard Woodcock as ambassador to China, in the *Congressional Quarterly Weekly Report*, January 20, 1979, p. 97.

32. Our discussion of Congress's reliance upon the power of the purse to influence American foreign policy relies upon the more extended discussion in the *Congressional Quarterly Almanac 1982*, pp. 6-9, 136-147, 151-156, 160.

33. See the discussions of legislative activities affecting various aspects of American foreign relations in the *Congressional Quarterly Almanac 1977*, p. 347.

34. For an illuminating analysis of the role of the House of Representatives in the appropriations process, see Richard F. Fenno, Jr., "The House Appropriations Committee as a Political System," *American Political Science Review* 56 (June 1962): 310-324; and Jeffrey L. Pressman, *House vs. Senate: Conflict in the Appropriations Process* (New Haven, Conn.: Yale University Press, 1966).

35. See Jeffrey L. Pressman, "Focus on the Combatants: The Appropriations Committees," in Sidney Wise and Richard F. Schier, eds., *Studies on Congress* (New York: Thomas Y. Crowell Co., 1969), pp. 141-164.

36. Baton Rouge *Morning Advocate,* March 3, 1979, dispatch by Peter Finney, Jr.; and Elizabeth B. Drew, "Mr. Passman Meets His Match," *The Reporter* 31 (November 19, 1964): 40-43.

37. For the text of the Budget and Impoundment Control Act of 1974, see P.L. 93-344. An illuminating discussion of the problems encountered by Congress in the attempt to introduce more centralized decisionmaking on budgetary issues may be found in John W. Ellwood and James A. Thurber, "The New Congressional Budget Process: The Hows and Whys of House-Senate Differences," in Lawrence C. Dodd and Bruce Oppenheimer, eds., *Congress Reconsidered* (New York: Praeger Publishers, 1977), pp. 163-192. Indicative of the existing confusion over budgetary procedures in Congress was the fact that in mid-1981 a 4,000-page budget reconciliation bill emerged from legislative deliberations, but very few legislators were familiar with its provisions! Dissatisfaction with congressional budgetary procedures remains widespread on Capitol Hill. See the analysis by Frank C. Ballance in the *New York Times,* July 23, 1980; the discussions of budgetary procedures in the *Congressional Quarterly Weekly Report,* April 9, 1983, p. 694, and May 14, 1983, pp. 924-931.

38. See, for example, the discussion of the reaction on Capitol Hill to President Reagan's message to a joint session of Congress on April 27, 1983, calling for a bipartisan approach to the problems of political ferment and Marxist gains in Central America, in *U.S. News & World Report,* May 9, 1983, pp. 30-34. President Reagan's view was that the White House may legally "reprogram" funds already appropriated by Congress (in effect, shifting funds from one budget category to another) without explicit legislative authorization to do so. Needless to say, Reagan's critics on Capitol Hill believed such reprogramming was illegal and was an overt attempt by the president to evade legislative restrictions upon his diplomatic moves in Latin America. For more detailed discussions, see the *Congressional Quarterly Weekly Report,* March 19, 1983, p. 552, and April 2, 1983, pp. 667-668.

39. For more detailed discussion of the right of the chief executive to impound funds provided by Congress, see "Controversy over the Presidential Impoundment of Appropriated Funds," *Congressional Digest* 52 (April 1973): 65-96.

40. See the *Prize Cases,* 67 U.S. (2 Black) 635 (1863).

41. The text of the War Powers Resolution may be found in P.L. 93-148, H.J. Res. 52 (November 7, 1973); and for the views of recent presidents concerning their authority over the armed forces, see Senate Foreign Relations Committee, *Hearings on War Powers Legislation,* 93d Cong., 1st sess., 1973, pp. 167-172.

42. Thus Sen. Jacob Javits was convinced that it would have been "most unfortunate" if Congress had declared war in the Vietnam conflict; this act would have had "unforseeable consequences." See Jacob K. Javits, "The Congressional Presence in Foreign Relations," *Foreign Affairs* 48 (January 1970): 226.

43. See, for example, viewpoints expressed in the House and Senate on President Reagan's proposed new MX missile system in the *New York Times,* May 25, 1983, dispatch by Steven V. Roberts; and in the *Congressional Quarterly Weekly Report,* May 14, 1983, p. 933.

44. The context of the War Powers Resolution is discussed more fully in Gerald R. Ford, *A Time to Heal* (New York: Harper and Row, and the Reader's Digest Association, 1979), pp. 249-252, 280-283.

45. Former President Ford's views on the War Powers Resolution are contained in his memoirs, *A Time to Heal*, pp. 251-253, 279-283. President Jimmy Carter's account of the Iranian hostage crisis indicates little or no concern about the provisions of the War Powers Resolution. For example, late in 1979 Carter determined to "make a direct military attack" against Iran if the American hostages were harmed. See Jimmy Carter, *Keeping Faith: Memoirs of a President* (New York: Bantam Books, 1982), p. 466. According to one legislator, President Ronald Reagan effectively nullified the provisions of the War Powers Resolution when he ordered the marines into Lebanon, by asserting that there was no intention or prospect that American forces would become involved in hostilities. Yet even he concedes that if President Reagan had asked for congressional approval of this step, the House and Senate would have granted it. See the views of Sen. Thomas F. Eagleton in the *New York Times*, November 17, 1982, and the discussion of congressional viewpoints toward the Lebanese crisis in the *Congressional Quarterly Weekly Report*, April 23, 1983, p. 777.

46. This point of view was exemplified in the approach of Sen. J. William Fulbright to American foreign policy. Fulbright believed that the nation's diplomatic success depended "on the strength and character of our society, which in turn depend on our success in resolving the great social and economic issues of American life." See his *Old Myths and New Realities* (New York: Random House, 1964), pp. 109, 138. A more detailed analysis of recent neo-isolationist thought is provided in Cecil V. Crabb, Jr., *Policy-Makers and Critics: Conflicting Theories of American Foreign Policy* (New York: Praeger Publishers, 1976), pp. 214-299.

47. *New York Times*, February 10, 1979, dispatch by Clyde H. Farnsworth.

48. See, for example, the investigations conducted by the Senate Foreign Relations Committee, *Multinational Corporations and United States Foreign Policy*, 93d Cong., 1st sess., March 20-April 2, 1973, pts. 1 and 2, focusing upon the activities of the International Telephone and Telegraph Co. in Chile; and 94th Cong., 2nd sess., February 4-6 and May 4, 1976, pt. 14, dealing with the overseas activities of the Lockheed Aircraft Corporation.

49. For an informative discussion of Congress's use of its economic powers to promote human rights abroad, see Richard H. Ullman, "Human Rights and Economic Power: The United States versus Idi Amin," *Foreign Affairs* 56 (April 1978): 528-543.

50. Ralph K. Huitt, "Congress, the Durable Partner," in *Studies on Congress*, p. 45.

51. For a detailed study of this committee's influence, see Wayne S. Cole, *Senator Gerald P. Nye and American Foreign Relations* (Minneapolis: University of Minnesota Press, 1962).

52. See Donald H. Riddle, *The Truman Committee: A Study in Congressional Responsibility* (New Brunswick, N.J.: Rutgers University Press, 1964); and Wilfred E. Binkley, *President and Congress* (New York: Alfred A. Knopf, 1947), pp. 268-269.

53. A useful source on congressional investigations is Arthur M. Schlesinger, Jr., and Roger Burns, eds., *Congress Investigates: A Documented History, 1792-1974*, 5 vols. (New York: Chelsea House Publishers, 1975). For a discussion and documentary materials on Congress's investigation of Communist influences on the State Department and other executive agencies during the early 1950s, see vol. 5, pp. 3729-3923.

54. See, for example, the discussion of the action by the Foreign Operations Subcommittee of the House Appropriations Committee in reducing funds for El Salvador and its insistence that the White House seek peaceful negotiations in Central America, in the *Congressional Quarterly Weekly Report,* April 30, 1983, pp. 819-823, 938.

55. See the discussion of the nuclear freeze resolution adopted by the House of Representatives on May 4, 1983, by a vote of 278-149, in the *Congressional Quarterly Weekly Report,* May 7, 1983, pp. 868-869; and the resolution passed by the Senate Foreign Relations Committee limiting American troops stationed in Honduras, in the *New York Times,* May 27, 1983, dispatch by Philip Taubman.

56. Baton Rouge *Morning Advocate,* May 30, 1983, dispatch by UPI correspondent Ira R. Allen. For an example of Congress's use of foreign travel to influence foreign policy, see Senate Foreign Relations Committee, *Congress and United States-Soviet Relations,* 94th Cong., 1st sess., 1975. This report summarizes a conference between members of the Senate and of the Supreme Soviet in which a variety of diplomatic issues were discussed.

57. From 1973 to 1979, for example, President Anwar Sadat of Egypt encouraged visits to his country by American legislators; Sadat had great confidence in his ability to influence congressional opinion favorably toward the Arab point of view. During this six-year period some 400 senators and representatives visited Egypt. See Stanley F. Reed, "Dateline Cairo: Shaken Pillar," *Foreign Policy* 45 (Winter 1981-1982): 176.

58. The key role played by Senator Vandenberg in the foreign policy programs of the Truman and early Eisenhower administrations is highlighted in Arthur H. Vandenberg, Jr., ed., *The Private Papers of Senator Vandenberg* (Boston: Houghton Mifflin Co., 1952).

59. See, for example, Senator Fulbright's widely publicized speech criticizing the Johnson administration's diplomacy in the Dominican Republic, in the *Congressional Record,* 89th Cong., 1st sess., 1965, 3, pp. S23855-S23865.

60. See the profile of Sen. John Tower in the *New York Times,* April 29, 1983, dispatch by Steven V. Roberts. In the House, Rep. Clarence Long, D-Md., chairman of the House Foreign Operations Appropriations Subcommittee, had also become a highly influential voice affecting American foreign policy toward Central America. See the *Congressional Quarterly Weekly Report,* May 7, 1983, pp. 887-888.

61. For a detailed discussion of the impact of Wilsonianism upon the conduct of American foreign relations, see James L. McCamy, *Conduct of the New Diplomacy* (New York: Harper and Row, 1964), pp. 141-163.

62. Senator Taft's views are cited in Norman A. Graebner, "Isolationism," *International Encyclopedia of the Social Sciences* (New York: Crowell Collier and Macmillan, 1968); and see Vandenberg, *The Private Papers of Senator Vandenberg,* p. 1.

63. For the text of Truman's address see *Public Papers of the Presidents of the United States: Harry S Truman, 1947* (Washington, D.C.: Government Printing Office, 1963), pp. 176-180.

64. McHenry and Bird, "Food Bungle in Bangladesh," pp. 83-85.

65. Douglas L. Bennet, Jr., "Congress in Foreign Policy: Who Needs It?" *Foreign Affairs* 57 (Fall 1978): 43.

66. An extremely critical account of the Johnson administration's relations with Congress during the crisis is provided in Sen. J. William Fulbright, *The*

Arrogance of Power (New York: Random House, 1966), pp. 50-53.

67. Senator Vandenberg's complaint was expressed with regard to the Truman administration's presentation of the Greek-Turkish Aid Program to Congress in 1947. See the *New York Times,* March 14, 1947, dispatch by James Reston.

68. See the views of Ross K. Baker on the decline of the seniority system in Congress and the tendency of legislators today to act as "a soloist who plays for his own fans in the audience rather than acting in concert with the other players," in the *New York Times,* November 13, 1979. See also *Congressional Quarterly Weekly Report,* January 27, 1979, p. 154.

69. For background discussion, see Warren H. Butler, "Administering Congress: The Role of the Staff," *Public Administration Review* 26 (March 1968): 3-13; and the more recent analyses of the impact of a greatly expanded legislative staff on Congress's foreign policy role in Wayne Valis, "A Reagan Presidency: The Congress and the Courts," in Wayne Valis, ed., *The Future under Ronald Reagan* (Westport, Conn.: Arlington House, 1981), p. 45; and the discussion of the influence of the staff of the House Armed Services Committee in the *New York Times,* June 28, 1982, dispatch by Richard Halloran.

70. See Ross Y. Koen, *The China Lobby in American Politics* (New York: Harper and Row, 1974); and Stanley D. Bachrack, *The Committee of One Million: "China Lobby" Politics, 1953-1971* (New York: Columbia University Press, 1976).

71. Several diverse approaches to American foreign policy in the post-Vietnam War era are identified and discussed in Crabb, *Policy-Makers and Critics.* For an informative discussion of the problem of arriving at a new foreign policy consensus, see James Chace, "Is a Foreign Policy Consensus Possible?" *Foreign Affairs* 57 (Fall 1978): 1-17.

72. See Sen. J. William Fulbright, *The Crippled Giant: American Foreign Policy and Its Domestic Consequences* (New York: Random House, 1972); and Stanley Hoffmann, *Gulliver's Troubles, or the Setting of American Foreign Policy* (New York: McGraw-Hill Book Co., 1968).

73. Informative studies of American public opinion toward foreign affairs in the early 1980s may be found in Theodore C. Sorensen, "The Absent Opposition," *Foreign Policy* 47 (Summer 1982): 66-82; John E. Rielly, "American Opinion: Continuity, Not Reaganism," *Foreign Policy* 50 (Spring 1983): 86-105; and the analysis of conflicting public attitudes on foreign policy questions by former Secretary of State Henry Kissinger in the *New York Times,* January 18, 1982.

PART II

Congress Confronts the Issues

We now turn our attention from the general pattern of interaction between Congress and the president in the foreign policy process to five specific case studies of policy areas. The concrete issues selected for examination illustrate Congress's changing perceptions of its role in foreign policymaking and how the executive branch and public opinion shape these perceptions.

Chapter 3 examines congressional action on the Panama Canal treaties approved by the Senate March 16 and April 18, 1978. This case study demonstrates how the Senate deals with the political dynamics of a highly controversial issue. It is a classic example of the Senate's participation in the treaty-making process and of its exercise of the constitutional advice and consent prerogative. Treaty provisions require follow-up legislation and appropriations, which involve the House in the treaty process as well. In the case of the Panama treaties especially, the House jealously guarded its own prerogatives.

Chapter 4 deals with the Arab-Israeli conflict by focusing upon the Reagan administration's decision to supply AWACS and other advanced military aircraft to Saudi Arabia. The AWACS case is an illuminating example of congressional reliance upon the power of the purse to influence the foreign policy process. It also highlights the role and activities of pressure groups in American foreign relations.

Chapter 5, "The Armed Forces," recounts ways in which Congress has attempted to draw the line between the constitutional power of the president as commander in chief and the constitutional power of the Congress to declare war and "to make Rules for the Government and Regulation of the land and naval Forces." The chapter highlights the essential pragmatism of the congressional approach. When Congress has agreed with a president's use of the armed forces, it has acquiesced without asserting its constitutional prerogatives. When it has disagreed, it has attempted to oppose presidential policies.

In Chapter 6, we examine the legislative oversight role of Congress with particular reference to the intelligence community. Perhaps nothing better illustrates the changed attitudes in Congress toward its role in foreign policy than the change in its relationship to the intelligence community. The congressional approach went from almost total neglect following the creation of the Central Intelligence Agency in 1947 to line-item scrutiny of the intelligence budget by committees in both the House and the Senate in 1977.

Finally, in Chapter 7, congressional initiatives concerning human rights in American foreign policy are examined. Congressional dissatisfaction with the lack of attention given to human rights in foreign policy-making under the Nixon administration sharpened national focus on this hotly disputed issue. But Congress continued to press human rights in American foreign policy beyond the desires, at times, of even the Carter adminstration. Chapter 7 also illustrates the limitations on the means available to Congress to implement human rights objectives.

The Panama Canal Treaties 3

The Senate's consideration of the Panama Canal treaties in 1977-1978 is more than a classic example of the Senate's constitutional role in the treaty-making process: it marks a watershed in American foreign policy. It also provides an illuminating case study of the Senate as an institution and of how individual senators can maneuver through the political minefields of a highly controversial issue and turn it to their advantage. Further, House action on the implementing legislation in 1979 illustrates the different views of the two bodies about how the treaty-making process ought to work; specifically, the episode demonstrates the determination of the House to become a more influential body in dealing with major foreign policy issues. The story began years before the treaties reached the Senate.

Background

Strategic is a word that is frequently misused to exaggerate the importance of an area, but it applies literally and forcefully to the 50-mile-wide Isthmus of Panama, which joins the North and South American continents. Panama has lived off its geography from the time the first European, Vasco Núñez de Balboa, crossed the isthmus in 1513. In the sixteenth century Spaniards used the isthmus to transship the gold and silver they took out of Peru and Bolivia. In the nineteenth century Americans used it as the quickest route to the California gold fields; American interests even built a railroad across it.

In the late nineteenth century a French company undertook to dig a canal across the isthmus, a project that ended in such dismal failure that the French began looking for a way to unload it and recoup at least some of their losses. The United States had been rather languidly interested in just such a project for a number of years, and this interest was now whetted not only by the French, but especially by the experience of the Spanish-American War in 1898—it had taken more than two months to move warships from the Pacific to the Atlantic around the tip of South America.

At this time Panama was a part of Colombia. When the Colombian senate, in August 1903, rejected a treaty giving the United States the right to build a canal across Panama, President Theodore Roosevelt and the French interests took matters into their own hands. The result was a revolution in Panama on November 3; on November 18 the Hay-Bunau-Varilla Treaty between the United States and Panama was concluded. With unprecedented speed the Senate approved the pact on February 23 by a vote of 66-14. The new treaty provided for the American construction of a canal. Significantly, the Panamanian negotiator of this treaty was not Panamanian at all, but the Frenchman Philippe Jean Bunau-Varilla, the agent of the French canal company! The French company received $40 million from the United States.

The new treaty was much more favorable to the United States than had been the treaty rejected by Colombia. It gave the United States both the control "in perpetuity" over a Canal Zone 10 miles wide and the authority to act "as if it were sovereign." The United States also got the right to use, occupy, and control any other lands or waters necessary or convenient for the construction and maintenance of the canal; the right of eminent domain in the cities of Panama and Colón and adjoining areas; and the right to intervene for the general maintenance and protection of the canal. What Panama got was $10 million plus annual payments of $250,000 that would begin in nine years. It was also given by the United States a guarantee of its independence, such as it was.[1] Roosevelt later bragged, "I took the canal zone."[2]

This set the stage for a clash of the national pride of both countries. For the United States the canal became a symbol of American achievement in making a centuries-old, seemingly impossible dream come true. The United States overcame every imaginable kind of obstacle. Americans were proud of the smooth functioning of the locks and gates; after more than three-quarters of a century the original engineering has not been improved on.

For Panamanians the canal—and more especially, the Canal Zone—became a symbol that Panama was something less than a whole country. The United States always recognized that the 1903 treaty left residual or titular sovereignty over the Zone in Panama. But since the United States had the right to act "as if it were sovereign"—even though it was not—this recognition had more importance as a legal theory than as a practical reality.

In response to Panamanian pressure, the United States renegotiated the 1903 treaty in 1936 and again in 1955. The annual payment was increased to reflect the devaluation of the dollar, and some concessions were made with respect to the Zone commissaries, U.S. exercise of eminent domain outside the Zone, and the right of intervention. But nothing fundamental was changed.

All this time the canal continued to operate smoothly and efficiently in the service of world commerce. It speeded the flow of supplies and the passage of the American navy through the two world wars, the war in Korea, and the war in Vietnam. It was taken for granted as fundamental to American national security. Most Americans saw no reason to change something that was working so well.

Confrontation

Thus the stage was set for confrontation, and it was in the nature of things that trouble would erupt over the symbolic issue of the flag.

One of Panama's objectives in the 1955 negotiations for revision of the 1903 treaty was that ships transiting the canal should fly both the Panamanian and the U.S. flags in recognition of the maritime tradition that ships fly the flag of the country through whose territorial waters they are passing. The United States refused this demand.

There was also Panamanian agitation, sometimes riotous, to fly the Panamanian flag in the Zone. This began to make an impression in the United States. Following particularly severe riots in Panama in November of 1959, President Eisenhower announced in a news conference in December, "We should have visual evidence that Panama does have titular sovereignty over the region." [3] Privately, he remarked that he had no objection to flying the Panamanian flag, but "I'll be goddamned if I'm going to do it with a gun at my head." [4]

At the same time, however, in the United States the hard-core resistance to any change was strengthened. On February 2, 1960, by a vote of 382-12, the House of Representatives passed a concurrent resolution declaring that "any variation in the traditional interpretation" of treaties with Panama, "with special reference to matters concerning territorial sovereignty, shall be made only pursuant to treaty"—that is, with a two-thirds vote in the Senate.[5] The resolution did not obtain the concurrence of the Senate and therefore never took effect. This signaled the executive branch that the Senate was less determined to maintain the status quo than the House and thus might be willing to give it room to maneuver.

Bit by bit, the executive branch made concessions, leading to a 1963 agreement that the Panamanian flag would be flown together with the American flag wherever the latter was flown on land in the Canal Zone by civilian authorities. This new policy was disliked by the American residents of the Zone. When it was ordered that neither flag should be flown at Balboa High School, the students took matters into their own hands on January 7, 1964, and raised the American flag. They repeated this the next day.

On the afternoon of the following day, January 9, a group of approximately 200 Panamanian students from the National Institute in Panama

City entered the Canal Zone with the intention of raising a Panamanian flag on the Balboa High School flagpole. They were confronted by at least twice as many American students. Some scuffling ensued, and the Panamanians withdrew. Within a few hours, riots involving thousands of Panamanians and directed against the Zone erupted in Panama City and across the isthmus in Colón, at the Atlantic terminus of the canal. By the time order was restored on January 13, 21 people had been killed and 120 injured.

On January 10, while the riots were at their height, Panama took the drastic step of breaking diplomatic relations with the United States; Panama made "complete revision" of the existing treaties a condition for resuming relations. After almost three months of tedious negotiations, both parties agreed "to seek the prompt elimination of the causes of conflict between the two countries, without limitations or preconditions of any kind" and to pursue the objective "of reaching a just and fair agreement which would be subject to the constitutional processes of each country." [6]

The Negotiations

There now began, with glacial speed, the tedious work of negotiation, which extended from the spring of 1964 to the summer of 1977. By 1967 the negotiators had reached agreement, subject to the approval of their governments, on a set of new treaties—one dealing with a new regime for the canal, one dealing with the possible construction of a sea-level canal in the indeterminate future, and one dealing with American defense base rights. The texts were leaked prematurely in Panama to the *Chicago Tribune;* the resulting hue and cry in both countries, but especially in Panama, was so great that the Panamanian government felt compelled to repudiate the work of its negotiators.

In Panama opponents of the draft treaties thought the United States had not made enough concessions; in the United States opponents thought it had made too many. The negotiations began again, with starker focus on the problem: to devise treaties that could be ratified in one country without being rejected in the other.

This proved to be an extremely difficult and time-consuming problem. Panamanian negotiators were subjected at home to intense pressures by nationalist elements, which opposed any concessions to American demands. For their part, American negotiators had to carry on, in effect, two sets of negotiations—one with their own government and one with Panama. The first set of negotiations arose out of the diversity of American bureaucratic interests in Panama. The State Department, responsible for relations between the United States and the Republic of Panama and sensitive to world opinion, tended to argue for a more flexible U.S. position. The U.S. Army, which operated the canal and governed the Zone, tended to reflect the views of the American residents of the Zone, views strongly in favor of maintaining the status quo. The Joint Chiefs of

Staff, charged with the responsibility of defending the canal and the Zone, were concerned principally with military base rights, with access, and with jurisdiction over American military personnel. Many of the delays in the negotiations were caused not only by the disarray of the Panamanians (who went through various changes of government during this period), but also by the time-consuming task of bringing the United States government itself to a unified position.

The Role of Congress. Each of the contending bureaucratic groups had its friends in Congress, generally corresponding to committee jurisdictions. The Senate Foreign Relations and House Foreign Affairs committees tended to be linked with the State Department, the Armed Services committees with the army and the Joint Chiefs of Staff, and the House Merchant Marine and Fisheries Committee (which, through a quirk in House rules, had jurisdiction over the canal and the Zone) with the Panama Canal Company and the Canal Zone government.

The Senate Foreign Relations Committee had the most direct interest because it would consider whatever treaty resulted. Some members of the committee privately advised the Johnson administration to begin the negotiations and to make some concessions. But generally the committee limited itself to keeping quietly informed while maintaining a low profile and leaving negotiations to the executive branch. The political instincts of its members told them that any treaty that made significant concessions would be unpopular.

During most of the period of the negotiations, the chairman of the House Merchant Marine and Fisheries Committee (Leonor K. Sullivan, D-Mo.) and the chairman of its subcommittee on the Panama Canal (John M. Murphy, D-N.Y.) were among the most vocal opponents of change. Mainly through hearings and reports, the committee sought to lay the groundwork for the argument that American property in the Canal Zone could be disposed of only through legislation approved by both houses, not through a treaty.

The basis for this argument lies in Article IV, Section 3 of the Constitution, which gives Congress the "Power to dispose of and make all needful Rules and Regulations respecting the Territory or other Property belonging to the United States." There are, however, a number of precedents whereby territory has been disposed of by treaty, and there is also a question of whether the Canal Zone, for which residual sovereignty remained in Panama, was ever American territory in the first place. The Department of Justice found a treaty to be a legal way to handle the matter. A number of members of Congress and the attorneys general of four states brought suit challenging the validity of the treaties under Article IV of the Constitution. All of these attempts failed in the Supreme Court.

The first legislative involvement by Congress in the negotiations came in 1975, when it appeared that they might be drawing to a conclusion. Rep. Gene Snyder of Kentucky, the ranking minority member of the

Panama Canal Subcommittee, offered an amendment to the fiscal year 1976 State Department appropriations bill to prohibit the use of funds for negotiating "the surrender or relinquishment of any United States rights in the Panama Canal Zone." It passed the House by a vote of 246-164.

The Senate dropped the amendment, and the conferees agreed to a compromise that "any new Panama Canal treaty or agreement must protect the vital interests of the United States in the operation, maintenance, property and defense of the Panama Canal." In a startling demonstration of antitreaty sentiment, the House rejected this compromise by a 197-203 vote.

The second conference added a reference to the protection of "vital interests . . . in the Canal Zone," and the House approved this by a shaky vote of 212-201.[7] Similar efforts by opponents of the still-prospective treaties were made in 1976 and 1977, but these failed by larger margins.

The Treaties. Finally, in the summer of 1977, negotiations ended. The treaties were signed by President Carter and Brig. Gen. Omar Torrijos Herrera on September 7 in an unprecedented ceremony attended by representatives of 26 Western Hemisphere nations, including the presidents or prime ministers of 17.

The two treaties in a single document were formally transmitted to the Senate September 16. One was called simply the Panama Canal Treaty. The other was called, more awkwardly, the Treaty Concerning the Permanent Neutrality and Operation of the Panama Canal (hereafter referred to as the Neutrality Treaty).

The Panama Canal Treaty terminated and superseded the treaty of 1903 and subsequent agreements. Thereby at one stroke it abolished the Canal Zone. The United States retained the right to manage, operate, and maintain the canal and to provide for the movement of ships. This was to be done, however, not through the old Panama Canal Company, but through a new agency, the Panama Canal Commission, which was to have a board of nine members, four of whom would be Panamanians. After December 31, 1999, total control of the canal would pass to Panama.

Until that date the United States retained military base rights, as well as the primary responsibility for defense of the canal for the duration of the treaty. Panama was given a fixed payment of $10 million a year, plus 30 cents for each ton of shipping transiting the canal, plus an additional sum of up to $10 million a year if there was a surplus of operating revenues over expenditures. In addition, there were numerous administrative provisions.

The Neutrality Treaty established a permanent regime of neutrality for the canal "in order that both in time of peace and in time of war [the canal] shall remain secure and open to peaceful transit by the vessels of all nations on terms of entire equality, so that there will be no discrimination against any nation, or its citizens or subjects, concerning the conditions or charges of transit, or for any other reason." The same regime of neutrality was to apply to any other canal that might be built in Panama. After termination of the Panama Canal Treaty in 1999, no nation other than Panama could operate the canal or maintain military installations in Panamanian territory. Finally, the warships of the United States and Panama were to be entitled to transit the canal "expeditiously." [8]

Advice and Consent of the Senate

With the treaties now formally before the Senate, the long preliminaries were over at last and the political process of Senate action could begin. The administration and the Democratic leadership in the Senate had already started to lay the groundwork. In April the Senate Foreign Relations Committee had been informed that a breakthrough in the negotiations was imminent. The focus of executive-Senate contacts then shifted from the committee to the office of Majority Leader Robert C. Byrd, D-W.Va. During the summer Byrd arranged a series of quiet meetings with senators of differing viewpoints. These informal meetings marked a departure from what had been the customary leadership of Foreign Relations. Byrd was more assertive of his prerogatives as majority leader than had been any of his recent predecessors, with the exception of Sen. Lyndon B. Johnson. The Foreign Relations Committee was perceived to be less influential than it once had been. And, in any event, the White House and Byrd were not worried about how members of Foreign Relations would vote; they were worried about other senators.

The arithmetic was predetermined by the constitutional requirement that the treaties had to be approved by two-thirds of the senators present and voting. This meant that if all 100 senators voted (which they, in fact, did), supporters of the treaties needed 67 votes and opponents needed only 34. In November a United Press International (UPI) poll showed 37 senators uncommitted, 36 either for or leaning toward the treaties, and 27 either against or leaning away from. The number shown uncommitted was almost surely exaggerated. Most senators who said they were undecided probably had a pretty good idea of how they would vote but did not want to say so publicly at too early a stage.

A more realistic way of measuring senatorial opinion at this point would have been as follows:

Those who passionately believed that the treaties were in the best interests of the United States and that rejecting them would be calamitous for the American position in the world

Those who were predisposed to support the president, but not at the risk of their own political careers

Those who did not care very much one way or the other and who approached the issue looking for what they could get out of it in help in the Senate or support from the administration on some other issue that they did care about

Those who did not like the treaties very much but who were reluctant to oppose the president

Those who passionately believed that the treaties were bad for the
United States and would lead to disaster

Within each of the groups except those at the extremes, there were, of
course, a multitude of shadings and gradations. Some senators voted
solely on the basis of their mail and the polls. Although Sen. Edward
Zorinsky, D-Neb., personally favored the treaties, his constituents opposed them; in the end Zorinsky opposed them, too. It is probably safe to
say that most senators would have been grateful if they had not had to
face the issue at all.

The competing strategies of the contending forces were dictated by
these feelings and were essentially mirror images of each other. Supporters of the treaties had to make it politically safe for senators to vote yes,
or failing this, at least to limit the political damage as much as possible.
Opponents had to make the risk of voting yes politically unacceptable.

Each side pursued its strategy at several levels simultaneously. At
one level there was the battle for public opinion. At another there were
maneuvers to change the treaties. The objective of the opponents was
simple: to change the treaties so much that even if they were approved by
the Senate, they would be rejected by Panama. The objective of the
supporters was more subtle: to reap the political benefit of something
that could be presented as an improvement in the treaties without
changing them so fundamentally as to lead to their rejection by Panama.
At yet a third level, there was old-fashioned logrolling and vote trading
among senators and between senators and the White House. The question of the merits of the treaties themselves was the final debating point.

At this last level, the proponents of the treaties had to demonstrate
to the satisfaction of reasonable but skeptical people that the treaties at a
minimum protected, and at a maximum advanced, the national interests
of the United States. The opponents had only to create doubts that this
was true. If they could, in addition, demonstrate that the treaties raised
the possibility of a threat to those interests, that was so much the better.

These strategies required time to work themselves out. The Foreign
Relations Committee held 16 days of hearings on the treaties in September and October of 1977 and January of 1978. The published record
comprises four volumes, which total 2,423 pages. The committee heard
more than 90 witnesses on all sides of the issue, perhaps as impressive an
array as has ever been assembled for a congressional hearing. They
included not only the negotiators of the treaties, but also the secretaries
of state, defense, and transportation; the attorney general; the chairman
of the Joint Chiefs of Staff; and distinguished representatives of acade-
mia, business, and labor. Former secretaries of state Dean Rusk and
Henry Kissinger testified, as did two former chairmen of the Joint Chiefs
of Staff, Admiral Thomas Moorer and General Maxwell Taylor. During
December and January, 10 of the 16 members of the committee also

visited Panama. Every aspect of the treaties was examined in exhaustive, repetitive detail. This was the indispensable foundation for the forthcoming Senate debate. After its hearings the Foreign Relations Committee spent three days discussing the treaties, and on January 30 the committee ordered them reported favorably by a vote of 14-1. The dissenter was Sen. Robert P. Griffin, R-Mich. He thought the treaties should be returned to the president for renegotiation.

Senate debate began February 6 and continued, to the virtual exclusion of all other business, until April 18—the longest Senate debate on a treaty since the Treaty of Versailles, which ended World War I. The Senate gave its advice and consent to ratification of the Neutrality Treaty on March 16 by a vote of 68-32. The Panama Canal Treaty was approved April 18 by an identical vote. Democrats voted for the treaties 52-10; Republicans voted against them 16-22. Leading the opposition were James B. Allen, D-Ala., and Paul D. Laxalt, R-Nev. The leaders of the protreaty forces, besides Majority Leader Byrd and Minority Leader Howard H. Baker, Jr., R-Tenn., were members of the Senate Foreign Relations Committee Frank Church, D-Idaho (later to become chairman), and freshman Paul Sarbanes, D-Md.

The Battle for Public Opinion

Despite the outcry from conservative and veterans groups following the disclosure of the 1967 draft treaties, many senators were astonished by the depth of the response Ronald Reagan evoked in campaigning against concessions to Panama in 1976. The objective of opponents of the treaties was to convert this response into massive antitreaty mail to the Senate. Hundreds of thousands of letters and postcards poured in, at one point in ratios as great as 300-1 against the treaties. Some of them were nasty. One received by Sen. Thomas J. McIntyre, D-N.H., said the writer and 200 million other Americans hoped that McIntyre and all the rest would be assassinated if the treaties were ratified.[9]

The opposition strategy was based on a principle of congressional political behavior: one gets elected not so much by pleasing people as by not offending them. This principle has become more important with the growth of single-issue politics—that is, with the growing numbers of people who judge candidates not on their overall record or platform but on their stand with respect to a single issue, such as abortion or gun control. The Conservative Caucus, one of the groups that were most active in opposition to the treaty, had a program with the goal of getting pledges from 10,000 voters in each state that they would "never vote for any person who votes for the treaties."

Although the proponents, whose efforts were coordinated in the White House, did not neglect the public at large, their campaign was directed specifically to individuals who could mold public opinion. To counter the perception of the treaties as a sellout or a giveaway, the White House secured endorsements from broadly representative, respected community or national leaders whose prestige, it was hoped, would make it respectable to support the treaties. To this end, a series of intimate briefings was organized to take place in the White House itself, with appearances by the president, his national security adviser Zbigniew Brzezinski, the secretary of state, the secretary of defense, and one or more members of the Joint Chiefs of Staff. Candidates for invitations to these meetings were frequently suggested by senators who wanted to vote for the treaties and needed outside help in convincing important constituents.

Twenty-four senators who voted on the treaties sought reelection in 1978. Of those who voted for the treaties, 7 were reelected and 8 defeated. Of those who voted against the treaties, 8 were reelected and 1 was defeated. There is no way to determine with any precision the weight that should be assigned to the controversy over the treaties in assessing these results; but it seems safe to say that the result of a Senate vote on the treaties might well have been different in 1979 than in 1978.

There was a lingering effect even in the election of 1980. In that year 28 senators who had voted on the treaties ran for reelection. Of those who voted for the treaties, 11 were reelected and 12 were defeated. Of those who voted against the treaties, 5 were reelected and none was defeated. Nineteen eighty was, of course, an unusual political year in which there was generally a marked conservative swing, and in most of these senatorial races several issues were at work. But votes for the treaties figured prominently in at least two Senate campaigns—in Florida, where Richard Stone lost in the Democratic primary, and in Idaho, where Frank Church lost in the general election. President Carter also thought the treaties contributed to his defeat.[10]

By 1982 it was no longer possible to see a political effect of the votes on the treaties. In that year 28 senators who voted on the treaties sought reelection. Of those who voted for the treaties, 18 were reelected and 1 was defeated. Of those who voted against, 8 were reelected and 1 was defeated.

Changing the Treaties

The administration's effort to bring public opinion around was a necessary, but not a sufficient, condition for Senate approval of the treaties. It was also necessary that senators be in a position to take credit for improving the treaties in one way or another.

Senators by and large react negatively when confronted with a take-it-or-leave-it proposition, and changing the treaties was a way to avoid looking like a rubber stamp for the president. It was also a way to have something with a senator's name on it written into the treaties. Not only was this important to senatorial egos; it also tended to make a senator view the treaties (with his or her handiwork in them) more sympathetically. Furthermore, proposals to change the treaties gave the leadership a potent weapon. It is always easier for a senator to get an amendment adopted if it is accepted by the leadership, and in many cases the leadership decides whether or not to accept an amendment on the basis of how the senator will vote on final passage. Finally, changing the treaties contributed—or so senators thought—to a public perception that although the treaties might have been defective as they had been negotiated, the Senate had changed them to remedy those defects and protect the national interest. This provided an opportunity for senators to begin by criticizing the treaties and to end by supporting them.

The amendment process is one of the ways the Senate skirts an issue rather than meeting it head on; it is one way of defusing single issue politics. In this case, it enabled a senator to avoid coming out foursquare for the treaties as negotiated. The senator might win this argument on the basis of logic and the facts, but not in political terms. The alternative was to argue, not in favor of the treaties as signed, but in favor of the treaties as they had been changed by the Senate, preferably by adoption of an amendment or reservation proposed by the senator making the argument.

The real issue in the Senate became the degree of change. Supporters of the treaties had to limit the changes to what would be acceptable to Panama; opponents had to push them beyond those limits. The lengths to which both sides went in pursuing these tactics are to be seen in the numbers of changes proposed. In all, senators offered 145 amendments, 26 reservations, 18 understandings, and 3 declarations—a grand total of 192 changes of one kind or another. Some of these were incorporated in the resolutions of ratification as *conditions*—a new terminology for Senate action on treaties, perhaps important to somebody semantically, but not legally. (The distinctions among amendments, reservations, understandings, declarations, and conditions are murky at best, as explained in Chapter 1.)

A large number of the proposed changes duplicated in some way or superseded others. In the course of the Senate debate, 88 were actually voted on. All the approved changes were acceptable to the leadership. The most important concerned the neutrality and defense of the canal and transit rights for the U.S. Navy.

Neutrality and Expeditious Transit. The provision regarding neutrality of the canal, Secretary of State Cyrus R. Vance told the Foreign Relations Committee, "means that there is no limit under the treaty on the freedom of the United States to assure permanently the canal's neutrality." And in response to a question from Sen. Clifford P. Case, R-N.J., he was even more specific: "I think our right [to intervene] is clear, and there can be no question about it." [11]

Panamanians, of course, had a different view. Even before the treaties had been signed, chief negotiator Rómulo Escobar Betancourt said, "We are not giving the United States a right of intervention. What we are giving is an assurance that the Canal will be permanently neutral." [12]

The matter was enlivened a bit more when Sen. Robert Dole, R-Kan., made public a confidential telegram from the American Embassy in Panama to the State Department reporting a conversation with negotiator Carlos López Guevara in which López had told an Embassy officer, "Panama cannot agree to the right of the U.S. to intervene." [13]

Of course, no Latin American government can agree to such a right and expect to survive. But opponents of the treaties now had an issue that cast doubt on the right of the United States to defend the canal's neutrality in the indefinite future. From this, it did not take much imagination to conjure up a situation in which the canal could conceivably be seized by forces hostile to the United States and then closed to American shipping.

Vance said that the right of U.S. and Panamanian naval vessels to "transit the Canal expeditiously," meant "our ships can go to the head of the line." Escobar and López said that the U.S. Navy would not be given "preferential rights" and that such language had been proposed and rejected during the negotiations. Although it seemed reasonable to suppose that the right to transit the canal expeditiously meant the right to do so without waiting in line, there was enough confusion about the matter to allow for the specter of the American navy waiting on one side of Panama while the world was in flames on the other side.

In a letter to the Senate Foreign Relations Committee on October 5, the State Department sought to deal with the problem of ensuring the canal's neutrality, but it succeeded only in muddying the waters further:

> Panama and the United States each will have the right to take any appropriate measures to defend the Canal against any threat to the regime of neutrality established in the Treaty.
> The Treaty does not give the United States any right to intervene in the internal affairs of Panama, nor has it been our intention to seek or to exercise such a right. [14]

The State Department did not say the United States had the right to take "any measure"—only "any appropriate measures." Nor did the department deal with what would happen if a threat to the canal arose from an internal situation in Panama.

The uproar over the ambiguities concerning the canal's neutrality and the transit of the U.S. Navy alarmed both governments and appeared to be a genuine threat to the treaties in the Senate. General Torrijos at this time was in Europe on a tour (which also included Israel) designed to drum up international support for the treaties. On his way home he stopped for a day in Washington to see President Carter. From this meeting there emerged a "statement of understanding," which said, with respect to neutrality:

> The correct interpretation of this principle is that each of the two countries shall, in accordance with their respective constitutional processes, defend the Canal against any threat to the regime of neutrality, and consequently shall have the right to act against any aggression or

threat directed against the Canal or against the peaceful transit of vessels through the Canal.

This does not mean, nor shall it be interpreted as, a right of intervention of the United States in the internal affairs of Panama. Any United States action will be directed at insuring that the Canal will remain open, secure and accessible, and it shall never be directed against the territorial integrity or political independence of Panama.

With respect to the passage of American and Panamanian warships, the statement of understanding asserted:

> This is intended, and it shall so be interpreted, to assure the transit of such vessels through the Canal as quickly as possible, without any impediment, with expedited treatment, and in the case of need or emergency, to go to the head of the line of vessels in order to transit the Canal rapidly.[15]

This statement of understanding calmed the uproar, but it did not wholly eliminate the problem, which was enmeshed in the larger strategies of the contending forces in the Senate. Nobody understood the delicacy of the situation better or maneuvered more skillfully to win passage of the treaties than Senate Minority Leader Howard Baker. From the beginning of Senate consideration of the treaties, Baker kept his own counsel and studiously presented an open mind to the public. At the opening of hearings in September, Baker announced, "For the time being I have decided not to decide what I think about the treaties." [16]

On a tour of Latin America in January, Baker spent five days in Panama. It is indicative of the importance the White House attached to Baker's trip that he was accompanied by Frank Moore, the president's chief congressional liaison officer. While in Panama, Baker and his group, which also included Sen. Jake Garn, R-Utah, and Sen. John H. Chafee, R-R.I., spent one day and part of another with General Torrijos. In the course of these conversations, Baker negotiated with Torrijos some changes in the treaties. As the group's report explains:

> The delegation advised General Torrijos that the treaties as submitted to the Senate had no chance of obtaining the Senate's consent to ratification. He was further advised that there might be enough flexibility in the Senate to secure consent to ratification were guarantees of United States rights more clearly spelled out in the treaties by way of amendment. In particular, reference was made to the need to incorporate the language of the Statement of Understanding previously issued by General Torrijos and President Carter into the text of the treaties with regard to the United States' right to defend the Canal after the year 2000 and to secure priority passage in time of emergency. Torrijos indicated that he was open-minded with regard to modification of the treaties and that it was his belief that no additional plebiscite would be necessary under the Panamanian Constitution if modifications of the treaties were limited to the incorporation of the Statement of Understanding, as that statement had been fully explained to the Panamanian people prior to their October plebiscite.[17]

Amendments were drafted to incorporate in the treaties the text of the statement of understanding. With Byrd as the principal sponsor and Baker as the driving force, the Senate adopted the provision on neutrality by a vote of 84-5 and the provision on expeditious transit by a vote of 85-3. If these amendments did not set at rest all doubts, they at least went far enough to give a large measure of protection to senators voting for the treaties.

Pursuing the strategy of giving senators the maximum opportunity to associate themselves with changes in the treaties, within limits acceptable to Panama, Byrd urged the Foreign Relations Committee not to incorporate changes of its own but rather only to recommend changes to the Senate. This would give senators a way to cosponsor amendments in the Senate and thereby have their names identified with specific changes. It was also a sharp departure from the usual practice, in which a Senate committee actually makes the changes it desires and sends a finished product to the Senate. This finished product is, of course, subject to amendment; but if a senator agrees with the changes made by a committee, the only way to identify himself or herself with them is by making a speech. The senator cannot get into the record by name as having been one of those suggesting the change. Some members of the Foreign Relations Committee, including its chairman, John Sparkman of Alabama, did not like Byrd's suggested procedure very much. Nevertheless, in the interests of advancing the treaties, they cooperated.

Defense of the Canal.   On March 15 freshman Sen. Dennis DeConcini, D-Ariz., met with President Carter and received his support for an amendment (which became a condition) allowing the United States "to use military force in Panama" or to take such other steps as deemed necessary to keep the canal open after the year 2000.[18] With administration support, this was adopted in the Senate with respect to the Neutrality Treaty on March 16 by a vote of 75-23.

The Panamanians, as should have been foreseen, took strong exception. With a vote nearing on the second treaty, this development threw the administration and the Senate leadership into consternation. There was nothing to be done about the Neutrality Treaty; the Senate had already completed action. Unless a way was found to modify this action in the Panama Canal Treaty, however, the clear likelihood existed that the whole painstakingly put together package would be rejected by Panama. But if the condition were modified so much as to cause the defection of DeConcini on the second vote, the package might well be defeated in the Senate.

Frantic negotiations ensued within the Senate, between the Senate and the administration, between the Senate and the Panamanians, and between the administration and the Panamanians. William D. Rogers, a Washington lawyer and former assistant secretary of state for inter-American affairs, was brought in as an unofficial catalyst and go-between.

(Rogers is not to be confused with William P. Rogers, the former secretary of state and also a Washington lawyer.)

Well known for his expertise with respect to both Latin America and the ways of Washington, Rogers was approached by the Panamanian government to represent it in the affair in an attorney-client relationship. He consulted the State Department, which advocated his involvement, and the Justice Department, which warned of a possible conflict of interest stemming from his previous service as assistant secretary. The problem was resolved by Rogers using only his good offices—an arrangement, as he ruefully pointed out, that meant he could not be paid. The condition he laid down was accepted by both governments: he would be the sole channel of communication between them. This meant not only that he could be sure of being fully informed, but also that he would be in a position to advise each government with respect to the substance of the communications. It was a position he could not have been in if he had been representing the government of Panama as an attorney. It was also, he said later, a condition he would not have accepted if it had been proposed by an outside party while he was in the State Department.

In the end—on Sunday morning, April 16, preceding the final Senate vote on Tuesday the 18th—the matter was resolved in a meeting in Frank Church's Capitol hideaway office among Church, Byrd, Paul S. Sarbanes (chairman of the Foreign Relations Committee's Latin American subcommittee), Rogers, Panamanian ambassador to the United States Gabriel Lewis, and Deputy Secretary of State Warren Christopher.

The compromise text was in the form of a new condition omitting the reference to the use of force and stating that any action the United States might take to keep the canal open "shall not have as its purpose nor be interpreted as a right of intervention" in Panama nor of "interference with its political independence or sovereign integrity." [19]

Ambassador Lewis checked this new condition with his government. Panama approved it later that day; Senator DeConcini approved it the following day. The Senate leadership had successfully extricated itself from the dilemma brought about by Carter's agreement to the DeConcini amendment in the first place. This agreement is explicable only in terms of the president's anxiety to nail down at any price an additional vote for the treaty. He got the additional vote, but he almost lost the treaty.

The effort to vitiate the effect of the DeConcini amendment without appearing to do so brought out another aspect of the Senate's consideration of the Panama treaties, one that was unprecedented in the long history of the Senate's role in the treaty-making process. This was the degree of involvement of senators in direct negotiations with foreign officials about a treaty after it had been negotiated and signed by the executive branch.

During the period between the signing of the treaties in September and the opening of Senate debate in February, almost half the Senate visited Panama and talked to General Torrijos and other Panamanian officials. For most of these senators it was a fact-finding and orientation trip. Some went because they were genuinely interested in obtaining on-the-scene impressions, some because they felt their political future required it. But some of them—Senator Baker, for example—discussed with Torrijos and others prospective amendments to the treaties, at least in general terms. This process culminated in the frantic negotiations over the DeConcini amendment in which the Panamanian ambassador himself took part.

With respect to a wide range of matters, senators have always had a variety of social and other informal contacts with the Washington diplomatic corps and with foreign officials. Frequently senators have been members of American delegations to international meetings. But the extent to which senators became directly involved with Panamanian officials raised new questions for foreign governments: Are they dealing with one United States government or with two—or with even more, considering that the Senate rarely takes a unified approach? In making a treaty, do they have to go through a process of multiple negotiations—one with the executive branch and a second (or third or fourth) with the Senate? And if it is a multiple negotiating process, how much reliance can foreigners put on the first stage? The questions recurred in connection with the SALT II agreement with the Soviet Union.

Quid Pro Quos: The Politics of the Senate

As the time for the final vote on the first treaty approached, the administration increased its pressure on uncommitted senators—pressure that was by no means wholly unwelcome and that no doubt explained why some senators had remained uncommitted as long as they did. It gave them more bargaining power with the administration.

After the Democratic senators from Georgia, Herman Talmadge and Sam Nunn, announced their support on March 14, Washington abounded with so many reports of quid pro quos that Talmadge felt compelled to deny that the administration had agreed to support his farm bill. The administration did, however, support a Nunn-Talmadge reservation the same day. The Georgia senators started out wanting a reservation that gave the United States the right to keep military forces in Panama beyond the expiration of the Panama Canal Treaty in 1999, arguing that this might be necessary to defend the canal under the permanent Neutrality Treaty. They ended up accepting one that merely stated the obvious—that nothing in the Neutrality Treaty precluded the United States and Panama from reaching a further agreement or arrangement to station American forces in Panama.

Sen. Richard S. Schweiker, R-Pa. (who voted against the treaties), remarked, "If you want a bridge or road or other federal project, it [being uncommitted] might help, but I don't think you should decide this issue on what you can get for your state." And Douglas J. Bennet, the assistant secretary of state for congressional relations, declared, "I don't know of a single vote which has been decided by non-germane considerations." [20]

Perhaps not, but there are plenty of cynics around the Senate office buildings who were convinced—at least until the Reagan administration's budget-cutting spree—that a part of the price of the Panama Canal treaties would still be tucked away in the federal budget (probably under public works) in the fiscal year 1983. Some of these cynics were senators who announced their support of the treaties early, thereby, as they saw it, losing bargaining power with the president.

Whether these kinds of explicit quid pro quos existed or not, there were many other, more subtle ones, such as seeing to it that senators were kept informed about administrative actions affecting their states. Failure to do this on the part of the Carter administration was a source of great irritation to some senators, particularly those who had no enthusiasm for the treaties anyway and felt they were running a political risk in voting for them. "They keep expecting us to fall on our swords," said Sen. Jim R. Sasser, D-Tenn., "but there's been very little reciprocity." [21]

In other cases, the administration cooperated with senators' efforts to protect their political flanks in connection with policies related indirectly (if at all) to Panama. In response to a complaint by Sen. Richard Stone, D-Fla., about "retreat in our hemisphere," the president promised to "oppose any efforts, direct or indirect, by the Soviet Union to establish military bases" in the hemisphere and to "maintain our bases in the Caribbean necessary to the defense of the Panama Canal and the security of the United States." Given the careful qualifications in this statement, it is difficult to imagine any president doing anything else, but Stone seized on it as an important policy clarification that would permit him to vote for the treaty. [22]

Two cracks appeared in the tenuous protreaty coalition in the days before the final vote. They were due in no small part to the administration's own desperation. As senators saw, or thought they saw, increasing concessions being made to those who held out the longest, some who had already committed themselves began to waver, thereby seeking to reestablish their bargaining power.

On April 13 Sen. James Abourezk, D-S.D., linked his support of the treaty to the administration's energy policy. In October of 1977 Abourezk, a quixotic liberal, had led an unsuccessful Senate filibuster against the deregulation of natural gas prices. He lost in the Senate, but antideregulation forces had won in the House, and the matter had to be resolved in a conference committee that had been deadlocked for months. In an effort to find a way out of the impasse, some of the conferees had been holding private meetings; Abourezk took these meetings as a violation of the spirit, if not the letter, of a recent requirement that conference committee meetings be held in public. Now he threatened to withhold his support of the treaty if these private meetings continued and if the president agreed to the deregulation of natural gas. Under pressure from his fellow liberals in the Senate, Abourezk finally relented. The last senator to speak before the final vote, he salvaged what he could by announcing he had learned from the White House that the administration intended "to try to encourage an open democratic process" in the energy conference.

On April 14, the day after Abourezk had linked the treaty to energy policy, Sen. S. I. Hayakawa, R-Calif., linked it to the American position in the world generally. This is what treaty supporters had been doing all along. They argued that rejection of the treaty would damage America's world position, but Hayakawa put a new twist on the matter. During his campaign for the Senate in 1976 Hayakawa said that he favored keeping the canal, because "we stole it fair and square"—one of the year's memorable quotations. Hayakawa voted for the Neutrality Treaty in March, but in April he announced he was reconsidering his support. The president's decision not to build the neutron bomb and the U.S. negotiating position on SALT, among other things, reinforced the objection to the treaties as "a revelation of American weakness." [23]

The freshman senator's change of heart won him a private meeting with the president and a chance to issue immediately after the final vote a previously prepared press release, in which he stated that Carter had offered to meet with him regularly to discuss important foreign policy and defense issues before he made final decisions on them.

Implementing Legislation

Legislation was now required to implement the treaties. Supposedly, this involved no more than housekeeping details—providing for the administration of the new Panama Canal Commission, setting tolls, paying claims, adjusting laws pertaining to employees and courts in the Canal Zone, and generally disentangling the United States after 75 years of acting "as if it were sovereign." But carrying out these actions involved the House in the treaty process; opposition to the treaties had always been stronger there than in the Senate.

Action in the House

Jurisdiction over the implementing legislation in the House was shared by four committees: Foreign Affairs, Merchant Marine and Fisheries, Post Office and Civil Service, and Judiciary. Primary jurisdiction belonged to Merchant Marine and Fisheries, whose chairman, Rep. John M. Murphy of New York, had long been a vocal and adamant opponent of a new treaty relationship with Panama. The adminstration wanted the implementing legislation to be flexible and to operate automatically; Murphy's inclination was to require further congressional consideration of successive steps.

The administration wanted the Canal Commission to be a government corporation (like the old Panama Canal Company), which would pay its expenses out of the tolls it collected. Representative Murphy wanted it to be a government agency, with tolls deposited in the treasury and expenses paid out of appropriations, so that an annual opportunity would exist to fight over the treaty-mandated payments to Panama.

The administration wanted property transferred to Panama automatically, as provided in the treaties; Murphy wanted each transfer subject to congressional approval—another opportunity for obstruction.

In determining whether canal revenues were sufficient to permit the $10 million annual payment to Panama provided by the treaty in years of surplus, the administration wanted to count only the normal expenses of operating and maintaining the canal. Murphy wanted to include interest on the American investment in the Panama Canal Company, with the result that Panama probably would not get the money.

In April 1979 the House Merchant Marine and Fisheries Committee reported a bill that generally reflected Murphy's views. Bad as it was from the administration's point of view, there arose an even worse alternative in a bill sponsored by Rep. George Hansen, R-Idaho. Hansen wanted to require that Panama pay the costs of implementing the treaties; in addition, the United States would be reimbursed for the entire net investment cost of construction of the canal. He estimated the total of these charges at $4 to $5 billion. Hansen's bill picked up 180 cosponsors, much to the administration's dismay.

Ironically, the administration abandoned its own bill and settled on the Murphy bill as its chosen instrument in the House. This was a little like a chicken seeking refuge in a fox's den to escape a lion.

On May 17 the House agreed to consider the legislation by the narrow margin of 200-198. This so alarmed the House leadership that it postponed further votes until a campaign could be mounted to solidify the administration's position. In the meantime, House opponents of the treaties took advantage of unrelated events in Central America and the Caribbean. The civil war in Nicaragua in July led to the downfall of President Anastasio Somoza, thereby ending a family dynasty of more than 40 years over two generations. Representative Murphy had gone to school with Somoza and had maintained a close personal friendship with him over the years.

Two weeks before the House voted on the implementing legislation, the Panama Canal Subcommittee of Murphy's Merchant Marine and Fisheries Committee held hearings on allegations of Panamanian gun smuggling to Somoza's opponents. Lt. Gen. Gordon Sumner, who had resigned in May as chairman of the Inter-American Defense Board because of his differences with the Carter administration over Central American policy, charged that Torrijos was under the influence of "Communists-Marxists" and that Panama was "an unreliable and indeed dangerous partner." [24] Witnesses included Luis Pallais, the vice president of the Nicaraguan congress. (It is exceedingly rare for a congressional committee to take formal testimony from a foreign official. Historically, this has been considered poor diplomatic practice, because it impinges on the separation of powers: only the executive branch is supposed to have *formal* communications with foreign governments. It also means that

Congress opens itself to demands to be heard from contending foreign political factions, and this takes it down the slippery slope of intervention in foreign politics.)

The House took its crucial votes on June 20 and 21. On the first day, Hansen offered the gist of his bill as an amendment to the Murphy bill. Murphy countered with a substitute amendment, which for practical purposes restated the provisions of his bill as reported by the Merchant Marine and Fisheries Committee. The Murphy substitute prevailed by a vote of 220-200. The next day a motion to recommit the bill, with instructions to include the Hansen amendment, was rejected by the even closer vote of 210-216; then the bill was passed 224-202.

Action in the Senate

After biting the bullet and passing the treaties in 1978, the Senate approached the implementing legislation with all the enthusiasm of a man playing Russian roulette for the second time. In contrast to the House, where four committees shared jurisdiction, in the Senate the problem was all dumped into the lap of the Armed Services Committee. This came as a vast relief to the Foreign Relations Committee, which had borne the brunt of the battle the year before and whose new chairman, Frank Church, was threatened with conservative opposition in the 1980 election in Idaho, coincidentally the home state of Representative Hansen also.

In the Senate Armed Services Committee, 9 of the 10 Democratic members exercised the prerogatives of seniority to avoid handling the bill, leaving that task to the most junior member, Carl Levin of Michigan. (Levin was the only senatorial candidate in 1978 to defeat an incumbent who had voted against the treaties.) Hearings were held by the committee the week after the House passed its bill, and on July 17 the bill was ordered reported by a favorable vote of 9-8. The committee accepted the administration's proposal to make the Canal Commission a government corporation; it rejected House provisions that called for putting the commission under the Defense Department, setting conditions on the $10 million annual contingency payment to Panama, giving the U.S. military control of the canal in wartime, and requiring congressional approval of property transfers. The committee report called the provisions of the House bill "inconsistent with the treaty." [25] President Aristides Royo of Panama also complained that the House bill would violate the treaty.

On July 26, by a 64-30 vote, the Senate passed the bill in substantially the form recommended by the Armed Services Committee after rejecting several amendments that would have brought the bill closer to the House version.

The Conference Report

Adjusting the differences between House and Senate versions in conference committee was not easy. In agreeing to send the bill to conference, the House had voted 308-98 to instruct its conferees to insist on the House provisions relating to the Canal Commission, transfers of property, conditions on the payments to Panama, and Defense Department control. The conferees perforce settled on an agreement that generally followed the House bill with only minor changes. This still did not satisfy the hard-core opponents in the House, who used the additional argument of the presumed threat posed by the newly discovered presence of a Soviet combat brigade in Cuba. On September 20 the House rejected the conference report by 192-203. (The Senate had passed it a few hours earlier by 60-35.)

Now, with time growing short, the exercise of trying to reach House-Senate agreement had to be repeated. New conferees were appointed, and on September 24 they reached a new agreement. It contained a few new concessions to the House, mainly in the form of nonbinding language in the statement by the conferees. This provided that the president could put the canal under military control if foreign combat troops deemed to be a threat to the canal were stationed in Panama. The second conference report was agreed to in the Senate 63-32 on September 26; the House approved it the following day by a vote of 232-188. One of the main arguments used in the House was that no matter what happened to the implementing legislation, the treaties were going into effect October 1. In voting to approve the legislation, the House avoided taking the extreme position of the opponents to make implementation as difficult as possible. But it gave the opponents many other days in court.

As it turned out, neither side had the stomach to reopen the debate. Although the implementing legislation provided for annual authorizations of the appropriations for the Canal Commission, in none of the next three years did Congress pass an authorization bill; it provided the necessary appropriations, without benefit of authorization, in the regular Department of Transportation appropriations bill. Neither side wished to go through another major debate. Ronald Reagan had made the treaty negotiations an issue in his campaign for the presidency in 1976 (as he said in 1978, "We built it. We paid for it. It's ours, and we are going to keep it.") But he accepted the fait accompli when he reached the White House in 1981. Representative Murphy was defeated in 1980, a victim of the Abscam bribery scandal. His successor as chairman of the Panama Canal Subcommittee was Rep. Carroll Hubbard, Jr., D-Ky., who had also strongly opposed the treaties in 1978-1979. By 1982, however, Hubbard was calling the treaties successful.

In fact, the canal continued to operate smoothly under the new regime. Further, with the canal issue settled, U.S.-Panamanian relations greatly improved. And although a few years is too short a time to be confident of long-term political trends, Panama—despite its turbulent history—in the mid-1980s presented a picture of stability. This was especially noteworthy in contrast to most of its neighbors in Central America.

Postscript

As noted earlier, the administration's posture throughout this case was one of making steady, incremental concessions, not only with respect to the substantive provisions of the treaties and the implementing legislation, but also with respect to unrelated matters of political importance to individual members of Congress. One of the last victims of this process might have been the snail darter, the small fish threatened with extinction by construction of the Tellico Dam in Tennessee. Two nights before the House vote on the second conference report on Panama, Carter signed the energy and water appropriations bill for fiscal 1980, which contained a provision, opposed by the administration, ordering completion of the dam. Carter had vetoed a bill with a similar provision the year before and had been sustained. Now, he said, "I believe that avoiding a divisive veto battle will help focus congressional efforts on priority concerns." [26] One of these priority concerns was reported to be the Panama implementing legislation and the desire to avoid retaliation by representatives who favored the dam. Even this story had a happy ending. By February 1983 Fish and Wildlife Service biologists had found populations of the snail darter in six tributaries of the Tennessee River, and the Interior Department changed its status from endangered to threatened.

As a case study illustrating the new assertiveness of Congress in the foreign policy field, the Panama Canal treaties call attention to several significant tendencies. First, they highlight the growing decentralization of the House and Senate and of Congress collectively. As we have seen, several influential congressional committees played leading roles in the processes of ratifying the treaties and of providing the implementing legislation needed to make the new agreements effective. Second, the case study provides an excellent example of the determination of the House of Representatives to become an equal partner with the Senate in congressional action on major foreign policy issues. Third, the intrusion of legislators into the realm of diplomatic negotiations—once a province reserved solely for the president or those acting under his authority—is dramatically illustrated.

Finally, perhaps no episode from recent American diplomatic experience more forcefully communicates Congress's determination to appear as the defender of the nation's diplomatic and security interests than this case. The way in which the Senate debated and changed the treaties is a classic demonstration of the political process at work. Most senators came to feel that the national interest required ratification of the treaties, unpopular though they might have been. The Senate then proceeded to reduce the issue by prolonged debate and by amending the treaties. Owing to changes made to them on Capitol Hill, the new Panama Canal treaties were successfully presented to the American people as consonant with the security demands of the United States. Without that assurance, it is doubtful that the new treaties could have been ratified.

Notes

1. The Isthmian Canal Convention, popularly known as the Hay-Bunau-Varilla Treaty, was signed in Washington November 18, 1903, and entered into force February 26, 1904 (33 Stat. 2234, Treaty Series 431). The text, as well as a wealth of other documentary material, is included in Senate Foreign Relations Committee, *Background Documents Relating to the Panama Canal* (Washington, D.C.: Government Printing Office, 1977). Hereafter cited as *Background Documents*.
2. *New York Times*, March 24, 1911, quoted in Henry F. Pringle, *Theodore Roosevelt: A Biography* (New York: Harcourt, Brace and Co., 1931), p. 330.
3. *Background Documents*, p. 1047.
4. As quoted to the author in a personal conversation with a senator.
5. U.S. Congress, House, 86th Cong., 2d sess., 1960, H. Con. Res. 459.
6. *Background Documents*, p. 1093.
7. Ibid., p. 1499.
8. *Panama Canal Treaties*, Executive N, 95th Cong., 1st sess., 1977.
9. Ward Sinclair, "The Closing of the Senate Club," *Washington Post Magazine*, April 23, 1978.
10. "Subdued and Thoughtful, Carter Plans a Quiet Life," *Washington Post*, November 13, 1980.
11. U.S. Congress, Senate Foreign Relations Committee, *Hearings on Panama Canal Treaties*, 95th Cong., 2d sess., 1978, pt. 1, pp. 12, 30. Hereafter cited as *Hearings*.
12. *Statement to National Assembly of Panama*, August 19, 1977, quoted in *Hearings*, pt. 1, p. 77.
13. Ibid., pt. 2, p. 214.
14. Ibid., pt. 1, p. 488.
15. Ibid., pt. 1, p. 454.
16. Ibid., pt. 1, p. 7.
17. U.S. Congress, Senate, *Report of Delegation Studying the Panama Canal Treaties and Other Matters of Interest to the U.S. in Latin America*, 95th Cong., 2d sess., 1978, S. Doc. 80, pp. 5-6.
18. U.S. Congress, Senate Foreign Relations Committee, *Senate Debate on the Panama Canal Treaties: A Compendium of Major Statements, Documents, Record Votes and Relevant Events* (Washington, D.C.: Government Printing Office, 1979), p. 404. This volume is an encyclopedic collection of the official records.
19. Ibid., p. 485.
20. *Congressional Quarterly Weekly Report*, March 18, 1978, pp. 675-678.
21. For an illuminating account of Sasser-White House relations, see "The Sasser Disaffection: How Not to Win Friends," *Washington Post*, April 19, 1978.
22. *Hearings*, pt. 5, pp. 57, 100-102. See also "The Realpolitic of the Panama Canal Treaties," *Washington Post*, February 2, 1978.
23. Letter, Hayakawa to Carter, April 13, 1978. Text in *Congressional Record*, 95th Cong., 2nd sess., 1978, vol. 124, pp. 10474-10475.
24. *Washington Post*, September 26, 1978.
25. U.S. Congress, Senate Armed Services Committee, *Implementing the Panama Canal Treaty of 1977 and Related Agreements*, 96th Cong., 1st sess., 1979, S. Rept. 225, pp. 5, 9.
26. *Washington Post*, September 26, 1979.

The Arab-Israeli Conflict and the AWACS Controversy 4

American Diplomacy in the Middle East

One of the most intractable problems of the post-World War II era has been the Arab-Israeli conflict. It has been particularly difficult for the United States because of contradictory interests—on the one hand, a deep commitment to the idea and the reality of a Jewish state; on the other, the importance of the Arab states because of their geography, their leadership of the Moslem world, U.S. fears of Soviet influence, and especially Arab oil reserves.

American foreign policy toward the Arab-Israeli conflict may be conveniently envisioned in four stages.[1] In the first, from the founding of the Zionist movement in the late nineteenth century until World War II, the United States had no official involvement in the Arab-Israeli controversy. Yet private citizens and groups—whose views were often supported by resolutions passed by the state legislatures and Congress—were active in behalf of Zionist goals.

In the second stage—during and after World War II, until the creation of the State of Israel on May 14, 1948—the Roosevelt and Truman administrations energetically supported the establishment of a Jewish state in the ancient land of Palestine, and they endorsed other Zionist goals, such as expanded Jewish immigration to Palestine after the war.

For almost 20 years after Israel came into existence, American foreign policy in its third stage was overtly pro-Israeli: economic and technical aid by the United States, along with military assistance and arms sales (often on highly advantageous terms for the Israelis), enabled Israel to survive, to absorb a steady stream of Jewish refugees, and to create a high standard of living for its citizens. Official American aid and loans to Israel were supplemented by a high level of private donations, loans, and other forms of assistance to Israel by Jewish groups and others in America who supported the Zionist cause.

Sometime after the third round of military hostilities between Israel and the Arab states in 1967, American policy toward the controversy entered the fourth stage. The transition in American diplomacy did not become evident perhaps until the period of the Nixon administration, beginning in 1969; and it was accelerated by the events of the fourth round in the Arab-Israeli conflict, which erupted in 1973. In this stage, while by no means abandoning its longstanding ties of friendship with Israel, the United States did endeavor to assume a more evenhanded or impartial position toward the Arab-Israeli disagreement; more than at any time in the past, American policy reflected awareness among policymakers and informed citizens that "the Arab case" deserved more sympathetic consideration and that a number of Arab grievances against Israel were well founded. By the mid-1970s even Israeli officials had become disturbed about this change in official and public attitudes in the United States.

Two developments symbolized this transition in the direction of American diplomacy. One was the close rapport that developed between American officials (President Jimmy Carter was a notable example) and President Anwar Sadat of Egypt. More than any other single Arab leader, Sadat was responsible for engendering goodwill and sympathy in the United States for the Arab position. One of the Carter administration's leading diplomatic accomplishments, the Camp David peace agreements between Israel and Egypt in 1979, epitomized America's role as a peacemaker in the Arab-Israeli imbroglio. This goal was continued by the Reagan administration, which endeavored to pacify strife-torn Lebanon and to discover some basis for peace between the other Arab states and Israel, although many Arab states believed that Reagan's peace-keeping activities continued to favor Israel's interests.

The other development was the event that has been selected as a case study in this chapter: the Reagan administration's decision to sell AWACS aircraft to Saudi Arabia. As with all other aspects of the Arab-Israeli conflict, this step proved to be highly controversial in Washington. It also illustrated several key problems and issues related to executive-legislative relations in the foreign policy field.

Background

The State of Israel is the fulfillment of Zionism, or the idea of a Jewish state. Zionism as a political idea was developed and elaborated by Theodor Herzl at the end of the nineteenth century in his influential book *The Jewish State* (1896). For Herzl, a native of Hungary who spent most of his life in Austria and France, Zionism was the answer to the pervasive anti-Semitism that, in his view, made the assimilation of Jews in Europe impossible.[2]

The World Zionist Organization, with Herzl as its president, was established by a conference he organized in Switzerland in 1897. Herzl entered into unsuccessful negotiations with the Turkish government for lands in Palestine and with the British for lands in the Sinai Peninsula. Britain instead offered some territory in Uganda, which Herzl favored accepting but which the Zionist Congress of 1903 turned down.

World War I gave momentum to Zionism, and World War II gave it fulfillment. In 1917 Lord Balfour, the British foreign minister, issued the now famous Balfour Declaration:

> His Majesty's Government view with favour the establishment in Palestine of a national home for the Jewish people, and will use their best endeavors to facilitate the achievement of this object, it being clearly understood that nothing shall be done which may prejudice the civil and religious rights of existing non-Jewish communities in Palestine, or the rights and political status enjoyed by Jews in any other country.[3]

A similar statement was adopted by the United States Congress as a joint resolution in 1922. Two points are to be noted. First, the reference in the Balfour Declaration was to a "national home for the Jewish people"—which was not necessarily the same thing as a Jewish state. Second, there was also a proviso against prejudicing the rights of the Arabs in Palestine, who comprised a substantial majority of the population.

The Balfour Declaration was also incorporated into the British mandate for Palestine under the League of Nations. Resistance from the Arab population of Palestine (which had previously been part of the Ottoman Empire) was almost immediate, and the British government soon became involved in a conflict, which continued until Israel was established in 1948, over the levels of Jewish immigration that would be permitted and over other issues that engendered controversy in Palestine.

The Palestinian question became acute in the aftermath of World War II. Pressure mounted for the survivors of the holocaust—Nazi Germany's campaign to exterminate the Jews—not only to immigrate to Palestine, but also to establish a Jewish state there. On November 29, 1947, the United Nations General Assembly voted for a plan to partition an independent Palestine into separate Jewish and Arab states, tied together in an economic union, with the city of Jerusalem under direct U.N. trusteeship.

The United Nations plan satisfied neither Arabs nor Zionists; each group wanted all of Palestine. On December 3, 1947, the British announced that they would consider their mandate from the League of Nations terminated on May 15, 1948. Both Jews and Arabs prepared for a war that, in fact, did not wait until May. The State of Israel was proclaimed in Palestine at midnight May 14. President Truman recognized it 11 minutes later.[4]

Throughout this period Truman acted largely on his own, although he received encouragement from many legislators. Truman accorded increased Jewish immigration to Palestine priority over establishment of a Jewish state, but he was a Zionist from personal conviction. The State Department—viewed by Truman as dominated by "Arabists" who were under British influence—advised against his policy. Dean Acheson, undersecretary of state at the time, frankly stated in his memoirs, "I did not share the President's views on the Palestine solution." [5] Pro-Zionist pressures were coming from Capitol Hill, notably from Sen. Robert F. Wagner and Rep. Emanuel Celler, both prominent New York Democrats. Secretary of Defense James V. Forrestal, concerned even then over access to Arab oil, supported the State Department. Postmaster General Robert Hannegan, charged with arranging Truman's reelection, supported the Zionists—who were themselves extraordinarily active. "I do not think I ever had as much pressure and propaganda aimed at the White House as I had in this instance," Truman wrote later.[6]

For whatever reason or combination of reasons, the deed was done; the State of Israel was created. Then began the continuing effort by the United States to balance its diverse interests in the Middle East.

The Actors

Israel. In many respects it is remarkable that Israel even exists, and it is perhaps even more remarkable that it came into being only half a century after Herzl articulated modern Zionism. For many Israelis and other Jews as well, the State of Israel is the fulfillment of an ancient dream, one that has been present since biblical times.

The dream has been made a reality only after a long and torturous history, which culminated in the horror of Hitler's holocaust and in four wars with the Arabs—the War of Independence (1948-1949), the Suez War (1956), the Six-Day War (1967), and the Yom Kippur War (1973). Throughout its short existence Israel has been surrounded by hostile neighbors. On a map of the Middle East it is a tiny blip; until it occupied the West Bank of the Jordan River in the 1967 war, it was only eight miles wide at its narrowest point. By the early 1980s it still had a population of only 4 million; there are more than 125 million Arabs, almost 60 million of them in countries bordering Israel. Furthermore, Israel is a country almost totally lacking in natural resources. In view of these facts, private and official American aid has been vital to Israel's survival.

Israel's defense strategy, which has paid off in the four wars against the Arabs, has been based on mobility, a high state of readiness, and superiority of weapons and training to offset Arab superiority in numbers. Nevertheless, Israel's military victories have not brought the country security, which remains as elusive in the 1980s as in the late 1940s. Israel's extraordinarily high level of military expenditures (on a per capita basis, the highest in the world); its determination to acquire the latest and best military equipment; its insistence upon retaining control of Jerusalem, the West Bank territories, and the Golan Heights in Syria; and its maintenance of a large military force in Lebanon—these provide tangible evidence of Israel's continuing sense of military vulnerability and isolation. Adding to Israel's predicament is a formidable array of internal problems, despite a high standard of living. In contrast to the biblical depiction of Palestine as a "land flowing with milk and honey," in reality it is largely desert or semidesert, with few mineral resources. Since 1948 Israel has consistently incurred a foreign trade deficit, which continues to mount; double- and triple-digit inflation is endemic; taxes are among the highest in the world; and Israel remains heavily dependent upon official and private American aid, a condition which shows no sign of changing in the years ahead.[7]

The Arabs. While the Israelis, despite their nation's insecurity, are today brimming with pride over their accomplishments, the Arabs have long felt a sense of humiliation, outrage, and injustice. First of all, they saw foreigners take over lands in Palestine that they viewed as rightfully theirs, driving the inhabitants into a wretched existence as refugees. Secondly, despite their overwhelming numbers, they suffered four crushing military defeats.

On top of all this, there has been a feeling of hopelessness. In the Arab view, for many years Israel had the unflinching, unquestioning support of the United States for whatever it wanted. As Arabs saw it, the Israeli government, through the pro-Israeli lobby in the United States, controlled American foreign policy in the Middle East. A new element was injected into this picture, however, with the Arab embargo of oil exports to the United States at the time of the Yom Kippur War in 1973. The demonstration of the dependence of the United States, Western Europe, and Japan on Arab oil has considerably brightened the Arabs' view of their long-term prospects.

Beyond this, however, it is unwise to generalize about the Arabs. Nine different countries are considered Arab—Egypt, Syria, Jordan, Lebanon, Iraq, Saudi Arabia, the Yemen Arab Republic, South Yemen, and Kuwait—as well as a series of tiny sheikdoms along the Persian Gulf and four North African states known collectively as the Mahgreb—Algeria, Morocco, Tunisia, and Libya. There are many other distinctions to be made: between rich (those who have oil) and poor (those who do not); between those who are adjacent to Israel and those who are not; and among conservative, moderate, and radical regimes. The Arabs do, of course, share a common religion (Islam) and a common language (Arabic), but this common ground has resulted in no more unity than have Catholicism and Spanish in Latin America. Divisions within the Islamic faith itself were never more apparent than in November 1979, when Moslem fanatics took over the Grand Mosque in Mecca; the move was forcefully suppressed by the government of Saudi Arabia.

Throughout most of the period since 1948, opposition to Israel has been the principal unifying force throughout the Middle East, to the extent that there has been unity at all. Yet differences have also existed, ranging from intransigent radicalism to cautious moderation, even with respect to Israel. Indeed, one of the most serious splits in the Arab world since 1948 came about in 1979, when the other Arab states joined to ostracize Egypt because it had signed a peace treaty with Israel (then in 1983 Egypt was again welcomed into the Arab fold). A crucial economic difference, of course, has existed between the Arab nations (such as Saudi Arabia, Kuwait, Libya, and Iraq) that possess substantial oil resources and those (such as Lebanon, Jordan, and Syria) that do not. With the exception of the major oil-producing states of the Middle East, the Arab nations continue to suffer from pervasive poverty, a high incidence of disease and malnutrition, widening income disparities, and high levels of population growth that offer little hope of a significant improvement in their standard of living. For Americans, another pivotal difference between Israel and its Arab neighbors has been that the latter have usually been governed by authoritarian (sometimes fanatically anti-American) regimes, whereas Israel has a democratic system.[8]

The United States.   In their approach to the Arab-Israeli conflict, American policymakers have exemplified three different points of view toward the issue. The bureaucracy of the executive branch—represented principally by the State and Defense departments—has tended to favor either a pro-Arab or an evenhanded approach to the question. State Department specialists in the Middle East tend to view the area in terms of international, rather than domestic, politics. They envision the Middle East as mainly an Arab region, whose political systems are unstable and often subject to Soviet influence. Since 1973 especially, they have been concerned about the continued access of the United States and its allies to the region's oil reserves; and since 1979, after the Iranian revolution and the Soviet thrust into Afghanistan, Defense Department officials have been apprehensive about the security of the Middle East.

The orientation of the White House has reflected the fact that (with the vice president), the president is elected by the entire nation. Inevitably perhaps, White House viewpoints have been more sensitive to domestic political considerations than have attitudes in the State or Defense departments. Yet since the early 1970s incumbent presidents have seen the necessity to maintain a more balanced approach to the Arab-Israeli problem and to preserve at least minimally cooperative relations with most Arab governments in the Middle East. President Ronald Reagan's proposal to sell AWACS aircraft to Saudi Arabia—in the face of vocal opposition by Israel and its supporters—illustrated this transition in White House attitudes.

Congress has been, and it remains, the most pro-Israeli actor of all in the American foreign policy process. This result derives from several factors: the strength of the pro-Israeli lobby in the United States; the deep and sincere convictions of many legislators on the Palestine question; the impact of American public opinion, which has as a rule been overwhelmingly sympathetic to the Israeli position; and the general ineffectiveness of Arab attempts to influence American public opinion favorably.

In attempting to understand the Arab-Israeli conflict, it is essential to bear in mind that not all Jews are Zionists; and, of course, not all supporters of the Zionist cause are Jewish. Although the Zionist movement has its roots in the Judaic religious tradition, Zionism is essentially a *political* movement: its dominant goal has been the creation and (after 1948) the support and protection of the State of Israel. In the United States and other countries, Zionism has drawn support from people of many religious backgrounds. Nevertheless, the basic strength of the pro-Israeli lobby rests in the American Jewish community, whose continuing support of Israel has been vital to that country's survival as an independent nation.

Although the American Jewish community numbers only some six million people (nearly 3 percent of the American population), its political influence—especially on Capitol Hill—is greatly disproportionate to its numbers. By many criteria, the pro-Israeli lobby has been one of the most conspicuously successful pressure groups in the postwar American political system, serving as a model of effective lobbying activities. Many Arabs and their supporters in the United States believe that America's consistent support of, and identification with, Israel for over a generation has been "dictated" by the influence of the Zionist lobby in the news media, with American public opinion, and in Washington (particularly on Capitol Hill).[9]

In reality, the relationship between the activities of the Zionist lobby and American diplomacy in the Middle East is a highly complex one, involving a number of diverse elements. One of these is unquestionably the fact that Jewish individuals and groups in America tend to be politically active and involved; furthermore, their interest is frequently translated into tangible and financial support for candidates, especially those favoring Israel's position. Morris Amitay, the former executive director of the American Israeli Public Affairs Committee and principal spokesman for the lobby, puts it this way:

> A lot of these [uncommitted] Senators are from the Midwest, West, down South, and these [Jews] are some of the elite types of people that these Senators like to be with and talk to, besides the pull of actual contributions. I do not think anyone ever likes to be approached on the very gut political level. You look around at who the Jewish constituents are from sparsely inhabited states. They are teachers, they are doctors, they have invariably been involved some way in politics. They are usually respected people in the community, so you do not have to pitch it at the level of, "I contributed ten thousand dollars to your campaign— unless you do this you will make me unhappy and I will contribute to your opponent next time." At most it's implicit, and it is not even implicit a large percentage of the time.[10]

As explained in Chapter 3, politicians generally get elected and reelected less by pleasing people than by not offending them. It follows that a vocal, dedicated, and well-organized minority has more influence politically than an apathetic or indifferent majority. The success of the pro-Israeli lobby provides a striking illustration of the emergence and growing importance of single issue politics in the American system.

The strength of the Zionist lobby in America also illustrates the concept of ethnicity in the political system of the United States. In demanding support for Israel, Jewish groups within the United States have followed the path taken by Polish-Americans, Greek-Americans, Irish-Americans, and other ethnic minorities in seeking to influence governmental policy toward the "old country." As in the case of American foreign policy toward Israel, sometimes the demands of these special interest groups promote the diplomatic goals of the United States, and sometimes they do not.

In addition to these factors, the success achieved by the pro-Israeli lobby in the United States can be in part accounted for by an old axiom with which students of propaganda have long been familiar: the most effective propaganda motivates those toward whom it is directed (the target) *to believe and act as they are already inclined to do.* In propaganda strategy, this concept is known as *reinforcement.* As applied to American attitudes toward the Arab-Israeli conflict, this concept means that the pro-Israeli lobby has operated in an environment highly congenial to the achievement of its objectives. The values and norms of American society, for example, are derived from the Judeo-Christian tradition (there is no comparable Islamic-Christian tradition). As the only Western-style democracy in the Middle East, Israel draws many of its political traditions and practices from the United States and Europe. The pioneers who founded the State of Israel (the Ashkenazim, or those of European origin) came from the West and believed in maintaining close ties with the United States and other Western nations. The accomplishments of the Israeli society since 1948 in "making the desert bloom" seem to many Americans a reenactment of their own frontier experience in the face of great odds and dangers. If Israel has received untold billions of dollars in official and private aid from the United States, for their part the Israelis have used this assistance effectively to achieve a high standard of living, to improve agricultural output dramatically, to raise industrial productivity, and to achieve other goals favored by Americans. As Israeli officials have reiterated many times since 1948, Israel is one of the few nations in the Middle East that has not at some stage developed close ties with the Soviet Union—another key factor that enhances Israel's appeal for Americans. Except for an interest in Israel—and since the 1973 war in the Middle East, for concern about the price and availability of petroleum products—most Americans otherwise have little knowledge of the Middle East and minimal interest in it. For over three decades these factors combined to create a milieu in the United States considerably more favorable to the Israeli than to the Arab cause.

The Israeli government, through its embassy in Washington as well as directly from Jerusalem, maintains close contacts with Congress and with pro-Israeli lobbying groups, principally the American Israel Public Affairs Committee (AIPAC), and an umbrella organization called the Conference of Presidents of Major American Jewish Organizations (Conference of Presidents, for short). Israeli prime ministers, foreign ministers, defense ministers, and other officials visit Washington frequently; Capitol Hill is a routine stop on their rounds for informal meetings with key committees or with the House and Senate membership in general. More senators used to turn out to have their pictures taken with Golda Meir when she was prime minister of Israel than would show up for an important Senate debate.

These visiting officials almost always confer, as well, with the Conference of Presidents and with other prominent American Jewish leaders. During a particularly tense period in the negotiations for the Israeli-Egyptian peace treaty, Prime Minister Begin met with 2,000 Jewish leaders in New York on his way back to Jerusalem from Washington. He drew cheers with the charge that Carter had asked him to sign a "sham" treaty. Begin then said to his audience, "You have great influence. Do not hesitate to use that influence." [11]

The Arab-Israeli conflict has been a singular episode in American postwar foreign policy in another respect: in illustrating the phenomenon of lobbying by foreign governments to influence American diplomacy. Historically, American policymaking toward the issue has followed a familiar and often predictable pattern. An incumbent president has overruled the executive bureaucracy; then Congress has overruled the White House, compelling the president to do more for Israel or in some cases preventing the chief executive from putting pressure on Israel. Israeli officials have known that they could often successfully appeal the decisions of executive officials to Congress. Visits by the Israeli prime minister and other high-level officials to the United States have frequently had this objective as a primary goal. As the AWACS case illustrates, in some instances these Israeli appeals to Congress have been directed at preventing or circumscribing American diplomatic and military moves deemed favorable to the Arabs.

A striking example of the tactics and influence of the Israeli lobby was afforded in 1975, when the Ford administration announced it was engaging in a reassessment of American foreign policy toward the Middle East. (The unmistakable implication was that some reduction in American aid to or support of Israel would be forthcoming.) In response, the Zionist lobby mounted a campaign in the Senate opposing this idea. In time 76 senators signed a letter addressed to President Ford affirming their support of Israel. As one senator subsequently observed, this expression of senatorial opinion was offered to the White House, although "no hearings had been held, no debate conducted, nor had the administration been invited to present its views" on American policy toward the Middle East. Another senator admitted that "the pressure was too great" to avoid joining his colleagues in signing the letter. In this and other cases, a legislator commented, widespread awareness exists in Congress that "political sanctions will be applied to any who fail to deliver" in ostensibly supporting the Israeli cause.[12]

The Context of the AWACS Proposal

A few weeks after he entered the Oval Office, President Ronald Reagan proposed to Congress that the United States sell five AWACS (Airborne Warning and Control System) aircraft to Saudi Arabia. Reagan's request, which precipitated one of the most intense debates over American policy toward the Middle East witnessed since World War II, must be understood against a background of major tendencies and developments in the region, as these affected American diplomatic interests.

Since the late 1940s Israel had been involved in four major military conflicts with the Arab states. The first round of fighting grew out of the establishment of the State of Israel in 1948. Miraculously, the outnumbered Israelis defeated several Arab military forces, successfully founded the State of Israel, and greatly enlarged its borders. In the process, some 900,000 Arab refugees were displaced from Palestine—a group which remained intensely antagonistic toward Israel and which in later years supplied many of the recruits for the Palestine Liberation Organization (PLO) and other groups that forcibly opposed Israel's existence. The refugee problem became one of the intractable issues that produced fundamental disagreement between Israel and its Arab neighbors.[13]

The Suez crisis of 1956 was the second round in the Arab-Israeli contest. Anglo-French-Israeli troops invaded Egypt, quickly defeated its armed forces, and sought to depose President Gamal Abdel Nasser's government. Owing to the firm opposition of the Eisenhower administration, however, in time these foreign troops were withdrawn from Egyptian soil, and Israel was compelled to relinquish territory occupied by its armed forces in the Sinai area. Nasser's regime emerged from the conflict more popular—and more determined to vindicate Arab rights in Palestine—than before. As a result of this clash, the United Nations Emergency Force (UNEF) was established to preserve peace along the Israeli-Egyptian frontier.[14]

Animosity between Israel and the Arab states continued; they reached a new level of violence in the third round of hostilities, which erupted on June 5, 1967. The ensuing Six-Day War was an overwhelming military triumph for Israel. Relying upon a preemptive strike, Israel's air force largely wiped out the Egyptian air fleet on the ground, leaving Egyptian armored forces in the Sinai defenseless against Israeli air and ground attacks. Israeli military superiority also defeated the smaller armed forces of Syria and Jordan.[15]

The Six-Day War had far-reaching consequences for nations inside and outside the Middle East. As a result of the conflict, Israel greatly expanded its borders, extending them to the Suez Canal and to the strategic Golan Heights in the north. Another outcome of this conflict was that the Arab enemies of Israel—after sustaining three defeats in orthodox military engagements—now relied increasingly upon guerrilla warfare to achieve their goals. After 1967, Al Fatah and other organizations comprising the PLO resorted to hit-and-run tactics, terrorism, and other forms of violence to express their opposition to Israel. Among some groups belonging to the PLO, fomenting revolution *against established Arab governments* whose zeal in opposing the Zionist enemy was questionable also ranked as a primary goal.[16]

Two other developments growing out of the Six-Day War directly involved Saudi Arabia and its relations with the United States. As a result of its spectacular military victory, the government of Israel officially annexed the city of Jerusalem (from 1948 until 1967 the Old City had been under Jordanian authority). In the months that followed, Israeli officials asserted that the annexation of Jerusalem was a fait accompli that was nonnegotiable with its Arab adversaries. Later Israel went further and proclaimed Jerusalem its capital. While Arabs generally were incensed by Israel's action, it was especially offensive to Saudi Arabia. Controlled by the rigidly orthodox Wahhabi sect of Sunni Islam, its government had long served as the custodian of the most sacred religious shrines venerated by Sunni Moslems. Next to Mecca and Medina, Jerusalem (according to the Sunni tradition, the site from which Mohammed ascended into Paradise) is the third holiest shrine in Islam. Following the 1967 war, therefore, for the first time Saudi Arabia became actively involved in the Arab-Israeli conflict. Saudi Arabia does not directly border Israel; and its relatively small military establishment would be no match for the armed might of Israel. After 1967 the Saudi contribution to the Arab campaign against Israel consisted mainly of subsidies provided to the Palestine Liberation Organization and certain Arab governments (such as Jordan, and during some periods, Syria). The PLO, for example, was massively dependent on funds that were supplied by Saudi Arabia, Kuwait, and other oil-rich states and that were needed to acquire arms and supplies for pursuing the struggle against Zionism. This fact made groups like the PLO and Arab states that were financially dependent upon Saudi Arabia extremely sensitive to the attitudes of Saudi officials on regional and global issues.[17]

Another far-reaching consequence of the Six-Day War was the discovery of what came to be called oil power and reliance upon it to achieve Arab diplomatic objectives. Although Arab oil producers ceased production during the 1967 war in an attempt to bring pressure to bear upon the United States and other Western nations viewed as sympathetic to Israel, this initial reliance upon oil power had only very limited success. The United States (along with Venezuela and Indonesia) increased its production to supply the petroleum needs of its principal allies. Yet the discovery of oil power in 1967 was important for two reasons: it established a precedent that the oil-producing states of the Middle East were to use with telling effect in their next confrontation with Israel (1973); and it underscored the mounting vulnerability of the United States, Western Europe, Japan, and other advanced nations to an oil boycott that would deny them access to the petroleum supplies of the Middle East.

After the 1967 conflict tensions between Israel and its Arab adversaries continued to engender instability, violence, and the prospect of a fourth round of direct military hostilities in the Middle East. Despite its decisive military victories, Israel still found the peace and security it sought elusive. Arab governments showed no inclination to accept Israel or to arrive at a resolution of outstanding differences with it. The PLO and other anti-Israeli political movements continued to rely upon guerrilla attacks and terrorist incidents to express their militant opposition to Israel. In addition, for several years after the 1967 war the Soviet Union found new opportunities for expanding its ties and influence with the Arab states. By the early 1970s, for example, it was estimated that upward of 15,000 Soviet officials, technicians, and advisers were resident in Egypt; this large Soviet presence was finally expelled from Egypt by President Sadat in 1972. Countries like Syria and Iraq had become heavily dependent upon Soviet arms aid to rebuild and modernize their military establishments.[18] Conversely, the influence of the United States—which was widely viewed by Arabs as Israel's mentor and as responsible for its territorial expansionism—was perhaps at the lowest ebb reached in the post-World War II period.

As time passed, most informed observers predicted that a new wave of hostilities would engulf the Middle East. It came on October 6, 1973, when the fourth round (called by Israelis and Americans the Yom Kippur War and by Arabs the Ramadan War) in the Arab-Israeli conflict erupted. In well-executed surprise attacks, Egyptian forces struck the Bar Lev Israeli defense line in the Sinai region, while Syrian troops attacked Israeli defense forces in the Golan Heights; in these initial thrusts, the Arabs inflicted heavy losses on the Israeli military establishment. After their tank losses were replaced by a massive American airlift, ultimately Israeli troops reversed the tide of battle. In the final stage, Israeli officials were restrained by Washington from threatening the Syrian capital, Damascus, and from mounting attacks aimed at Egyptian territory west of the Suez Canal.[19]

In the sense that Israeli forces were ultimately victorious on the battlefield, the Yom Kippur War again demonstrated Israel's military superiority over its Arab enemies. Yet in several respects the conflict was a highly traumatic episode for Israel and its supporters in the United States. The war had shattered several myths: that Arab troops would not fight; that Arab governments were incapable of planning a surprise attack which would escape early detection by Israel's vaunted intelligence service; and that Israeli forces were invincible on the battlefield. Although their forces were ultimately defeated, for Arabs the 1973 war immensely bolstered their self-confidence and morale. For Israel the conflict had economic and political repercussions that would be felt within the country for many years. Most fundamentally perhaps, it highlighted the facts that Arab opposition to Israel remained intense and that with each passing year the Arabs were improving their military capabilities. For the United States the fourth round in 1973 underscored the continued volatility of the Middle East, the danger of a direct Soviet-American military encounter within the region, and the necessity for renewed efforts to resolve Arab-Israeli differences without resort to violence.

For Americans, perhaps the most far-reaching consequence of the Yom Kippur War, however, was that the Arab states had effectively employed oil power against the United States and other industrialized nations.[20] After hostilities erupted in 1973, the oil exporting states of the Middle East—which collectively produced over one-third of the oil needed by the non-Communist world—imposed a boycott upon oil shipments. Saudi Arabia alone accounted for nearly half (42 percent) of the region's output; the Saudi government's decision to join in the boycott was a crucial factor in its success. The five-month oil embargo cost the United States between $10 and $20 billion in income lost because of decreased production, and because of it some 500,000 Americans became unemployed. Western Europe and Japan—which derived 75 percent or more of their oil from the Middle East—were even more adversely affected by the boycott. If it had continued for several more months, the embargo would have produced severe economic dislocations in these regions, possibly engendering political crises and seriously impairing the defense efforts of America's principal allies. After the 1973 war the price of oil on the world market reached a new high ($20 per barrel); and in the years that followed it moved steadily upward, reaching $36 per barrel by the early 1980s before dropping back to $29. The Yom Kippur War served as a pointed reminder to Americans of their growing dependence upon oil imports and of the key role of Saudi Arabia in the decision by the Arab states to use oil power as a diplomatic weapon.

The Elusive Search for Peace

The 1973 war in the Middle East did little to remove the underlying sources of tension between Israel and the Arab states. In retrospect, the conflict did, however, have three results that induced American officials to try once again to resolve Arab-Israeli differences. In the first place, its victory was extremely costly for Israel in terms of the casualties sustained and of the financial burden of the war. After the fighting stopped, Israeli officials might well have recalled Napoleon's observation after one of his triumphs on the battlefield: "Many more victories like that, and I am undone!" After the successful Egyptian and Syrian attacks, the Israeli government was now required to maintain its military establishment in an advanced stage of readiness to repel a new attack by a capable and determined Arab enemy. As Israel discovered, this proved to be an extremely expensive undertaking, impairing the nation's economic viability and perpetuating its dependence upon the United States.

In the second place, some Arab nations—and President Anwar Sadat's Egypt was the leading example—concluded on the basis of the 1973 war that another direct military encounter against superior Israeli military power was futile and irrational. For over 25 years the confrontation with Israel had drained Egypt financially and had diverted attention from the country's increasingly acute domestic problems. As the leader of the nation that had borne the brunt of the military effort, Sadat concluded that Egypt and Israel must resolve their differences so that the Egyptian government could devote its attention primarily to internal needs.

In the third place, the Yom Kippur War unquestionably affected official and popular American attitudes toward the Israeli and Arab positions—a change induced in no small degree by the embargo imposed upon Middle East oil exports during this conflict. By the mid-1970s, as even the Israelis and some Arabs ultimately acknowledged, American opinion had become less overtly pro-Israeli, more critical of specific Israeli policies and behavior, and more inclined to demand flexibility from Israel's leaders in efforts to stabilize the Middle East. Egyptian president Sadat made a consistently favorable impression upon American public opinion. President Jimmy Carter, for example, believed that Sadat was one of the most outstanding political leaders of his era.[21]

These developments created an environment conducive to intensive American peace-making efforts in the Middle East. Under the Nixon and Ford administrations, Secretary of State Henry Kissinger engaged in a prolonged series of negotiations—which involved so much travel between countries that his method became known as *shuttle diplomacy*—in an effort to discover a basis for a peaceful resolution of Arab-Israeli differences. Kissinger was finally successful in achieving agreement between Egypt and Israel on troop disengagement (on January 18, 1974); but his efforts to broaden this accord to include other Arab countries and other outstanding issues between the belligerents ultimately failed. As the months passed, it became evident that President Sadat of Egypt was largely alone among Arab leaders in his desire to arrive at a peaceful settlement with Israel. Meanwhile, in 1975 President Ford did not conceal his belief that Israeli intransigence was one factor blocking the path to peace; and, as we have already noted, he called for a reassessment of American policy toward the Middle East in order to induce greater Israeli flexibility in the peace discussions. By September 4, 1975, Israel and Egypt had concluded another agreement, which called for the withdrawal of Israeli troops from the Sinai region and the return of the Abu Rudeis oil fields to the Egyptian government. In return, Egypt agreed not to resort to force to block Israel's access to the sea and to lift its longstanding blockade against shipping through the Suez Canal to and from Israeli ports.[22]

These accords paved the way for intensive efforts by the Carter administration to arrive at a peace treaty between Israel and Egypt. Prospects became even more favorable for achieving the goal following President Anwar Sadat's historic visit to Jerusalem on November 19, 1977. This meeting was followed by bilateral discussions between Israeli and Egyptian officials and by Prime Minister Menachem Begin's visit to Egypt at the end of 1977. Once more, little substantive agreement was achieved in these discussions, leading President Jimmy Carter in mid-1978 to invite Sadat and Begin to the presidential retreat at Camp David to resume the peace talks under American auspices.

For almost two weeks—in some of the most complex and difficult diplomatic negotiations in modern history—Sadat, Begin, and Carter, with their aides, endeavored to resolve Israeli-Egyptian disagreements. On several occasions, the Camp David conference seemed on the verge of failure; it was largely saved from that fate by President Carter's determination to make it succeed. Time and again, Carter reminded Sadat and Begin of the possibly dire consequences of failing to reach a peaceful settlement. Finally, two draft accords were signed between Sadat and Begin on September 17; but not until March 26, 1979, was a treaty of peace between the two countries signed, thereby inaugurating an era of peaceful relations between them.

Although the Camp David talks had made considerable progress toward stabilizing the Middle East, events soon made it clear that the Arab-Israeli conflict had by no means ended. Two things were memorable about President Sadat's role in the discussions. First was his courage in being the first Arab leader to join Israel in formal peace negotiations. Second, as quickly became apparent—and as was dramatically highlighted by President Sadat's assassination on October 6, 1981, by Moslem extremist elements—Sadat had become isolated from the other Arab states; they were unwilling to become associated with his peace-making activities.[23]

In spite of the confident expectations of the United States, the Camp David meeting was not followed by other, more comprehensive accords between Israel and its Arab adversaries. PLO-sponsored attacks against Israel showed no sign of diminishing; the Arab Rejectionist Front—chiefly Syria, Iraq, and Libya—denounced Sadat and called him a traitor to the Arab cause; political disturbances and unrest became an almost daily occurrence among the Arab population of the Israeli-occupied West Bank territories. Still distrustful of Arab intentions and apprehensive about its security, the government of Israel became increasingly reluctant to adhere to written and verbal understandings with Egypt and the United States concerning a Palestinian homeland and other provisions of the peace treaty with Egypt. Perhaps most disturbing of all to Washington was the fact that "moderate" Arab governments—such as Saudi Arabia, Kuwait, and Jordan—remained highly critical of the Camp David accords and refused to associate themselves with them. By the Reagan administration, the peace process in the Middle East was clearly stalled and showed little sign of being revived. Meanwhile, the civil war that had engulfed Lebanon served as a new source of regional, and possibly international, conflict. The anti-American government of Iran created new instability in the Persian Gulf area. Syria was becoming increasingly militant and had developed close ties with the Soviet Union. Israel's security remained precarious. Overall, American influence with the Middle East was at a low ebb.

The Saudi-American Diplomatic Connection

By the 1980s three major segments of Arab opinion toward Israel and toward what Arabs viewed as its sponsor, the United States, could be identified. As we have already observed, one point of view was exemplified by Sadat's Egypt—the only Arab nation willing to sign a peace treaty with Israel. With the passage of time, Egypt's prestige and influence within the Arab world deteriorated markedly. A second group of Arab states and political movements comprised the Rejectionist Front, which consisted of the Arabs who remained implacably opposed to Israel, refused to recognize its existence, and were unwilling to enter into peace negotiations with it. Led by Syria, Iraq, Libya, and several factions within the PLO, this group tended to be overtly anti-American; and often they were also recipients of massive Soviet economic, military, and other forms of assistance, which Moscow willingly extended to governments and rebel political movements throughout the Middle East. With rare exceptions, American officials in effect assumed that efforts to bring spokesmen for the Rejectionist Front into peace negotiations had little or no chance of success. (Yet in some cases, as in Libya and Iraq, American business firms did find limited opportunities for investments, which were sometimes solicited by these governments.)

The third group consisted of moderate Arab opinion, as symbolized by the position of Saudi Arabia on the Arab-Israeli conflict and related regional issues. The attitude of members of this group can be summarized by saying that they would envision the ultimate possibility of peace with Israel, provided that the government of Israel made a number of fundamental concessions designed to satisfy Arab grievances and to vindicate Arab rights. (It was of course highly questionable whether Israeli authorities would *ever* make the kind of concessions demanded by this segment of Arab opinion.) For this group, key questions related to Israel's readiness to grant true political autonomy to the Arab inhabitants of the occupied West Bank territories; to return the Old City of Jerusalem to Arab jurisdiction; and above all perhaps, to accept the idea of a Palestinian homeland whose borders would include some Israeli territory. American officials knew that unless Arab moderates could be induced to support any new peace initiative in the Middle East, it was bound to fail. They were no less aware that because of its strategic location, its enormous oil reserves, its income from petroleum sales, and its leadership role in the Organization of Petroleum Exporting Countries (OPEC), the attitudes of Saudi Arabia were vital in determining the political future of the Middle East.

The key role of Saudi Arabia in achieving American diplomatic objectives in the Middle East was heightened by another climactic event: the collapse of the Iranian monarchy in January 1979. This event ranks as one of the most serious American diplomatic reverses in the postwar period; it was followed by the emergence of an outspokenly anti-American regime in Iran, headed by the Ayatollah Khomeini, whose power base was the Shi'ite clergy. Viewing America as "the Great Satan" and encouraging violent anti-American outbursts in the population, Khomeini's government permitted a revolutionary student group to seize 52 American diplomatic hostages, who were incarcerated in the American Embassy for over a year (the hostages were finally released on January 20, 1981).[24]

Under Khomeini Iran lapsed into a prolonged period of internal upheaval and repression. In foreign relations, the Islam-based government called for revolution in other states throughout the Persian Gulf area; supported the PLO and other enemies of Israel (while concurrently selling oil to the Israeli government); denounced Soviet intervention in Afghanistan and Communist machinations within Iran; and fought an exhausting war against Iraq, whose forces invaded Iran in September 1980. Prolonged political turbulence in Iran, coupled with the Soviet invasion of Afghanistan at the end of 1979, called into question the future stability of the entire Persian Gulf area and of Western access to its vital oil reserves.

Confronted with this new danger, President Jimmy Carter issued the Carter Doctrine in his State of the Union Message to Congress on January 23, 1980. This pronouncement declared the defense of the Persian Gulf area vital to the security and well-being of the United States, and it pledged America to defend the area from forces that might endanger its security. While the Carter Doctrine was directed specifically at the Soviet Union—it was an explicit warning to Moscow not to extend its hegemony in Afghanistan to adjacent countries—informed students of the Middle East were aware of two other forces that might jeopardize the security of the Persian Gulf area.

One of these was the revolutionary movements (sponsored by Iran, the Ba'ath Party in Iraq, and other sources) aimed at radicalizing the governments adjoining the Persian Gulf. A prime target for such revolutionary activities was the monarchy of Saudi Arabia. The other potential threat was the possibility of a fifth round in the Arab-Israeli conflict, which might result if the strife in Lebanon widened into a regional war, or even a global one. With the collapse of the American position in Iran— and in the light of the ensuing Iraqi-Iranian war—Washington was induced more than ever to maintain close ties with the government of Saudi Arabia.[25]

American ties with Saudi Arabia of course antedated the Iranian revolution and the issuance of the Carter Doctrine. Before 1932, when the Kingdom of Saudi Arabia was proclaimed under its first ruler, Ibn Saud I, the traditional homeland of the Arabs was little more than a collection of primitive Bedouin tribes, whose main pursuits appeared to be nomadism and warfare.[26] Ibn Saud succeeded in uniting the tribes under his leadership and in defeating his rivals (such as the Hashemites, who governed Jordan and Iraq after World War I). Yet throughout his long rule (Ibn Saud died in 1953), the kingdom was largely governed according to tribal customs and traditions and in accordance with the fundamentalist Wahhabi religious principles professed by its leaders and the vast majority of its people.* The most crucial development during his reign was the discovery of oil in Saudi Arabia in the early 1930s and the development of this oil by the Arabian-American Oil Company (ARAMCO). Saudi Arabia was officially neutral in World War II, although it did assist the Allied cause during that conflict. From the end of the war through the early 1960s U.S. air bases in Saudi Arabia contributed to the defense of the Middle East; then, mindful of adverse Arab reaction, the Saudi government requested that the bases be closed. When Ibn Saud I died, he was succeeded by his son, Ibn Saud II. The new king's extravagances and lack of interest in the welfare of the country finally led the Saudi royal family late in 1964 to depose him in favor of Crown Prince Faisal, who ruled until his assassination early in 1975.

Under King Faisal, who was a devout Moslem and devoted to his country's welfare, Saudi Arabia's growing oil revenues were allocated primarily to modernization and national development. For the period 1980-1985, the development program called for the expenditure of some $300 billion on social programs, education, health, industrial development, and other projects, some of which were designed to prepare the country for the eventual depletion of its oil reserves. Faisal and his successors also introduced limited political reforms, though without fundamentally changing the monarchical character of the government. After Faisal's death, the infirm King Khalid ruled until his death in June 1982, when he was succeeded by the de facto ruler, Crown Prince Fahd. In Saudi Arabia's ambitious modernization program American business firms and advisers continue to play a leading role.[27]

In recent years American ties with Saudi Arabia have been strengthened for other reasons: the country's pivotal position among Middle Eastern oil producers and its role in the deliberations and decisions of the Organization of Petroleum Exporting Countries (OPEC). In the early 1980s Saudi Arabia's oil reserves were believed to exceed 160 billion barrels; since much of the country remained unprospected, some estimates placed these reserves at 500 billion barrels or more! Saudi Arabia's oil resources were approximately three times those of the United States, making the country the largest oil producer in the Middle East. At full production, Saudi Arabia was capable of shipping 9 to 10 million barrels of oil daily into the world market. Income from the petroleum industry

---

* The Wahhabi sect of Sunni Islam (with the Shi'ite branch, one of the two great divisions of Islam) derived from the life and thought of Muhammed ibn Abd al-Wahhab (1703-1787). His movement represented a reaction against the corruption and adulteration of the pure and revealed Islamic faith by foreign religious ideas and philosophical concepts, and even by Islamic movements (like Sufism) deemed at variance with the Koran. Thus Wahhabism demanded a return to the original and literal tenets of Islam; Wahhabis have been called the Puritans of Islam and the custodians of religious fundamentalism. In practice, as it has evolved in Saudi Arabia, Wahhabism calls for literal adherence to Koranic requirements in such spheres as religious rites, treatment of criminals, and the status of women. See Bayly Winder, *Saudi Arabia in the Nineteenth Century* (New York: St. Martin's Press, 1965), pp. 8-15; and John B. Christopher, *The Islamic Tradition* (New York: Harper and Row, 1972), pp. 158-162.

provided some 90 percent of the government's total revenues, including the funds needed to finance its ambitious national development program.

As the country that exemplifies Arab oil power, Saudi Arabia's voice has more often than not been decisive in the policies adopted by OPEC. In the American view, Saudi officials have had a moderating influence upon the organization. For example, Saudi Arabia did not favor the imposition of an oil boycott against the West in 1967; and except during the war of 1973, it has usually urged other OPEC members not to use this diplomatic weapon frequently or recklessly. Saudi attitudes within OPEC have been heavily conditioned by awareness of three key realities. One reality is that the oil-producing states of the Middle East are as dependent upon income from the sale of petroleum products to the United States and other advanced nations as the latter are upon purchases of oil from the Middle East. Another reality is that the economic and political destinies of the oil-rich states of the Middle East are crucially affected by economic tendencies in the United States, Western Europe, Japan, and other industrialized nations. The Saudi government, for example, has invested many billions of petrodollars in bonds and other securities of the United States government, in corporate American stocks and bonds, and in other ventures in the West. Better than most other Arab leaders, Saudi officials understand their country's stake in the continued stability and prosperity of the industrialized nations. A third reality affecting Saudi viewpoints within OPEC is the realization that if OPEC priced its oil products at exhorbitant levels, the inevitable result would be—and has been—a more intensive search by OPEC customers for substitutes, with a corresponding decline in income from oil sales by all of OPEC's members. In turn, this development would almost certainly in time set in motion disruptive and radical political forces within Saudi Arabia and other oil-producing states of the Middle East.[28]

Executive-Legislative Relations and the AWACS Case

Reagan Proposes the AWACS Sale

In what was to become the first major test of his authority in the foreign policy field, President Ronald Reagan in April 1981 disclosed his administration's intention of selling five advanced AWACS aircraft, valued at $5.8 billion, to the government of Saudi Arabia. Under the terms of the Arms Export Control Act (P.L. 90-629), Congress had 30 days within which to disapprove of (or veto) foreign arms sales through resolutions passed by majority votes in the House and Senate. Following established custom, the Reagan administration had provided Congress with informal notification of the proposed AWACS sale; formal notification of this intention was sent to Capitol Hill on October 1. Congress, therefore, had until October 30 to disapprove the transaction or the president would be free to complete it. In addition to the AWACS planes, the White House proposed to sell Saudi Arabia equipment for F-15 fighter aircraft that would improve their capability; several KC-707 tanker aircraft, valued at some $2.4 billion; and 1,177 AIM-9L air-to-air missiles, costing approximately $200 million. Another item in the package (devices for improving the offensive striking power of the F-15s) was dropped after the government of Israel expressed outspoken opposition to it.[29]

In justifying the AWACs transaction, the president and his advisers emphasized its importance in promoting the diplomatic and security goals of the United States in the Persian Gulf area. On August 5, for example, President Reagan in a letter to Congress called the AWACS transaction one of the "essential elements" in American Middle Eastern policy. He and his staff were convinced that "providing Saudi Arabia with this equipment will improve the security of our friends, strengthen our own posture in the region, and make it clear both to local governments and to the Soviet leadership that the United States is determined to assist in preserving security and stability in Southwest Asia." [30]

A few days later, Under Secretary of State James Buckley referred to such recent developments as the Iranian revolution, the Iraqi-Iranian war, the Soviet invasion of Afghanistan, and Moscow's reliance upon proxies (like South Yemen) to promote its objectives in the Middle East. In the State Department's view, the AWACS transaction would contribute to achieving four major American goals in the Persian Gulf region. First, it would help preserve America's continued access to Middle East oil. Second, it would serve as a deterrent to Soviet influence in the area. Third, it would enhance the security of nations friendly to the United States, including Israel. Fourth, it would demonstrate America's "constancy" and its "resolve" in protecting the security of nations bordering the Persian Gulf. In brief, this official believed that this arms sales package made "a major contribution to Saudi security and to our vital regional security objectives." [31] On October 1, in testimony before the Senate Foreign Relations Committee, Secretary of State Alexander Haig urged favorable congressional action on the AWACS sale. If Congress vetoed the transaction, Haig contended, "Saudi confidence in the ability of the United States to conduct a coherent and effective foreign policy will be diminished." Quoting a comment by President Sadat of Egypt, Haig asserted that a congressional veto would raise "a huge question mark" about the reliability of American defense commitments in the Middle East.[32]

Lobbying Activities and the AWACS Case

The AWACS case precipitated some of the most intense lobbying activities witnessed on a foreign policy question since World War II. Major participants in this campaign were the government of Israel and its supporters in the United States, the government of Saudi Arabia and groups favoring its position, and officials of the Reagan administration.

Predictably, the response of the pro-Israeli lobby to the AWACS proposal was vociferously adverse. Israeli Prime Minister Menachem Begin informed State Department officials that making advanced AWACS aircraft available to Saudi Arabia would "present a very serious threat" to the security of his nation. Secretary of State Alexander Haig's offer to increase American assistance to Israel (as a grant, instead of the customary loan) did little to reassure Begin's government and its supporters in the United States.[33]

As the weeks passed, blocking the AWACS transaction became what one study called the primary goal of the Israeli lobby in the United States. Spearheaded by the American Israel Public Affairs Committee (AIPAC), the pro-Israeli lobby undertook a grass-roots campaign to rally public opinion against the sale and to direct popular sentiment against it to executive and legislative officials in Washington. Initially, opponents sought to prevent the Reagan White House from submitting the AWACS proposal to Congress. Failing to achieve that objective, the Israeli lobby concentrated upon convincing members of the House and Senate that the AWACS sale was in neither America's nor Israel's interests. At a minimum, Israel and its supporters called for the imposition of numerous conditions and restrictions upon the sale (some of which were clearly unacceptable to the government of Saudi Arabia and might induce its government to withdraw the request); they also advocated a public pledge by the White House that the military superiority of Israel would be maintained.[34]

Arguments advanced against the AWACS sale included the following. (1) In view of the political instability of the Persian Gulf area, these advanced American aircraft might fall into the hands of governments of political groups that would use them against Israel or the United States. (2) Saudi Arabia, with its limited armed forces, did not need sophisticated weapons like AWACS and the other advanced military hardware it had requested from the United States. (3) The provision of these weapons to Saudi Arabia could well add to its political instability, leading to the kind of domestic oppostion that had toppled the Iranian monarchy. (4) To match Saudi Arabia's intensified defense efforts, Israel would be required to embark on a new round of military spending that would further damage its economy.

A noteworthy feature of the AWACS case was that—perhaps for the first time in the history of the Arab-Israeli conflict—the pro-Israeli lobby found itself pitted against a skillful and effective pressure campaign conducted by the Arab lobby in behalf of the AWACS transaction. As emphasized earlier in the chapter, for many years pro-Israeli groups had been able to capitalize on public opinion in the United States, which was nearly always sympathetic to their cause.

By the 1970s, however, American attitudes toward the Arab-Israeli dispute had clearly begun to change. After four military victories since 1948, Israel no longer appeared to many Americans as the underdog in the Arab-Israeli contest. Arab imposition of an oil embargo during the

1973 war—followed by rapid increases in the price of oil imports from the Middle East—served as forceful reminders to Americans of their vulnerability and dependence upon the oil reserves of the region. By the end of the decade, Soviet gains in the vicinity of the Persian Gulf and its western flank (as in eastern Africa) focused American attention once more on the region's strategic importance. Moreover, many Americans in time concluded that Arab viewpoints, as articulated by Arab leaders like King Hussein of Jordan and President Sadat of Egypt, were often more reasonable, persuasive, and entitled to serious consideration than they had earlier believed. By contrast, Menachem Begin (who became Israel's prime minister in 1977, was reelected in 1981, and retired in 1983) frequently projected to Americans an image of ideological rigidity, militancy, and unwillingness to compromise in the interests of resolving Arab-Israeli differences. In this new environment, foreign governments and organizations in the United States that advocated the AWACS sale found conditions favorable for their activities.

For many years pro-Arab groups in the United States had found their lobbying activities hindered by several factors that diminished their political impact. Among these were the overall American ignorance of the Middle East and of important forces (such as modern Arab nationalism and the Islamic religion) that affected the region's political development; the continuing schisms that perpetuated suspicions and rivalries among Arab governments and political movements; the negative feelings of many Americans toward certain oil corporations and their links with the Arab states; and the relative smallness (some two million members, most of whom were of Lebanese extraction) of the Arab-American community.

Yet the Arab lobby also possessed strengths that had slowly enhanced its effectiveness as a pressure group. Led by the National Association of Arab Americans (NAAA), the Arab lobby had unquestionably become more skillful in its public relations and media campaigns designed to make Americans more receptive to Arab viewpoints. While still lacking the resources of the Israeli lobby, the NAAA's mailing list was growing steadily and its budget was increasing. Several Arab governments retained former legislators, such as former senator J. William Fulbright, D-Ark., to represent their interests in the United States. Saudi Arabia was represented by Frederick Dutton, who had been a State Department official during the Kennedy administration. For several years a few legislators, such as Sen. James Abourezk, D-S.D., had been willing to champion the Arab cause on Capitol Hill. Even so, developments such as the internecine strife among various Arab groups in Lebanon remained a serious obstacle to unified Arab lobbying activities in the United States. Nor had the Arab lobby been nearly as successful in its attempts to influence the outcome of elections as the pro-Israeli lobby had been in its political efforts.[35]

For several months the Arab lobby undertook a public relations and media campaign emphasizing the importance of the AWACS sale for cooperative Saudi-American relations, the defensive nature of the weapons scheduled for delivery to the Saudi government, and the role of a well-equipped Saudi military establishment in protecting the security of the Persian Gulf area. Certain actions by the government of Israel—such as its bombing attack against a nuclear installation in Iraq in the summer of 1981 and its intensive bombing of the city of Beirut several weeks later (in which some 300 people were killed)—reinforced the Arab contention that the Saudi military establishment needed the AWACS planes and related military equipment.

Congress Considers the AWACS Proposal

From the beginning, it was evident that the AWACS proposal faced formidable opposition in the House and Senate. As expected, opposition to the AWACS sale was especially intense in the Democratic-controlled House of Representatives, where pervasive fears existed that the move would endanger Israel's security. On October 14, 1981, by a vote of 301-111 the House passed a resolution (H. Con. Res. 194) disapproving the AWACS transaction. (In order to block the sale, it must be remembered, majorities in both the House and Senate had to vote *against* it; otherwise, the president was free to conclude the transaction.) Although prospects did not initially appear encouraging, the White House now turned to the Senate for the support it needed to complete the AWACS transaction.[36]

On October 15 the Senate Foreign Relations Committee voted 9-8 against approving the proposed AWACS sale. It is illustrative of the divisions within Congress on foreign policy issues that on the same day the Senate Armed Services Committee voted 10-5 *in favor* of providing the AWACS aircraft and other military equipment to Saudi Arabia. As events proved, sentiment in the Senate on the AWACS question was closely divided. Before the issue reached the Senate floor President Reagan and his aides renewed their efforts to gain the support of wavering senators. A presidential promise to provide Israel with radar-jamming equipment reassured several senators that the AWACS planes would not jeopardize Israel's security; and the White House also pledged that providing the AWACS planes to Saudi Arabia would not be followed by a large-scale military buildup in the Persian Gulf area. At the administration's initiative, three former chief executives—Presidents Nixon, Ford, and Carter—endorsed the AWACS proposal as a move that would promote American diplomatic interests in the Middle East and pose no threat to Israel's security.[37]

The climax came on October 28, when after prolonged and heated debate the Senate voted on the AWACS transaction. Ultimately, the outcome was an impressive, if narrow, victory for the Reagan administration, for the Senate failed (by a vote of 48-52) to join the House in disapproving the AWACS transaction. Crucial to the outcome was the fact that President Reagan and his aides had persuaded seven new Republican senators to change their positions and to support the White House proposal. In the end, President Reagan was granted the authority he requested to provide a $8.5 billion arms sales package, including the AWACS aircraft and related military equipment, to the government of Saudi Arabia.[38]

The AWACS Case in Retrospect

As a case study in the American foreign policy process, the AWACS issue calls attention to certain lessons and problems related to the conduct of foreign relations by the United States. From the perspective of substantive diplomacy, the proposal of the AWACS sale by the Reagan White House, together with Congress's eventual approval of it, provided dramatic evidence of the centrality of Saudi-American relations and of changes that had occurred in public and legislative sentiment concerning America's role in the Middle East. By the 1980s official and public opinion in the United States clearly did regard cooperative Saudi-American relations—and more generally, American efforts to retain the goodwill of moderate Arab governments—as an essential strand in its Middle Eastern policy. If the outcome clearly did *not* mean that the United States had abandoned Israel, it did signify awareness that the United States had, and needed, more than one friend in the region.

The AWACS question also highlights the importance of pressure group activity in the American foreign policy process. It raises questions about the links between domestic pressure groups and foreign governments, about alliances among pressure groups, and about cooperation between private organizations and governmental officials in favor of (or in opposition to) a particular diplomatic undertaking. The evidence presented in this case clearly indicates that the long virtual monopoly enjoyed by the pro-Israeli lobby on Middle Eastern aspects of American diplomacy has ended. The government of Israel, Zionist organizations, and their friends can no longer count upon the uncritical and automatic support of the American people and their legislative leaders for the Israeli position on regional and global issues. After the AWACS episode it was evident that a countervailing pressure group—the Arab lobby—had emerged as an effective competitor.

An interesting feature of the case was the de facto alliance that was forged between the Arab lobby and the executive branch in the effort to influence congressional opinion favorably. Comparable coalitions (as between the pro-Israeli lobby and religious and labor organizations in the United States) have existed on other questions involving American diplomacy in the Middle East. For pro-Israeli groups particularly, the question was raised in the debate over AWACS whether some techniques employed by lobbyists helped—or whether in fact they may have hindered—the Israeli cause.

The AWACS episode also communicated a number of useful lessons to the Reagan administration and other actors in the controversy concerning effective techniques of lobbying and of legislative liaison on major foreign policy issues. At one point, President Reagan pointedly admonished Prime Minister Begin's government not to attempt to interfere in the American political system (and yet the Reagan White House itself arranged a visit by a high-ranking Saudi official to influence opinion on Capitol Hill). For their part, the government of Israel and its supporters did not hesitate to suggest that those who criticized Israel's position on the AWACS question were anti-Semitic—a tactic that may well have hindered Israel's cause. A substantial number of legislators also believed that the consultations between executive and legislative policymakers on the AWACS issue had been inadequate; that the White House had not been receptive enough to suggestions from the House and Senate; and that executive officials had sometimes been poorly informed about the facts and implications of the AWACS sale. Many legislators also resented the pressure placed upon them by the White House to change their viewpoints.[39]

In the end, the Reagan administration substantially achieved its objective in the AWACS case. Although Congress had the prerogative of doing so, it refrained from exercising its legislative veto over the proposed military sales to Saudi Arabia; but after the Supreme Court's decision in 1983 this device for controlling presidential activity in the foreign policy field was no longer available to Congress.[40]

While the outcome in the AWACS case could be regarded as a presidential victory vis-à-vis Congress in the conduct of foreign relations, the outcome did not signify the end of legislative assertiveness in the foreign policy field. In the months ahead, for example, President Reagan encountered deep-seated congressional opposition to his diplomacy in Central America and rising anxiety on Capitol Hill about America's continued military presence in Lebanon. Even without the legislative veto, Congress possesses other, perhaps even more potent, techniques for determining the course of American diplomacy; as emphasized in Chapters 2 and 5, it retains the historical power of the purse along with its constitutional authority to determine the size and nature of the American military establishment. As in the AWACS controversy and other cases before and after it, however, the ability and will of Congress to utilize the prerogatives available to it for diplomatic purposes remains crucial in determining the outcome of the "invitation to struggle" over particular issues in American foreign relations. To anticipate a point discussed more fully in Chapter 8: in the final analysis, Congress's *capacity* for unified and coherent participation in the foreign policy process may be the key to whether it is able to serve as a partner with the executive branch in the conduct of American foreign relations. On the basis of the evidence supplied by the AWACS case, the question of whether Congress has that capacity remains unresolved.

Although the Reagan White House ultimately won its point in the AWACS dispute, the administration was compelled to accept several ideas and constraints that legislators demanded as a price for their support of the AWACS transaction. Moreover, executive officials could not help reflecting upon the price exacted by their victory over congressional critics of the AWACS sale. In order to win his case on Capitol Hill, President Reagan and his aides were required to undertake a five-month, intensive, and enervating campaign to influence Congress and public opinion—one of the most prolonged lobbying efforts witnessed since the end of World War II. According to House Speaker Thomas P. O'Neill, the campaign conducted in behalf of the AWACS sale by President Reagan and his supporters constituted a display of "awesome power" by the White House, involving a massive expenditure of the president's political capital with the legislative branch.[41] Reagan's diplomatic victory resulted from the kind of lobbying effort that can be employed most *infrequently* by executive officials and that must be reserved for diplomatic issues of the highest priority. As events in the months that followed were to prove, gaining congressional approval for the AWACS transaction was in many respects a costly victory for the Reagan administration; the episode left in its wake a considerable residue of congressional uneasiness about the direction of American foreign policy and about the means used by the president to gain legislative support for it. This sort of environment in executive-legislative relations was not likely to foster and maintain a spirit of genuine bipartisan cooperation in the foreign policy field. Without such bipartisan foundations, the Reagan administration's diplomatic efforts were not likely to endure.

Notes

1. Background on the evolution of American diplomacy in the Middle East is available in William R. Polk, *The United States and the Arab World* (Cambridge, Mass.: Harvard University Press, 1965); John S. Badeau, *The American Approach to the Arab World* (New York: Harper and Row, 1968); and Georgiana Stevens, ed., *The United States and the Middle East* (Englewood Cliffs, N.J.: Prentice-Hall, 1964).
2. The establishment, growth, and goals of the Zionist movement are discussed more fully in Soloman Grayzel, *A History of the Jews,* rev. ed. (New York: New American Library, 1968); Arthur Hertzberg, *The Zionist Idea* (Garden City, N.Y.: Doubleday and Co., 1959); and Oscar I. Janowsky, ed., *Foundations of Israel* (Princeton, N.J.: D. Van Nostrand, 1959).
3. The background and text of the Balfour Declaration may be found in Polk, *The United States and the Arab World,* pp. 108-112.
4. See Janowsky, *Foundations of Israel,* pp. 81-88, 157-173; and Grayzel, *A History of the Jews,* pp. 669-727.
5. Dean Acheson, *Present at the Creation: My Years in the State Department* (New York: W. W. Norton, 1969), p. 169.
6. Harry S Truman, *Years of Trial and Hope,* vol. 2 of *Memoirs* (Garden City, N.Y.: Doubleday and Co., 1956), p. 158.

7. More extensive discussion of internal developments and problems within Israel since 1948 is available in Gerald Kaufman, *To Build the Promised Land* (New York: Bantam, 1973); William Frankel, *Israel Observed: An Anatomy of the State* (New York: Thames and Hudson, 1980); and Michael Curtis, ed., *Religion and Politics in the Middle East* (Boulder, Colo.: Westview Press, 1981), pp. 163-217.

8. A useful symposium on the Arab states, focusing on their regional and global policies, is Tareq Y. Ismael, ed., *The Middle East in World Politics* (Syracuse, N.Y.: Syracuse University Press, 1974). Influential political ideas and movements in the area are identified and assessed in Daniel Bates and Amal Rassam, *Peoples and Cultures of the Middle East* (Englewood Cliffs, N.J.: Prentice-Hall, 1983); and Ray R. Anderson, Robert F. Seibert, and Jon G. Wagner, *Politics and Change in the Middle East* (Englewood Cliffs, N.J.: Prentice-Hall, 1983).

9. See *The Middle East*, 5th ed. (Washington, D.C.: Congressional Quarterly, 1981), pp. 63-68; and a detailed analysis of the political and lobbying activities by pro-Israeli groups in the United States may be found in Samuel Halperin, *The Political World of American Zionism* (Detroit: Wayne State University Press, 1961).

10. Quoted in Stephen D. Isaacs, *Jews and American Politics* (Garden City, N.Y.: Doubleday and Co., 1974), pp. 264-265.

11. Marquis Childs, "Stirrings against Carter," *Washington Post*, March 13, 1979.

12. See Gerald R. Ford, *A Time to Heal* (New York: Harper and Row and the Reader's Digest Association, 1979), pp. 245-248, 286-288.

13. The 1948 war in Palestine and the resulting refugee problem are analyzed more fully in Fred J. Khouri, *The Arab-Israeli Dilemma* (Syracuse, N.Y.: Syracuse University Press, 1968), pp. 68-102. See also Don Peretz, *Israel and the Palestine Arabs* (Washington, D.C.: Middle East Institute, 1958).

14. The origins, developments, and principal consequences of the Suez Crisis of 1956 are examined in Dwight D. Eisenhower, *Waging Peace* (Garden City, N.Y.: Doubleday and Co., 1965), pp. 20-58; Anthony Eden, *The Suez Crisis of 1956* (Boston: Beacon Press, 1960); and Peter Calvocoressi, ed., *Suez: Ten Years Later* (New York: Random House, 1967).

15. Informative treatments of the Six-Day War are Khouri, *The Arab-Israeli Dilemma*, pp. 242-292; and Col. Trevor N. Dupuy, *Elusive Victory: the Arab-Israeli Wars, 1947-1974* (New York: Harper and Row, 1978), pp. 221-343.

16. The goals, organization, and membership of the Palestine Liberation Organization are examined more extensively in Gerard Chaliand, *The Palestine Resistance* (Baltimore: Penguin, 1972). More contemporary information is available in Congressional Quarterly's *The Middle East*.

17. *The Middle East*, pp. 140-142; and see the more extended discussion in Nadav Safran, *From War to War: The Arab-Israeli Confrontation, 1948-1967* (New York: Pegasus Press, 1969), pp. 317-417.

18. Soviet diplomacy in the Middle East is analyzed more fully in R. D. McLaurin, *The Middle East in Soviet Diplomacy* (Lexington, Mass.: D. C. Heath, 1975); Robert O. Freedman, *Soviet Policy Toward the Middle East Since 1970* (New York: Praeger Publishers, 1975); and Alvin Z. Rubinstein, *Red Star on the Nile* (Princeton, N.J.: Princeton University Press, 1977).

19. The outbreak of the 1973 war, its principal stages, and its consequences are examined in *The Middle East*, pp. 20-26; Dupuy, *Elusive Victory*, pp. 387-

603; and Nadav Safran, "The War and the Future of the Arab-Israeli Conflict," *Foreign Affairs* 52 (January 1974): 215-237.

20. The concept of oil power and its implications for American foreign policy in the Middle East are appraised in Dankwart A. Rustow, "Who Won the Yom Kippur and Oil Wars?" *Foreign Policy* 17 (Winter 1974-1975): 166-176; the symposium on OPEC in *Foreign Policy* 13 (Winter 1973-1974): 123-139; and James Akins, "The Oil Crisis: This Time the Wolf Is Here," *Foreign Affairs* 51 (April 1973): 462-491.

21. See, for example, former president Jimmy Carter's comments about Egyptian President Anwar Sadat in his memoirs, *Keeping Faith: Memoirs of a President* (New York: Bantam, 1982).

22. Detailed accounts of Henry Kissinger's shuttle diplomacy are provided in Edward R. F. Sheehan, *The Arabs, Israelis, and Kissinger* (New York: Reader's Digest Press, 1976); and Kissinger's memoirs, *Years of Upheaval* (Boston: Little, Brown and Co., 1982).

23. The Camp David peace negotiations are described at length in Carter, *Keeping Faith*.

24. Comprehensive background on the Iranian Revolution and on American-Iranian relations are available in Fred Halliday, *Iran: Dictatorship and Development* (Baltimore: Penguin, 1979); Barry Rubin, *Paved with Good Intentions: The American Experience and Iran* (Baltimore: Penguin, 1981); and the account of the hostage crisis in Hamilton Jordan, *Crisis: The Last Year of the Carter Presidency* (New York: G. P. Putnam's Sons, 1982).

25. For an analysis of the origins, meaning, and implications of the Carter Doctrine, see Cecil V. Crabb, Jr., *The Doctrines of American Foreign Policy: Their Meaning, Role, and Future* (Baton Rouge: Louisiana State University Press, 1982), pp. 325-371.

26. Historical background on the emergence of Saudi Arabia and on its economic and political problems is provided in R. Bayly Winder, *Saudi Arabia in the Nineteenth Century* (New York: St. Martin's Press, 1965); Fred Halliday, *Arabia Without Sultans: A Survey of Political Instability in the Arab World* (New York: Random House, 1975); and David E. Long, *Saudi Arabia* (Beverly Hills, Calif.: Sage Publications, 1976).

27. Saudi goals and attitudes since the 1973 war are identified and assessed in William B. Quandt, "Riyadh between the Superpowers," *Foreign Policy* 44 (Fall 1981): 37-57; and in Ramon Knauerhase, "Saudi Arabia: Our Conservative Ally," *Current History* 78 (January 1980): 17-22.

28. For more extensive discussion of Saudi Arabia's behavior as a leading member of OPEC, see Quandt, "Riyadh between the Superpowers," pp. 42-43; and Dankwart A. Rustow, *Oil and Turmoil: America Faces OPEC and the Middle East* (New York: W. W. Norton, 1982).

29. *The Middle East,* p. 61. American assistance in helping the government of Saudi Arabia strengthen its air defense system had initially been extended late in 1973. In the months that followed, Riyadh purchased 115 fighter planes; subsequently, Washington sold Hawk missiles to Jordan and transport aircraft to Egypt. Early in 1978 the Carter administration proposed a "package" aircraft sale to Egypt, Saudi Arabia, and Israel. Early in 1980 Saudi officials asked Washington for AWACS aircraft and other modern equipment. See the *New York Times,* November 1, 1981, dispatch by Charles Mohr.

30. President Reagan's letter is reproduced in *Department of State Bulletin* 81 (October 1981): 52.
31. See the background paper on the AWACS proposal presented by Under Secretary of State James Buckley on August 24, 1981, in *Department of State Bulletin* 81 (October 1981): 52-57.
32. See the transcript of Secretary of State Alexander Haig's testimony to the Senate Foreign Relations Committee in the *Department of State Bulletin* 81 (November 1981): 60-67.
33. *Congressional Quarterly Weekly Report,* April 11, 1981, p. 632; *The Middle East,* pp. 61-62; *New York Times,* November 1, 1981, dispatch by Charles Mohr.
34. *The Middle East,* pp. 61-63.
35. Fuller discussion of the emergence, organization, and techniques utilized by the Arab lobby may be found in *The Middle East,* pp. 63-70; and *Congressional Quarterly Weekly Report,* April 22, 1981, pp. 1523-1530.
36. See *Congressional Quarterly Weekly Report,* October 10, 1981, p. 1942, and December 26, 1981, p. 2573.
37. The Reagan administration's lobbying activities in behalf of the AWACS proposal are described in the *Congressional Quarterly Weekly Report,* April 11, 1981, p. 632; September 26, 1981, p. 1868; October 10, 1981, p. 1942; October 31, 1981, p. 2095; and December 26, 1981, pp. 2577-2578; and in the *New York Times,* October 1, 1981, dispatch by Phil Gailey.
38. *Congressional Quarterly Weekly Report,* September 26, 1981, p. 1868; October 31, 1981, p. 2095; and December 19, 1981, p. 2514; and *Newsweek,* November 9, 1981, pp. 30-33.
39. *The Middle East,* pp. 66-70; *Congressional Quarterly Weekly Report,* September 26, 1981, pp. 1868-1869; and October 31, 1981, pp. 2096-2097; and the editorial in the *New York Times,* November 1, 1981.
40. See the text of the Supreme Court decision in the case of *Immigration and Naturalization Service v. Chadha,* 51 U.S.L.W. 4907 (1983).
41. *Congressional Quarterly Weekly Report,* December 26, 1981, p. 2576; *Reagan's First Year* (Washington, D.C.: Congressional Quarterly, 1982), p. 45; and *New York Times,* November 1, 1981.

The Armed Forces 5

Where to draw the line between the power of Congress to declare war (Article I, Section 8) and the power of the president as commander in chief (Article II, Section 2) is one of the most controversial issues relating to the Constitution. How far may the president go in ordering troops into combat, or into situations where combat is likely, in the absence of a declaration of war by Congress? How far may Congress go in restraining the president? How far may, or should, Congress go in determining where the armed forces are to be deployed, even in nonhostile environments? What is the proper role for Congress in dealing with the foreign policy consequences of such deployments, especially in regard to quid pro quos for the rights to foreign bases?

These questions have been the subject of scholarly and inconclusive exegesis, and it is not our purpose to review that voluminous literature here. Nor shall we review the long history of dispute over these questions, during which the pendulum has swung between the two ends of Pennsylvania Avenue. Rather, we shall look at examples of the use of the armed forces since World War II and examine some of the problems that have arisen.

What becomes clear from the post-World War II practice is that Congress pays much less attention to constitutional niceties or consistency than it does to pragmatic considerations. When Congress has agreed with the general thrust of a presidential policy, it has acquiesced in the use or even the enlargement of presidential power. When it has disagreed, it has asserted its own prerogatives.

Korea

American troops in Korea provide a good illustration of how Congress's attitudes toward its own powers change over time. In 1950 Congress was content to let the president act on his own authority in sending American troops to Korea. In 1977 Congress insisted on having a voice in deciding whether to bring them home.

Getting In

Korea emerged from World War II a divided country. Installed by the Soviet Union, a Communist regime (the Democratic People's Republic of Korea or North Korea) governed north of the 38th parallel. Below that line, the Republic of Korea (or South Korea) developed close ties with the United States. Growing tension characterized relations between the two Koreas.

On Sunday, June 25, 1950, North Korean troops crossed the 38th parallel in an evident attempt to overrun South Korea. In the week of frantic American decisionmaking that followed, Congress played no significant role, nor did it give much indication of wanting to. In large part, this was because most members of Congress supported, initially anyway, the adminstration's response to the crisis. Such disagreement as developed was over whether Congress should formally bestow its blessing on the administration's Korea policy and whether such a blessing was constitutionally necessary or politically desirable.

The first American response to the North Korean invasion was to call for an emergency meeting of the United Nations Security Council. On Sunday, with the Soviets absent, the Security Council voted 9-0 to order North Korea to cease the invasion and withdraw. That night, following a meeting with executive officials, President Truman ordered General Douglas MacArthur, the American commander in the Far East with headquarters in Tokyo, to evacuate Americans from Korea and to get ammunition and other supplies to South Korea, by airdrop if necessary. MacArthur was authorized to use air and naval power, but he was cautioned to keep it south of the 38th parallel. This precaution becomes more significant in the light of later events.

As the meeting broke up, Truman directed the State Department to prepare a statement for him to make on Tuesday, perhaps to Congress, although that was left undecided. He emphasized that no other statement was to be made in the meantime, not even by Secretary of State Dean Acheson or Secretary of Defense Louis Johnson, both of whom had previously been scheduled to appear the next day before the Senate Appropriations Committee in connection with the mutual defense assistance program.

Truman's injunction of silence reflected a typical and traditional executive branch preference—namely, to arrive at a finished policy before involving Congress in the decisionmaking process. The extent to which Congress was willing to acquiesce in this procedure is shown by Acheson's remark that the appropriations committee hearing, which was held in executive session, "went off without too much trouble." [1]

On that Monday, Truman himself had talked to the chairman of the Senate Foreign Relations Committee, Tom Connally, D-Texas. The president had inquired whether the senator thought a declaration of war would be necessary "if I decide to send American forces into Korea." Connally replied:

> If a burglar breaks into your house, you can shoot at him without going down to the police station and getting permission. You might run into a long debate by Congress, which would tie your hands completely. You have the right to do it as commander in chief and under the U.N. Charter.[2]

On Monday night Truman authorized MacArthur to use air and naval power in direct support of South Korea and again cautioned him to stay south of the 38th parallel. On Tuesday, June 27, the U.N. Security Council met again and called on all members of the United Nations to give assistance to the Republic of Korea. This was later used to give an added color of legitimacy to American actions.

The morning of that same day, Truman met with a bipartisan group of 14 members of Congress from both houses. Acheson summarized the situation in Korea. Truman read a press release (the statement he had asked on Sunday night to have prepared), announcing American air and naval support for South Korea. The president then requested the views of the congressional leaders; Truman later reported in his memoirs that they "approved of my action." [3] According to Acheson, "Senator Wiley seemed to express the consensus by saying that it was enough for him to know that we were in there with force and that the President thought the force adequate." [4] (It was not.) Connally recalls that he and others stressed the importance of the U.N. action and that "a few wondered if Congress should approve." [5]

Republican Sen. Robert A. Taft of Ohio, who was not in the group invited to the White House, did not wonder; he was convinced. In a speech in the Senate on Wednesday, June 28, Taft noted that the congressional leaders had no opportunity to change the president's statement and that "there has been no pretense of consulting the Congress." There was, he said, no legal authority for what the president had done, yet he added that "if a joint resolution were introduced asking for approval of the use of our Armed Forces already sent to Korea and full support of them in their present venture, I would vote for it." [6]

On Thursday, June 29, Truman expanded the involvement of U.S. air and naval forces to include military targets in North Korea, but not beyond. He also authorized the use of ground forces to secure the port, airfield, and communications facilities at Pusan on the southeast coast. On the morning of Friday, June 30, Truman gave MacArthur authority to use the ground forces under his command. The United States was then fully committed to the conflict.

That same day, a second White House meeting was held with members of Congress. Perhaps twice as many were present as on Tuesday. Truman reported to the legislators the orders he had issued about ground troops. There was, says Acheson, "a general chorus of approval," and Rep. Dewey Short, R-Mo., declared that "Congress was practically unanimous in its appreciation of the President's leadership." [7] But Senate Republican leader Kenneth Wherry of Nebraska questioned the president's legal authority. Sen. H. Alexander Smith, R-N.J., suggested a resolution approving the action. The president said he would consider this and asked Acheson to prepare a recommendation.

Acheson recommended against the resolution at a meeting with the president July 3, by which time Congress, incredibly, had recessed for a week over the Fourth of July. Senate Majority Leader Scott Lucas, D-Ill., was the only member of Congress present at the meeting, and he agreed with Acheson. Lucas argued that the vast majority of Congress was satisfied and the minority could not be won over but could keep debating and delaying a resolution so as to dilute much of its public effect.[8]

Getting In Deeper

During July and August the North Koreans swept down the peninsula and the U.N. forces, principally Americans, were hard pressed to hold a beachhead around Pusan. Then in September MacArthur made a surprise amphibious landing at Inchon on the northwest coast, cutting off the bulk of the North Korean forces to the south and rapidly driving the remainder north of the 38th parallel. This totally changed the military situation and led to a rethinking, both in Washington and in the United Nations, of American and U.N. objectives. The ultimate objective of U.S. policy in Korea since World War II had been the political reunification of the country under a democratic system.

As a consequence, what had started in June as a defensive operation aimed at restoring the status quo ante became in September and October an offensive operation aimed at achieving a united, independent, and democratic Korea. In June MacArthur had been instructed not to cross the 38th parallel; now he was authorized to do so. The U.N. General Assembly went further on October 7 in a resolution looking toward U.N.-sponsored elections in a unified Korea.

This was a radical expansion of military goals, and it led to disastrous consequences, but Congress had almost nothing to do with it. Two members of the Senate Foreign Relations Committee—Henry Cabot Lodge, Jr., R-Mass., and John Sparkman, D-Ala.—were serving as delegates to the General Assembly that year. Sparkman later confessed to doubts about the wisdom of the offensive operation; but if he expressed those doubts at the time, he certainly did so quietly.

That the doubts were well-founded became apparent in late November, when massive Chinese forces poured across the Yalu River boundary between China and Korea and drove the U.N. troops southward. In the course of the bitter winter of retreat, a long-simmering dispute erupted between MacArthur on the one hand and the Joint Chiefs of Staff, the president, and the State Department on the other. In brief, MacArthur wanted to widen the war by air attacks on China; the government in Washington, fearful of possible Soviet intervention and of becoming inextricably entangled on the mainland of China, wanted to fight a limited war in Korea.

MacArthur steadily became more strident in his criticism of the administration's policy, and on April 10, 1951, Truman relieved him of all his commands. This led Congress to inject itself into the Korean conflict for the first time in a major way. Two separate but related issues were involved: civilian control of the military (one of the bedrock principles of the American government) and the conduct of the war itself or, more broadly, the grand design of America's global strategy.

As has repeatedly occurred in connection with other cases, Congress involved itself in the controversy over MacArthur's dismissal on pragmatic grounds of policy, not on grounds of constitutional principle or procedure. Nobody questioned Truman's authority as president and commander in chief to relieve a general, but many people questioned his wisdom in doing so. At the bottom of this dispute was a fundamental difference over whether the United States should pursue a defensive or an offensive global strategy; in other words, the U.S. could attempt either to contain the Communist world or to put unrelenting pressure on it at all available points. This difference was epitomized in Korea. On one side, General MacArthur and his supporters wanted to pursue the offensive strategy—that is, to expand the war by carrying it to China. On the other side, President Truman, his principal advisers, and their supporters wanted to follow the defensive strategy—that is, to confine hostilities to Korea.

In the context of the recall of MacArthur, the debate over this broader issue took the form of a series of narrow, essentially tactical questions, such as whether to bomb north of the Yalu River. It was a classic example of the problem of where to draw the line between the day-to-day *conduct* of the war (which was the prerogative of the president as commander in chief), and the long-range *policy* of the war itself (in the determination of which Congress had a major role). The problem would arise again two decades later in connection with the bombing of Hanoi during the Vietnam War.

The outcry that followed the firing of MacArthur was immense, both in Congress and in the public at large. The general returned to the United States, for the first time in 14 years, more as a hero than as an officer disgraced for insubordination. He was met everywhere by wildly enthusiastic crowds. Congress took the astonishing step of inviting him to address a joint session and greeted him with an emotional ovation.

Pursuant to action by the Senate, the committees on Armed Forces and on Foreign Relations made a meticulous and exhaustive inquiry into MacArthur's dismissal under the general heading "Military Situation in the Far East." On 43 days, beginning May 3 and ending June 27, 1951, the two committees took testimony from 14 witnesses, including General MacArthur, Secretary of State Acheson, Secretary of Defense George

Marshall, and all the members of the Joint Chiefs of Staff. The record of the proceedings covers 3,691 pages. In the end, no report was issued and no further action taken, although different members of the committees delivered themselves of different conclusions.

The hearing served the purpose—intended by the Democratic leadership of the two committees—of defusing the Truman-MacArthur controversy by talking it to death. In large part because of the prolonged public airing the controversy received in Congress, popular and legislative support for General MacArthur's position declined significantly. The result was that the conduct of the Korean War was left where the Democratic leaders of Congress wanted it: in the hands of the president.

Following lengthy negotiations, an armistice in the Korean War was finally signed on July 27, 1953. No peace treaty between the belligerents was ever concluded, however; and relations between the two countries remained hostile throughout the years that followed. On October 1, 1953, the United States and South Korea concluded a mutual defense treaty, formally signifying America's commitment to the preservation of South Korea's independence.

Getting Out

A quarter of a century later, Jimmy Carter campaigned for the presidency advocating, among other things, withdrawal of some of the 41,000 American troops that remained in Korea in 1976. As Carter moved to execute this withdrawal in 1977, however, he ran into unexpected congressional opposition, opposition not unlike that encountered by President Truman in the MacArthur affair.

First, the same differences over global strategy that were so noticeable in 1951 still existed in 1977, but with a significant change. In 1951 it was the doves who wanted to maintain the status quo; in 1977 it was the hawks.

Second, on May 19, 1977, the *Washington Post* published an interview with Maj. Gen. John K. Singlaub, chief of staff of the American military command in Korea, in which the general was quoted as saying, "If we withdraw our ground forces on the schedule suggested, it will lead to war." Singlaub was recalled and reassigned by the White House. He was given a hearing by a congressional committee, this time the Investigations Subcommittee of the House Armed Services Committee. These hearings, like the MacArthur hearings, were marked by controversy and ended inconclusively.

Also in May, the Senate Foreign Relations Committee, at the instigation of Sen. George McGovern, D-S.D., added a policy statement about Korea to the bill authorizing appropriations for the State Department. The principal provision of this amendment was that "the United States should seek to accomplish, in accord with the President's announced intention, a complete withdrawal of United States ground forces from the Korean peninsula within four or five years." [9]

When the bill came before the Senate in June, this provision ran into a buzz saw of opposition. The debate was directed primarily to the merits of the issue—that is, whether withdrawing some or all of the troops from Korea was a sensible thing to do—but it also marked a new assertiveness by Congress with respect to the congressional role in deciding the issue. To avoid congressional repudiation of the president's policy, and more particularly to blunt an effort to enact some kind of prohibition on troop withdrawal, Majority Leader Robert C. Byrd, D-W.V., offered a substitute amendment that watered down McGovern's support of the president. As it finally passed the Senate, the Byrd amendment had Congress declaring that "U.S. policy toward Korea should continue to be arrived at by joint decision of the President and the Congress" and that "any implementation of the foregoing policy should be done in regular consultation with the Congress." [10]

In 1973, as will be discussed later, Congress had passed over President Nixon's veto the War Powers Resolution, which sharply circumscribed presidential authority to send troops abroad. Nixon based his veto on grounds of unconstitutional interference with the president's powers as commander in chief. Now Congress was going further and asserting its prerogative to circumscribe presidential authority to bring troops home. It argued in part from the precedent of the War Powers Resolution.

"I do not think this is strictly an executive branch decision," said Sen. Sam Nunn, D-Ga., a prominent member of the Armed Services Committee. "Under the War Powers Act [sic], we talked a long time about the commitment of troops abroad. I should think that, by implication, we would have some control over the withdrawal of forces that are in a dangerous spot in the world." And, "If it works one way, it works the other." [11]

Some senators who had opposed the War Powers Resolution now also opposed the president's authority unilaterally to withdraw troops from Korea. During the hearings on war powers, the following exchange occurred:

> Senator Javits. So really you are opposed to my bill because you have less faith in the Congress than you have in the President; isn't that true?
> Senator Goldwater. To be perfectly honest with you, you are right. [12]

Now Goldwater argued that the president should send his requests about Korea "to the proper committees of Congress, and then we can hold hearings." [13]

And Sen. James Allen, D-Ala., arguing against the Carter policy, said:

> We are turning our backs completely, as I see it, on the principle that was established in the Vietnam war debates, namely, that Congress have a right to participate in decisions regarding the waging of war or foreign policy in general.

But here, we are abdicating our role. A role that was fought for here in the Congress.

I did not always support that.... I thought the President as Commander-in-Chief of our Armed Forces should have a right to dictate the other policy, but the wisdom of the Congress, in which I now concur, prevailed and Congress did assert unto itself the right to participate in foreign policy decisions.[14]

Congress returned to the subject in 1978. Various proposals to put firm limits on the withdrawal were rejected, but the military assistance bill expressed the view that "further withdrawal of ground forces of the United States from the Republic of Korea may seriously risk upsetting the military balance in that region and requires full advance consultation with Congress." The act also says that the president "should" transmit to Congress, 120 days before each phase of troop withdrawal, "a report on the viability of the withdrawal." [15] The use of the word *should* is curious; most reporting requirements use the stronger *shall*.

In January 1979 new intelligence estimates showed greater North Korean military strength than had previously been thought. This finding increased doubts both in Congress and in the Pentagon. Finally, in July the White House announced that further implementation of Carter's plan was being postponed until 1981. By that time there was a new president in the White House, and the issue died by common consent. The total troop reduction from 1977 to 1979 was from 41,000 to 38,000.

Europe

Getting In

As part of its strategy of containing communism the United States joined 11 other Western nations in establishing the North Atlantic Treaty Organization (NATO) early in 1949. Then on September 9, 1950 (less than three months after American troops had been committed to the defense of South Korea with little objection from Congress) President Truman announced his approval of a "substantial increase" in American forces in Europe over the two American divisions already in Germany. On December 19 Truman said this increase would be carried out as soon as possible.

This decision provoked a great debate in the Senate, which began on January 5, 1951, with a major foreign policy speech by Sen. Robert Taft, R-Ohio:

As I see it [said Taft, foreshadowing the arguments that would be heard 15 years later with respect to Vietnam] members of Congress, and particularly members of the Senate, have a constitutional obligation to reexamine constantly and discuss the foreign policy of the United States. If we permit appeals to unity to bring an end to that criticism, we endanger not only the constitutional liberties of the country, but even its future existence.[16]

The president, Taft asserted,

> has no power to agree to send American troops to fight in Europe between members of the Atlantic Pact and Soviet Russia. Without authority, he involved us in the Korean war. Without authority, he apparently is now attempting to adopt a similar policy in Europe.[17]

Three days later, Senate Republican leader Kenneth Wherry of Nebraska introduced a sense of the Senate resolution (a resolution voted on by the Senate but without the president's signature and not having the force of law) that no American ground forces "should be assigned to duty in the European area for the purposes of the North Atlantic Treaty pending the formulation of a policy with respect thereto by the Congress."[18] This resolution was the subject of prolonged hearings by the Foreign Relations and Armed Services committees, in the course of which the administration put a figure of four divisions on its planned increase.

As had happened in the MacArthur controversy, the hearings and the Senate debate that followed were confused by the mixing of the issue of substantive policy and the issue of the proper role of Congress. Those who favored Truman's policy in Europe tended to take a broad view of the president's powers to act on his own. Those who opposed the policy tended to take a narrow view. The matter was complicated by the desire of the president's supporters to avoid any action on the part of Congress. They feared that, even if Congress approved the policy, the action might set a precedent that Congress had the right to do so. The end result was ambiguous and not wholly satisfactory to either side, though less so to those who supported a broad concept of presidential authority.

In March, following the hearings, the Foreign Relations and Armed Services committees reported two resolutions that were identical in language but different in form. One was a simple Senate resolution; the other was a concurrent resolution, that is, one requiring passage by both houses. The operative provisions of the resolutions approved the appointment of General Eisenhower as NATO commander and a "fair share" contribution of U.S. forces in NATO; asked the president to consult with the Senate Foreign Relations, House Foreign Affairs, and Armed Services committees in both houses before sending the troops abroad; and asked that the Joint Chiefs of Staff certify that other NATO countries were doing their share before U.S. troops were sent.[19]

The reasons for reporting two resolutions, though complicated in a technical parliamentary sense, reflected the underlying substantive issues. A Senate resolution requires action only by the Senate; a concurrent resolution requires action by the House as well. Neither is submitted to the president for his signature and neither has the force of law. They are only formal expressions of the sense of the Senate or the Congress, as the case may be. If the Senate passes both a Senate and a concurrent resolution in the same terms, the Senate resolution can stand alone if the House fails to act. A concurrent resolution, being an expression of both houses of Congress, carries somewhat more weight; but it also ruffles a latent senatorial jealousy of the House in matters of foreign affairs.

Some senators insisted that the action be taken in the form of a joint resolution. A joint resolution goes to the president for his signature and has the force of law. Thus, in the hierarchy of these things, a joint resolution is the most binding action; a simple Senate (or House) resolution, the least binding. Those who took the broadest view of the president's powers favored a Senate resolution; those who took the narrowest view favored a joint resolution.

These crosscurrents of opinion were reflected in the Senate votes. The simple Senate resolution passed by a vote of 69-21. The concurrent resolution passed by only 45-41 in the Senate and languished to its death in the House. The Senate rejected the idea of a joint resolution 31-56. The Senate also adopted an amendment offered by John McClellan, D-Ark., that no more than four divisions should be sent without the Senate's approval. The McClellan amendment was first rejected by 44-46. It was then reconsidered and agreed to, 49-43. The McClellan amendment had no force of law, but it was an assertion of Senate prerogatives that distressed the Truman administration.

Getting Out

Thereafter, discussion of the issue in Congress died out for a time. Over a period of years American troops in Europe were increased until they numbered approximately 300,000, accompanied by 225,000 dependents, most of them in Germany (which became a member of NATO in 1955). By 1966 there had begun to be agitation to bring some of them home. In a sense, it was a spillover of the nascent Senate disillusionment with Vietnam. More directly, it was a consequence of the French withdrawal from the military side of NATO and a generalized feeling that the United States contribution to NATO was more than its "fair share" (in the words of the 1951 resolution). Congressional sentiment for cutting American forces in Europe increased later as the dollar declined relative to the German mark, making it more expensive to maintain the troops in the NATO area.

The most articulate spokesman for reducing American troops in Europe was Senate Majority Leader Mike Mansfield, D-Mont. In 1966 Mansfield, joined by 12 other members of the Senate Democratic Policy Committee, introduced a resolution expressing the sense of the Senate that American forces in Europe should be reduced. Despite the prominence of its sponsors, no action was taken on the resolution, and the issue of troop reduction, although raised annually, did not come to a head until 1971.

In that year Mansfield shifted his strategy from Senate resolutions—in effect, recommendations to the president—to the power of the purse. In an amendment to a bill extending the draft, he proposed to limit funds to the amount necessary to support 150,000 troops. This would have meant a reduction of 50 percent, and it provoked a major debate in the Senate during which five alternative troop cut proposals were offered. All of them were less drastic than the Mansfield amendment, and all were defeated by a coalition of those who thought they did too little and those who thought they did too much. In the end, the Mansfield amendment itself was rejected by a vote of 36-61, but 60 senators voted for at least one of the proposals. The Nixon administration's all-out effort against troop reduction in Europe received a major assist from the Soviet Union in the form of the overture that led to Mutual Balanced Force Reduction (MBFR) talks in Vienna. This provided opponents of the reduction with the argument that the troops ought to be left in Europe as bargaining chips.

The Senate voted on the subject again in November 1971, when the Appropriations Committee added an amendment to the defense appropriation bill limiting funds to the level required for 250,000 troops. This was rejected 39-54.

Congress then let the issue drop for a decade, but returned to it in the early 1980s as concern mounted over the fairness of NATO cost sharing. In its report on the military construction authorization bill in 1981, the conference committee noted that the United States was paying all of the costs of the Rapid Deployment Force designed for use in the Persian Gulf and said that therefore it was imperative that other NATO members pay some of the costs of certain U.S. facilities in Europe. "Otherwise," the conferees warned, "the American people may force the Congress to consider reductions in U.S. defense commitments and such reductions could begin with a reduction in the number of U.S. military personnel deployed in Europe." [20]

In 1982, in the fiscal 1983 defense appropriations bill, the Senate Appropriations Committee limited troops in Europe to the level of fiscal 1980. It also provided for disbanding the Third Brigade of the First Cavalry Division. These provisions were weakened somewhat during Senate consideration of the appropriations continuing resolution, but the Pentagon felt sufficiently constrained that Defense Secretary Weinberger urged Congress to repeal the ceiling in fiscal 1984. Instead, Congress extended it.

The recurring efforts to reduce troops in Europe moved from numerical recommendations to limitations on money. These efforts thereby avoided the constitutional argument that was raised by the McClellan amendment to the original troops-to-Europe resolution in 1951 and repeated in the debate on the War Powers Resolution in 1973. This was whether Congress has a power, other than the power of the purse, to control troop deployments.

Eleven of the senators who voted on the McClellan amendment, including McClellan himself, were still in the Senate for the vote on Nixon's veto of the War Powers Resolution. A consistent view of the relative powers of the president and Congress over the armed forces would have required the same vote—yea on the part of those favoring a restriction of the president's powers and nay on the part of those opposing a restriction. Only two senators, McClellan and

Milton Young, R-N.D., voted the same way both times, yea in each case.

The Senate in 1951 also included two future presidents and one future vice president—Lyndon Johnson, Richard Nixon, and Hubert Humphrey. Although Humphrey voted against the limitation on the president's powers implied in the McClellan amendment, 22 years later he voted for the tighter limitation contained in the War Powers Resolution. Johnson and Nixon, each of whom as president was to assert sweeping executive powers, split on the McClellan amendment. Johnson—consistent with his later actions—voted against it. Nixon voted for it, then later vetoed the War Powers Resolution.

Other senators who voted on the McClellan amendment and the War Powers Resolution were John Sparkman, J. William Fulbright, Russell Long, James Eastland, John Stennis, John Pastore, George Aiken, and Warren Magnuson. (Technically, Magnuson did not vote on the McClellan amendment, but he was paired against it, which for practical purposes is the same thing.) [21] All of them changed from a less to a more restrictive view of presidential power.

Vietnam

What brought about this change was the war in Vietnam, which in the late 1960s and early 1970s became the most divisive issue in the United States since the Civil War. The period was marked by a growing split between Congress and two presidents, a schism that led to the enactment of the War Powers Resolution over Nixon's veto in November 1973 and finally to use of the ultimate congressional power—the power to withhold appropriations.

The differences between Congress and the president originated in the substantive policy of American involvement in Vietnam. The argument over relative constitutional powers came later. Congress itself, like the country at large, was divided over Vietnam. The curve of opinion in Congress, like that of public opinion, progressed from acceptance of presidential policies, through opposition by a minority, to opposition by an overwhelming majority. A farsighted member of the House saw this development coming at a time when the American buildup was just beginning. "We can take 1 casualty per congressional district," he said privately. "We can maybe even take 10. But if it gets to be 100, Congress will stop it." That is precisely what happened. By the time Congress stopped it, American deaths totaled about 50,000, or a little more than 100 per congressional district.

Getting In

Congress paid strikingly little attention to the steps taken by the Johnson administration in 1965 to convert the American role in Vietnam from support and advice to active participation. The first of these steps came in February, when Johnson ordered the bombing of North Vietnam in retaliation for a Viet Cong attack on an American barracks (housing personnel who were technically still advisers). The second came in July, when Johnson, after publicly agonizing over the decision, ordered an additional 50,000 American troops to Vietnam.

One reason for the almost silent congressional acquiescence was relief that those measures were not more far reaching. Before the July decision officials of the Johnson administration had talked about the possibility of calling up the reserves, raising taxes, and imposing controls on the economy. Compared to these proposals, sending 50,000 more regular army troops to Vietnam did not seem to be so drastic.

The same psychology had been at work to some extent the year before, when Congress, to its later regret, provided a statutory basis for the war through the Gulf of Tonkin resolution. This resolution was occasioned by a reported attack August 2, 1964, on the U.S. Navy destroyer *Maddox* while it was on what was described as a routine patrol in the Gulf of Tonkin off the North Vietnamese coast. On August 4 further attacks were reported on the *Maddox* and on the *C. Turner Joy,* which had joined it. There was no damage to the destroyers, but President Johnson ordered air strikes against North Vietnamese torpedo boat bases. The next day Johnson asked Congress for a joint resolution. In part, it read:

> That the Congress approves and supports the determination of the President, as Commander-in-Chief, to take all necessary measures to repel any armed attack against the forces of the United States and to prevent further aggression.
>
> SEC. 2. The United States regards as vital to its national interest and to world peace the maintenance of international peace and security in southeast Asia. Consonant with the Constitution of the United States and the Charter of the United Nations and in accordance with its obligations under the Southeast Asia Collective Defense Treaty, the United States is, therefore, prepared, as the President determines, to take all necessary steps, including the use of armed force, to assist any member or protocol state of the Southeast Asia Collective Defense Treaty requesting assistance in defense of its freedom.[22]

This resolution passed Congress August 7—two days after Johnson had requested it—by votes of 416-0 in the House and 88-2 in the Senate. Johnson was fond of carrying a tattered copy of it in his pocket and of showing it to anyone who questioned his authority, especially to members of Congress who had voted for it. He and other executive officials considered the resolution the "functional equivalent" of a declaration of war.

The immediate military response to the incidents of August 2-4 had been limited. This made Johnson look moderate, especially when compared to Sen. Barry Goldwater, his Republican opponent in the 1964 presidential election.

Later on, however, a serious question developed of whether the resolution had passed Congress under false pretenses. A review of navy documents by the Senate Foreign Relations Committee revealed that the *Maddox* had been not on a routine patrol, but rather on a sensitive and provocative intelligence mission. There was even some doubt as to whether one of the reported attacks even occurred.

Congress repealed the Gulf of Tonkin resolution in 1971. It may also be noted that this resolution was only one of five that Congress passed between 1955 and 1964 approving in advance the use of force to achieve specified American objectives in various parts of the world. The other resolutions concerned Formosa (passed 1955, repealed 1974), the Middle East (1957), Cuba (1962), and Berlin (1962).

Getting Out

For a number of years Congress did no more than argue, albeit with increasing stridency, the merits of presidential policies in Vietnam. In other words, it hoped to effect change through persuasion, rather than through legislation. In large part this was because until the 1970s the opposition was still not strong enough to muster a majority in Congress for legislation that would significantly restrict the scope of American involvement. Many members of Congress who had doubts about the wisdom of the involvement still felt compelled to support it because American troops had already been committed.

As opposition to the war increased, so did congressional frustration in trying to end it, and Congress turned to the power of the purse. A significant step in that direction was taken in 1970, when in the Cooper-Church amendment to the foreign military sales bill, Congress prohibited the expenditure of funds to support military operations in Cambodia after July 1, 1970. In a sense, this action was symbolic, inasmuch as by that cutoff date the Nixon administration had already withdrawn American ground forces from the country. It did, however, have the practical effect of preventing the reintroduction of American air and ground forces when the situation in Cambodia later deteriorated.

Throughout the months that followed, Congress utilized the same approach toward American involvement in Indochina. In 1973 and 1974, for example, no less than seven restrictions were placed on the use of funds appropriated by Congress for American military activities in the region. Typical of these restrictions was the language of the State Department Authorization Act of 1973:

> Notwithstanding any other provision of law, on or after August 15, 1973, no funds heretofore or hereafter appropriated may be obligated or expended to finance the involvement of United States military forces in hostilities in or over or from off the shores of North Vietnam, South Vietnam, Laos, or Cambodia, unless specifically authorized hereafter by the Congress.[23]

Again, as with the Cooper-Church amendment, the immediate practical effect of such measures was in a sense symbolic; the American involvement was winding down. The question was whether the disengagement would have occurred anyway or whether it was a response to growing congressional insistence. The congressional grip on the purse strings may also have prevented a reinvolvement in the hectic days of the final withdrawal in 1975.

The War Powers Resolution

Passing the Resolution

During the summer of 1973 Congress was in addition nearing the end of more than three years of consideration of the War Powers Resolution. The immediate inspiration for the early drafts of this measure was the American incursion into Cambodia ordered by President Nixon in May 1970.

As it finally emerged from the legislative process in November 1973, the War Powers Resolution was a complicated law in which a number of disparate strands of congressional thought were woven together. There was a general desire to restrain the president by ensuring a larger congressional role in war making, but the fulfillment of this desire was sought by various routes.

Some saw the resolution as a restatement of what the Founding Fathers had intended, an intent which in this view had been distorted through congressional abdication. It was a way of forcing Congress to share the responsibility for sending Americans into combat. Others viewed the resolution as a way to delineate the powers of the president as commander in chief. (And some, such as Sen. Thomas Eagleton, D-Mo., ended by opposing it because in their view it expanded those powers.) Still others, such as Sen. Jacob Javits, R-N.Y., viewed it as providing the basis for a compact between the president and Congress on how the totality of their combined powers would be exercised. (This concept was shattered when Nixon vetoed the resolution.)

The constitutional powers of the president as commander in chief to introduce the armed forces into hostilities "or into situations where imminent involvement in hostilities is clearly indicated by the circumstances" were defined by the War Powers Resolution. The powers "are exercised *only* pursuant to (1) a declaration of war, (2) specific statutory authorization, or (3) a national emergency created by attack upon the United States, its territories or possessions, or its armed forces." [Sec. 2(c). Emphasis added.] Note that the resolution excludes a national emergency created some other way—for example, an attack on American civilians abroad, or an attack on merchant shipping (as in the *Mayaguez* case), or the perceived threat of an attack (as in the Cuban missile crisis).

In any event, the president "shall" consult with Congress "in every possible instance" beforehand (Sec. 3).

In the absence of a declaration of war, the president is to report to Congress within 48 hours of deploying the armed forces in three kinds of situations: when the forces are sent into hostilities or into situations where hostilities are imminent; when forces equipped for combat are sent to any foreign country (except for supply, replacement, repair, or training); and when they are sent in numbers that "substantially enlarge" combat-equipped forces already abroad [Sec. 4(a)].

With respect to the last two of these three situations, the president's report is the end of the matter. With respect to the first, the law originally provided that Congress could order the forces withdrawn at any time by a concurrent resolution, which does not require the president's signature and is therefore not subject to his veto. This provision was invalidated in the summer of 1983 when the Supreme Court, in a case involving a different statute, ruled that the procedure—known as a legislative veto—is unconstitutional. (The legislative veto was discussed in more detail in Chapter 2.) The Court held that Congress instead must pass a law, that is, either a bill or a joint resolution, which must be presented to the president for his signature or veto.[24] In any event, under the War Powers Resolution the forces are to be withdrawn at the end of 60 days—in special cases, 90 days—unless Congress in the meantime has declared war, enacted some other specific authorization, extended the 60-day period, or is physically unable to meet (Sec. 5).[25]

In the form in which it became law, the War Powers Resolution passed Congress in October 1973. President Nixon vetoed it on October 24, calling it "unconstitutional and dangerous to the best interests of our Nation." [26] Nixon's objections were directed less to the concurrent resolution procedure (which would later be nullified by the Supreme Court decision) than to what he saw as infringement of the president's powers as commander in chief. Both houses voted to override the veto on November 7, the House by 284-135, the Senate by 75-18.

Gerald Ford shared Nixon's view that the resolution was unconstitutional and as a member of the House voted against it. Nevertheless, as president, Ford sent Congress the reports required by the resolution on four occasions: the evacuation of Danang, Phnom Penh, and Saigon in April 1975 and the rescue of the ship *Mayaguez* from Cambodian captors the following month. These four incidents were of short duration, ranging from less than three hours to eight days.

No question was raised about the operations in Danang and Phnom Penh. The evacuation of Saigon was controversial mainly because many in Congress thought it should have been carried out sooner than it was. The rescue of the *Mayaguez* was very controversial. Critics charged that the operation represented an overreaction by the Ford administration and that Congress had not been consulted. But nobody complained about the end result.

The Carter administration did not contest the constitutionality of the War Powers Resolution. On April 26, 1980 (within the 48-hour period provided by the resolution), President Carter submitted a report to Congress on the abortive mission to rescue the hostages in Iran. The president had not, however, consulted with Congress, as required by the resolution, before launching the mission. He did at least inform, if not consult, the Senate majority leader, Robert C. Byrd. Byrd apparently expressed no view as to the substance of the operation, but he did advise the president to consult more widely in Congress ("to bring Congress in as an equal partner," as Byrd later put it) [27] and particularly to consult with the minority. Carter's failure to consult was later upheld in a legal opinion by Lloyd Cutler, the president's counsel, as "a lawful exercise of his constitutional powers as President and Commander-in-Chief." [28]

The Reagan administration initially took the position that it would comply with the resolution without committing itself as to the binding nature of it. By 1983, however, the administration was caught up in controversies about the presence of American troops in Lebanon, Grenada, and Central America and was resisting what it saw as encroachment on the constitutional powers of the president.

Before we more fully describe these controversial deployments, we should note that President Reagan did make one war powers report that did not provoke controversy. This was in connection with Libyan attacks on Chad in 1983. In response to Chadian appeals for help, Reagan sent two AWACS and eight F-15s to stand by in Sudan. He reported this to Congress August 8. The French became even more heavily involved in Chad, and on August 23 the American planes began leaving Sudan.

The Resolution in Action

Lebanon. The presence of U.S. Marines in Lebanon was a part of the administration's efforts to bring peace and stability to that country and thus to lessen tension in the Middle East. The Lebanese difficulties were many and complex. The population is part Christian and part Moslem (Moslems are now in the majority), with both Christians and Moslems further subdivided into disputatious factions, many with their own armies. In addition, Lebanon has received waves of Palestinian refugees from Israel. And there was an influx of Palestine Liberation Organization fighters whom King Hussein ejected from Jordan in 1970. All of this erupted into a bitter and destructive civil war in 1975. In 1976 Syrian military intervention, carried out on behalf of the Arab League, temporarily ended the fighting, and the Syrian Army remained in Lebanon. Israel subsidized a Christian militia to keep the PLO away from northern Israel, but sporadic guerrilla raids on Israeli settlements continued.

Their patience exhausted, the Israelis invaded Lebanon in the summer of 1982, driving as far as Beirut. In August agreement was reached, with the crucial diplomatic assistance of the United States, for PLO withdrawal. A part of the agreement was that the evacuation would be observed by an international force of 800 Americans, 800 French, and 400 Italians. U.S. Marines began arriving August 25. Reagan had reported their arrival to Congress the day before—as he put it, "consistent with the War Powers Resolution." With this phrasing he avoided recognizing the validity of the resolution (as would have been the case if he had reported "under" it or "pursuant to" it) and at the same time made it difficult to charge that he was flouting the resolution. The evacuation was carried out successfully (though subsequently elements of the PLO began to infiltrate back), and the marines left Lebanon September 10.

They were back September 29, this time numbering 1,200 (the troops were subsequently increased to 1,700), and again in company with the French and Italians; later these forces were joined by a small British contingent. Their mission was to interpose themselves between various parties to the conflict—Israelis, Syrians, Lebanese government forces, and various other armed factions. On September 29 Reagan reported to Congress on their return, again "consistent with the War Powers Resolution." Initially it was hoped that the marines would stay no longer than 30 days and then that they would be gone by the end of 1982, but this hope was not realized.

Meanwhile, controversy grew over their presence and over whether the situation was one of "imminent" hostilities. If it was, then under the War Powers Resolution they could stay no more than 60 days—in exceptional circumstances, 90 days—unless Congress declared war or passed a specific, statutory authorization. Congress dealt with the problem tangentially in the Lebanon Emergency Assistance Act of 1983 (P.L. 98-43, approved June 27, 1983). This law provided, among other things, that the "President shall obtain statutory authorization ... with respect to any substantial expansion in the number or role in Lebanon of United States Armed Forces." This was a way of saying that Congress accepted, perhaps even approved, the policy thus far but was uneasy over where it might lead.

This uneasiness increased after August 29, when the marines had their first casualties—2 killed and 14 wounded, the consequence of nearby fighting between the Lebanese armed forces and various other factions. Marines returned the fire. Two more marines were killed September 6; the French also suffered casualties. On September 8 U.S. Navy guns offshore fired into the mountains, the source of the fire on the marines. On September 13, the White House announced that American air power and artillery might be used to defend positions of the Lebanese armed forces important to the defense of the marines. On September 17 there was more American naval fire, this time against guns in Syrian-held territory that were shelling the Lebanese defense ministry and the American ambassador's residence. On September 19 the navy opened fire to prevent the Lebanese army's loss of a strategic town in the mountains.

Thus in the space of three weeks there occurred a gradual, unannounced expansion of the American role from providing a buffer to taking sides in a civil war. The president reported the marine casualties to Congress August 30, but he still resisted describing the Americans as in hostilities.

The administration did, however, engage in extensive negotiations with congressional leaders, principally House Speaker Thomas P. O'Neill, Jr., D-Mass., and out of these talks emerged a compromise. This compromise passed the House September 28 and the Senate September 29. Reagan signed it October 12.[29] Its key provisions were:

> "United States Armed Forces ... in Lebanon are now in hostilities requiring authorization of their continued presence under the War Powers Resolution."
>
> "[T]he requirements of section 4(a)(1) of the War Powers Resolution became operative on August 29, 1983." This is the section applying to actual or imminent hostilities.
>
> "The Congress intends this joint resolution to constitute the necessary specific statutory authorization under the War Powers Resolution for continued participation by United States Armed Forces in the Multinational Force in Lebanon."
>
> "[S]uch protective measures as may be necessary to ensure the safety of the Multinational Force in Lebanon" are not precluded.

The authorization was good for 18 months, meaning that it would expire April 12, 1985.

In signing the resolution, Reagan said:

> ... I do not and cannot cede any of the authority vested in me under the Constitution as President and as Commander-in-Chief of the United States Armed Forces. Nor should my signing be viewed as any acknowledgment that the President's constitutional authority can be impermissibly infringed by statute, that congressional authorization would be required if and when the period specified in ... the War Powers Resolution might be deemed to have been triggered and the period had expired, or that [the 18-month authorization] may be interpreted to revise the President's constitutional authority to deploy United States Armed Forces.

The vote on the resolution in the Senate, 54-46, was sharply partisan, with all but three Republicans voting for it and all but two Democrats voting against it. A Democratic alternative to hold strictly to the 60-day limitation in the War Powers Resolution was defeated by a straight party vote of 45-55. In the House, the vote was 270-161. Democrats deserted the leadership and voted against the resolution, 130-134.

The argument in Congress was not so much over whether the War Powers Resolution should be invoked (there was general agreement that it should be) as over the duration and conditions of the marine presence. Many Republicans were prevailed on to support the Lebanon resolution by appeals to their loyalty to the president and the party. Many (but not quite most) Democrats in the House voted for it out of loyalty to the

Speaker, who had played a leading role in negotiating it with the White House. This role was counterproductive in the Senate, where many Democrats were miffed over being left out of the negotiations and over what seemed to them to be efforts by the House to usurp the Senate's foreign policy prerogatives. This was yet another example of sensitivity over these matters. It was analogous to House attitudes toward the Panama Canal treaties (see Chapter 3).

With respect to the substance of the resolution, many members of Congress thought that 18 months was far too long. The House Appropriations Committee went so far as to vote 20-16 to cut off funding for the marines in Lebanon after 60 days unless the president himself invoked the War Powers Resolution, but the committee backed down under pressure from the Speaker. On the other hand, there were two things to be said for the longer period. It avoided a showdown with the president, who had made it clear he would not accept a shorter time. And it meant that, barring an unforeseen change in circumstances, Congress would not have to face the issue again until after the 1984 election—and maybe the marines would be home in less than 18 months anyway.

Many members also could not accept the provision for "such protective measures as may be necessary to ensure the safety of the Multinational Force in Lebanon." Even without this chilling reminder of the Tonkin Gulf resolution, members had been comparing Lebanon to Vietnam. The provision could easily open the way to almost unlimited expansion of the marines' role. It was, said Senate Majority Leader Byrd, "a hole that you can run Amtrak through." [30] And Rep. Toby Roth, R-Wis., said, "If we keep the Marines in Lebanon, we're just waiting for a tragedy to happen." [31]

It happened October 23, when a suicidal terrorist crashed a truck laden with explosives into the lobby of the marine headquarters building at the Beirut airport and blew it up, killing 241. A nearly simultaneous bombing of French paratroop quarters killed 47. The incident produced yet another unsuccessful effort in the House to withdraw the marines. An amendment was offered to the defense appropriations bill by Clarence D. Long, D-Md., and Samuel S. Stratton, D-N.Y. The amendment would have cut off funding for keeping the marines in Lebanon after March 1984. The House defeated it November 2 by a vote of 153-274. In the Senate, Republicans used parliamentary maneuvers to avoid a vote in the Foreign Relations Committee on proposals to reduce from 18 months to 3 the authorization for the marines to remain in Lebanon.

Congress adjourned November 18 until January 23, but the restiveness of its members increased with three developments in December. (1) The fighting escalated. American navy planes bombed Syrian positions in Lebanon in retaliation for Syrian antiaircraft fire against reconnaissance planes. Two of the attacking planes were shot down, one crewman was killed, and one was captured. (The captive was freed by the Syrians after Democratic presidential candidate Jesse Jackson made a dramatic trip to Damascus to plead for his release.) The 16-inch guns of the battleship

New Jersey—the heaviest guns in the world—were also brought into play. (2) It was revealed that the Joint Chiefs of Staff had unanimously opposed sending the marines to Lebanon in the first place. (3) A Pentagon commission investigating the October bombing issued a scathing report criticizing the marines' security arrangements.

In early 1984 both the political and the military situation in Lebanon deteriorated markedly as Moslems (with Syrian support) pressed their campaign against President Amin Gemayel. On February 7 President Reagan removed the immediate issue of the marines' presence when he ordered them withdrawn to ships offshore. (The previous week he had still been saying that withdrawal would have "a pretty disastrous result" for U.S. foreign policy, and as late as February 5 Secretary of State George Shultz criticized Congress for generating discussions about withdrawal.) [32] Total U.S. casualties had been 264 killed and 134 wounded.

Larger issues remained concerning the American role in Lebanon and the application of the War Powers Resolution to the navy. Were American air or naval attacks on Moslem or Syrian positions purely in self-defense, or were they in support of the tottering Lebanese government? And what application, if any, did the War Powers Resolution have to warships in hostile or potentially hostile waters? The framers of the resolution had been concerned primarily with ground forces, but they wrote the law to apply all armed forces, including the much more mobile navy and air force. Precisely when the resolution came into play with respect to ships and planes, however, remained unanswered and became more urgent as air and naval involvement increased.

Grenada. On October 25, two days after the marines were bombed in Lebanon, other marines, accompanied by army units, invaded the tiny island of Grenada in the Caribbean. (Administration officials objected to descriptions of the action as an invasion. Rather, said Jeane Kirkpatrick, ambassador to the U.N., it was a liberation. The president himself called it a rescue mission.) Grenada has a land area of 133 square miles (just twice the size of the District of Columbia) and a population of 110,000. It became independent from Great Britain in 1974, contrary to the desires of many Grenadans who strongly opposed the government of Prime Minister Eric Gairy. Trinidad labor unions refused to handle cargos destined for Grenada, and neighboring Caribbean states boycotted the independence ceremonies.

Gairy was overthrown in 1979 in a coup led by Maurice Bishop, whose father, a labor leader, had been killed in the disorders accompanying independence. Bishop was the leader of the New Jewel Movement (Joint Endeavor for Welfare, Education, and Liberation). He shortly set the island on a radical leftward course and established close relations with Cuba. His accession was not welcomed by the Carter administration, and the Reagan administration was even colder.

In October 1983 Bishop was himself deposed in a rather unclear series of events. Reporting was sketchy because the United States did not maintain an embassy in Grenada, nor were there any foreign correspondents on the island. Bishop was at first arrested, then freed by a mob of his supporters, then shot. The principal figures emerging in power were General Hudson Austin, who had been chief of the army, and Bernard Coard, who had been Bishop's deputy prime minister. American officials feared that the new leadership would follow an even more leftist course and possibly provide a military base for Cuba, the Soviet Union, or both. In the light of the uncertain situation existing in Grenada, the Reagan administration was also worried about the safety of 1,000 Americans there, 700 of them students in an American-operated medical school.

Other Caribbean countries were also concerned about the course of events in Grenada, and the Reagan administration said that they had asked for U.S. assistance in occupying the island. There was, indeed, some Caribbean participation in the invasion, though by far the bulk of the force was American. The British refused to take part.

Reagan reported the invasion to Congress on October 25, the same day it occurred. He had provided an advance briefing for congressional leaders the night before. There was little resistance to the U.S. action, and within a week some of the troops were already back in the United States. On October 28 the Senate voted 64-20 that the 60-day clock of the War Powers Resolution had started running in Grenada on October 25. The provision was incorporated in an amendment to an unrelated bill which was subsequently defeated, but the strong Senate vote could not be ignored. The House voted 403-23 for a similar resolution November 1. By December only 300 military police, technicians, and support troops remained, and they were under the aegis of the Organization of East Caribbean States.

Central America.   Finally, there was controversy over the growing American involvement in Central America. Congress was extremely nervous about the military advisers helping the government of El Salvador fight an insurrection by leftist guerrillas. The advisers were limited administratively to 55, but were in fact fewer until the arrival in June 1983 of 25 medical personnel whom the Reagan administration did not count against the limit. Many in Congress saw the alignment of the United States with the Salvadoran government as a retreat from the human rights policy that had been first enunciated in Congress and then pursued by the Carter administration. (See Chapter 7 for more background on El Salvador and U.S. involvement there.) There was also a fear of a steadily deepening American entanglement from which it would become increasingly difficult to disengage and which might lead to an open-ended commitment. Parallels were drawn to Vietnam.

Concern over echoes of Vietnam was not allayed by the Reagan administration's repeated denials of any intention to send combat troops. Critics pointed out that the Johnson administration had also denied any intention to send troops to Vietnam. And they pointed out that American participation in the Vietnam War had started with advisers. This was one of the factors that—even before there were advisers in El Salvador—led the House Foreign Affairs Committee, in its report on the International Security and Development Cooperation Act of 1980, to spell out in great detail what it regarded as acceptable and unacceptable activities on the part of military advisers in all countries. These guidelines did not have the force of law; but considering their source, any administration had to take them seriously. In general they permitted assistance in organization, training, repair, and maintenance. They prohibited any Americans from accompanying units in combat, arming or fueling aircraft for combat sorties, or delivering equipment to units in combat.

The military presence that caused so much congressional apprehensiveness increased further in the summer of 1983. Lt. Gen. Wallace H. Nutting, head of the U.S. Southern Command, said in May that stopping Marxist expansion might ultimately require a willingness to use U.S. troops. Senator Goldwater agreed and urged Reagan to pledge to do so if such a move should prove to be necessary to save Central America from Soviet aggression. In July there was talk in the Pentagon of the need for more advisers—perhaps raising the total to 125—in El Salvador. Meanwhile, the administration announced American participation totaling 4,000 to 6,000 troops in joint military maneuvers with Honduras and sent a fleet of warships, including two aircraft carriers and one battleship, to maneuver off both coasts of Central America.

In September Under Secretary of Defense Fred C. Ikle called for a military victory and warned that lukewarm congressional support might force the deployment of American troops as in Korea or Germany. In February 1984 Sen. Jim Sasser, D-Tenn., in Honduras, expressed concern that the U.S. was building permanent military bases in that country.

Problems with the Resolution

The War Powers Resolution has not worked the way its sponsors intended. In part this is because no president has ever really accepted the spirit of the resolution. More important, Congress has not followed through with the same determination it showed when it passed the resolution. The only real test has come with respect to the marines in Lebanon, and on this Congress waffled. It waited a year after the marines were sent to Lebanon and then authorized their presence for an additional 18 months. It also opened the way to an expansion of their mission. Even with all this, Reagan's statement on signing the authorization sounded very much as though he did not accept any limitation and would do as he pleased. Said Senator Sasser, "The real casualty in this whole chain of events, beyond the young Marines who have lost their lives in Lebanon, has been the War Powers Resolution." [33]

The fundamental problem is that the War Powers Resolution does not contain any sanctions against a president who does not comply with it. There is always the implicit threat of impeachment, but this is so extreme that it has been seriously proposed only twice in 200 years. The real congressional power to control the deployment of troops abroad lies in withholding appropriations. Sen. Frank Church, D-Idaho, put it well in a 1977 hearing by the Senate Foreign Relations Committee to review the resolution:

> [I]f the President ... uses the Armed Forces in an action that is both swift and successful, then there is no reason to expect the Congress to do anything other than applaud.
>
> If the President employs forces in an action which is swift, but unsuccessful, then the Congress is faced with a fait accompli, and although it may rebuke the president, it can do little else.
>
> If the President undertakes to introduce American forces in a foreign war that is large and sustained, then it seems to me that the argument that the War Powers Resolution forces the Congress to confront that decision is an argument that overlooks the fact that Congress in any case must confront the decision, because it is the Congress that must appropriate the money to make it possible for the sustained action to be sustained.
>
> So I wonder really whether we have done very much in furthering our purpose through the War Powers Resolution.[34]

Congress has been extremely reluctant to use its power of the purse in these matters. The House rejected attempts to do so with respect to Lebanon while it was huffing and puffing about war powers. "In difficult foreign policy matters," Elizabeth Drew wrote in *The New Yorker*, "Congress often wants a role but not responsibility. It wanted to be consulted, and to have something to say, about the stationing of Marines in a situation where they were in obvious danger, but it didn't want to take it upon itself to decide when they should be removed." [35]

Base Rights

Decisions to deploy troops abroad—and the corollary, the acquisition and protection of foreign base rights—have been a continuing preoccupation of American foreign policy since World War II. Deployment decisions are usually made on the basis of military strategy, but they have much broader political effects as well, many involving Congress.

In the first place, the mere fact of the presence of large numbers of Americans in a foreign setting introduces an additional factor in the relations between the United States and the country in question. In many parts of the world, the Americans have more money and a higher standard of living than the local population. Some of them will run afoul of local laws or flout local customs. Their presence may become an issue in local politics and inevitably identifies the United States closely with the regime in power.

The decision to withdraw American troops and their dependents may have as many political ramifications as the decision to send them abroad initially. As in Korea and Germany, a proposed withdrawal may give the appearance of a lessening of U.S. interest in the country concerned and in its defense. Or, as in some other countries, it may signal the end of American aid programs to the governments. It will certainly signal the end of economic benefits to those who work for, or sell goods to, the Americans.

Quite apart from the issue of deployment, however, Congress has inextricably been involved in the question of base rights, if in no other way than through appropriating the money to build the bases. In addition, most base rights agreements involve some kind of quid pro quo that requires appropriations, either directly or indirectly. The question also arises of whether these agreements should have the dignity of treaties or whether they can properly be consummated by executive action.

By the mid-1960s the United States had 375 major foreign military bases and 3,000 minor facilities scattered around the world. In 1969-1970 a special subcommittee of the Senate Foreign Relations Committee made a major study of these bases and their political implications. In its report, the subcommittee pointed out:

> It is the day-to-day implementation of policy which frequently and sometimes almost imperceptibly provides the building blocks for future commitments.... Once an American overseas base is established, it takes on a life of its own. Original missions may become outdated, but new missions are developed, not only with the intent of keeping the facility going, but often actually to enlarge it.[36]

The record of congressional participation in decisionmaking about foreign bases has been mixed. Since the Foreign Relations Committee study—an outgrowth of concerns aroused by the Vietnam War—Congress has been somewhat more alert to the implications of its actions. But generally speaking, Congress has not been as inquisitive as it should have been, and the executive branch has not been as candid as it should have been. Consequently, neither has adequately thought through the implications of foreign military bases and attendant cooperation by the United States with foreign military forces and governments. Most of the time Congress has simply acquiesced in executive actions, in part because it has not been adequately informed and in part bacause it has been easier to acquiesce than to pick another fight with the executive branch.

The experience in Spain provides a good illustration of the complexity of the problem. The United States first obtained base rights in Spain in 1953 from the government of General Francisco Franco, who ruled the country from 1939 until his death in 1975. The original purpose of American air bases in Spain was to provide bases for the B-47 bombers, then the largest strategic bomber in the air force inventory; the plane's short range made foreign basing necessary. The United States also acquired a submarine base and navy communications facility at Rota. The base agreement was regularly renewed as it expired, even though the B-47 was replaced by the longer range B-52, which in turn was replaced by U.S.-based intercontinental ballistic missiles.

Not only did the United States provide military and economic assistance to Spain (some $3.3 billion), it also engaged in joint planning and joint military exercises with the Spanish government. In part, this was to meet the Spanish argument that the presence of American bases and U.S. forces made Spain a potential target for attack. But as the Senate Subcommittee on Security Agreements and Commitments Abroad pointed out:

> Overseas bases, the presence of elements of United States armed forces, joint planning, joint exercises, or extensive military assistance programs represent to host governments more valid assurances of United States commitment than any treaty or agreement. Furthermore, any or all of the above instances of United States military presence all but guarantee some involvement by the United States in the internal affairs of the host government.
>
> In November 1968, the then chairman of the Joint Chiefs of Staff, General Earle Wheeler, in a statement delivered in Madrid to representatives of the Spanish General Staff, formulated better than any statement by the subcommittee the concept being discussed here. At that time General Wheeler said, in a statement previously cleared by both the State and Defense departments, that the presence of United States troops on Spanish soil represented a stronger security guarantee than anything written on paper.[37]

The renewal of the Spanish base rights in 1970 through an executive agreement rather than a treaty provoked so much adverse comment in the Senate that the next extension in 1976 was submitted as a treaty. Although it did not embody a formal security commitment, the treaty went far beyond the previous executive agreements in terms of U.S.-Spanish cooperation. It provided military assistance, sales, and other benefits to Spain amounting to $1.2 billion over a five-year period—more than one-third as much as had been provided over the preceding 23 years. In addition, the treaty expanded, formalized, and provided an institutional framework for activities that had been carried on in the past with respect to defense, economic questions, education and cultural affairs, and science and technology.

Now the Senate critics of the nation's involvement in Spain found that they had painted themselves into a corner. They had loudly insisted that the new Spanish arrangements be submitted to the Senate as a treaty. When this was done by the White House, many senators felt inhibited from voting against the treaty, despite doubts about some of its provisions.

Complicating the issue was the fact that Franco had died in November 1975. Among executive and legislative officials there was a general uneasiness about rocking the boat during the delicate and unpredictable transition period in Spanish politics. As it turned out, the transition went relatively smoothly. At the end of 1978 a constitution was put in place and Spain became a parliamentary democracy. By the mid-1980s Spain had become a member of NATO and relations with the United States were stable.

Problems of the Congressional Role

Consultation

Quite apart from dealing with Congress because of statutory requirements such as those contained in the War Powers Resolution, presidents
are sensitive to congressional opinion for political reasons. Support in
Congress for the president's moves can broaden the base of public support for American policy in the United States as well as abroad. Conversely, congressional opposition can complicate and frustrate a president's policies.

Although presidents are jealous of their prerogatives as commander
in chief, they almost always go through the motions of consulting with
Congress about major decisions on the use of troops abroad. (A notable
exception was the Nixon incursion into Cambodia, and that was one of
the reasons it provoked such an outcry on Capitol Hill.) Chief executives
usually do this after the decision has been made so that it amounts to a
policy fait accompli. They generally limit themselves to giving selected
members information in advance of its public release.

This procedure is not at all what Congress has in mind when it
demands to be consulted. The House Foreign Affairs Committee in its
report on the War Powers Resolution reflected a widely held congressional view when it rejected "the notion that consultation should be
synonymous with merely being informed." The report said:

> Consultation in this provision means that a decision is pending on a
> problem and that Members of Congress are being asked by the Presi-
> dent for their advice and opinions and, in appropriate circumstances,
> their approval of action contemplated. Furthermore, for consultation to
> be meaningful, the President himself must participate and all informa-
> tion relevant to the situation must be made available.[38]

Even without these conceptual differences, the process of executive-
legislative consultation itself involves difficult problems. The initiative
almost always rests with the president, and the question immediately
arises of which legislators should be consulted. Especially during crises or
other occasions when time is a factor and when considerations of national
security information may be involved, it is obviously not practical to
consult with Congress as a whole—for example, through the device of a
presidential message to a joint session. There must be some selectivity in
choosing legislators to be included—an exceedingly delicate issue among
members of Congress. Most problems cut across rival committee jurisdictions, and the party leaders in the House and Senate must be included in
such consultations as well.

Thus the executive branch faces a dilemma. The fewer the members
of Congress involved in consultations, the less likely it is that there will be
leaks of sensitive information and the more likely it is that a consensus
will emerge from the discussions. But when consultations are limited to a

small group, the decisions made are less likely to be representative of opinion in Congress as a whole--particularly in this era of growing dispersion of power on Capitol Hill. Furthermore, the smaller the group consulted, the more likely there are to be hurt feelings on the part of those left out. Finally, if Congress is not in session, some or all of the members to be consulted may not be in Washington or even in the country.

As the House Foreign Affairs Committee pointed out, if there is to be meaningful consultation, there has to be a sharing with Congress of all relevant information. Not infrequently, the executive branch is reluctant to do this. In part, executive reticence stems from a fear of leaks; but more importantly, administrations are reluctant to share with Congress information that may be relevant but that does not support a particular policy. The problem of leaks may be more an excuse than a reason for not engaging in consultations. Over any given time period, Congress certainly leaks no more, and quite possibly less, than the executive branch. Most of the time, Congress has shown no disposition to insist on access to all relevant information, although its record in this respect has improved somewhat in recent years.

It is equally true that many members of Congress are unwilling to devote the time not only to absorb all the relevant information but to consider seriously all the policy options available to the United States. It took the Kennedy administration a week to decide on its policy in the Cuban missile crisis. The members of Congress who were then "consulted" had less than an hour; yet one can scarcely imagine any of them being willing, even if given the opportunity, to devote a week to the problem in the midst of a political campaign.

There is also a question of how much some members of Congress really want to be consulted, despite congressional fulminations on the subject. Particularly in crisis situations, there is a tendency in Congress to give the president the benefit of the doubt. There is also reluctance to take the political responsibility for potentially disastrous decisions. Better, in this view, that the president should get the credit for something that turns out well than that an individual member of Congress should share the blame for something that turns out poorly. It was not for nothing that Truman had a sign on his desk that read, "The buck stops here."

Policy versus Management

The increasing assertiveness of Congress about troop deployment raises the question of where to draw the line between broad policy on the one hand and day-to-day management or administrative decisions on the other. This not only involves constitutional problems that can be argued at length; it also involves the practical, more immediate problem of the allocation of time—a scarce commodity in Congress. The more Congress devotes itself to the minutiae regarding which troops are deployed where, the less it can address the larger policy questions with which it is better equipped to deal. The distinctions between these categories, however, are not always clear.

If Congress is to say, as the House Armed Services Committee did in 1978, that x thousand troops of the Second Division are to be kept in Korea, then there is no reason it cannot say that y thousand troops of the 82d Airborne Divison are to be kept at Fort Bragg, North Carolina, or transferred to Fort Knox, Kentucky, or that z ships of the Atlantic Fleet are to be based at Guantanamo, Cuba. No one has seriously suggested this level of congressional involvement in military decisionmaking, although Congress has come close to it in ordering certain domestic bases kept open against the wishes of the White House and Defense Department.

Declarations of War

Increasing legislative assertiveness over troop deployments overseas in part represents an attempt to compensate for the erosion of the power of Congress to declare war, as explained in Chapter 2. This erosion occurred primarily because of changes in international relationships, in military technology, and in the nature of modern warfare.

At various times during the Vietnam War, for example, several senators considered introducing a declaration of war to focus the issue of America's involvement in the conflict more sharply. The idea did not, however, gain support on Capitol Hill. Legislators who opposed it believed that a declaration of war would have given American involvement in the conflict a legitimacy it otherwise lacked; and the declaration might have escalated the war to an even higher level of intensity, possibly involving a direct Soviet-American or Sino-American confrontation. There was also the practical and perplexing question of whom to declare war against—North Vietnam or the rather shadowy Viet Cong, or both?[39]

The United States fought the Korean War under the aegis of the United Nations. A declaration of war by Congress in that conflict would have presented the risk of grave consequences by triggering North Korean-Chinese-Soviet defense alliances. In both the Korean and the Vietnam experiences, the absence of a declaration of war was one important way to keep a limited war limited. And in an age of megaton nuclear missiles, that is the only kind of war that can be tolerated.

Hawks versus Doves

"Where you stand," Sen. Hubert Humphrey once remarked, "depends on where you sit." Congress reasserts its powers over the armed forces, or acquiesces in the erosion of its powers, depending on its prevailing view of a particular presidential policy. Even those senators, such as Taft, who thought Truman exceeded his authority in Korea, muted their criticism because they approved of the substance of the policy if not of the procedure by which it was decided. A year later, during the MacArthur hearings, many of the same senators complained that Truman's conduct of the war was too restrained.

Most of the impetus behind the War Powers Resolution came from members of Congress who disapproved of the Nixon administration's policies in Indochina. And the members of Congress who were most vocal in asserting the power of Congress to keep troops in Korea were those who most strongly opposed the Carter policy of withdrawal.

Arguments over the proper role of Congress in connection with the armed forces usually center on the propriety of restraints on the president. As a legacy of Vietnam, and in the terminology of that era, the arguments tend to assume a division between doves in Congress and hawks in the White House and Pentagon. This does not necessarily accord with reality. There are numerous historical examples, going back to the War of 1812, when Congress has been more militant than the president in dealing with other countries.

History also provides abundant evidence that there is no monopoly on wisdom—or for that matter on bad judgment—at either end of Pennsylvania Avenue. Nor is there any guarantee that the president and Congress will not both be mistaken at the same time. It is the modest theory of the Constitution only that they are less likely to be.

Notes

1. Dean Acheson, *Present at the Creation: My Years in the State Department* (New York: W. W. Norton and Co., 1969), p. 407.
2. Tom Connally, as told to Alfred Steinberg, *My Name Is Tom Connally* (New York: Thomas Y. Crowell Co., 1954), p. 346.
3. Harry S Truman, *Years of Trial and Hope,* vol. 2 of *Memoirs* (Garden City, N.Y.: Doubleday and Co., 1956), p. 338.
4. Acheson, *Present at the Creation,* p. 409.
5. Connally, *My Name Is Tom Connally,* pp. 347-348.
6. *Congressional Record,* 81st Cong., 2d sess., 1950, 96, pp. 9319-9323.
7. Acheson, *Present at the Creation,* p. 413.
8. Ibid., p. 414.
9. U.S. Congress, House, 95th Cong., 1st sess., 1977, H.R. 6689, as reported in the Senate; see also S. Rept. 95-194, pp. 26-27.
10. *Congressional Record,* 95th Cong., 1st sess., pp. S9960, S9962, and S9963 (daily ed. June 16, 1977); the final version of the amendment is found in P.L. 95-105, sec. 512.
11. *Congressional Record,* 95th Cong., 1st sess., pp. S9946, S9948 (daily ed. June 16, 1977).
12. U.S. Congress, Senate Committee on Foreign Relations, *Hearings on War Powers Legislation,* 92d Cong., 1st sess., 1972, p. 393.
13. *Congressional Record,* 95th Cong., 1st sess., 1977, 123, p. 19457.
14. Ibid.

15. P.L. 95-384, sec. 23(d).
16. *Congressional Record,* 82d Cong., 1st sess., January 5, 1951, p. 55.
17. Ibid., p. 59.
18. U.S. Congress, Senate, 82d Cong., 1st sess., 1951, S. Res. 8.
19. U.S. Congress, Senate, 82d Cong., 1st sess., 1951, S. Res. 99 and S. Con. Res. 18.
20. U.S. Congress, *Military Construction Authorization Act, 1982,* 97th Cong., 1st sess., 1981, H. Rept. 97-362, p. 40.
21. A *pair* is a gentlemen's agreement between two lawmakers on opposite sides to withhold their votes on roll calls so the absence of one from Congress will not affect the outcome of record voting. If passage of the measure requires a two-thirds majority, a pair would require two members favoring the action to one opposed to it.
22. P.L. 88-408, August 10, 1964.
23. P.L. 93-126, October 18, 1973, sec. 13.
24. *Immigration and Naturalization Service v. Chadha,* 51 U.S.L.W. 4907 (1983).
25. P.L. 93-148, November 7, 1973.
26. U.S. Congress, House, 93d Cong., 1st sess., 1973, H. Doc. 93-171.
27. U.S. Congress, Senate Committee on Foreign Relations, *Hearings on U.S. Policy in the Western Hemisphere,* 97th Cong., 2d sess., 1982, statement by Senator Byrd, p. 190.
28. U.S. Congress, House Committee on Foreign Affairs, Subcommittee on International Security and Scientific Affairs, *The War Powers Resolution: Relevant Documents, Correspondence, Reports,* committee print, June 1981, p. 49.
29. Text in *Congressional Quarterly Weekly Report,* October 8, 1983, pp. 2101-2102. Text of Reagan statement on signature is in *Congressional Quarterly Weekly Report,* October 15, 1983, p. 2142.
30. T. R. Reid and Helen Dewar, "War Powers Deal Meets Resistance," *Washington Post,* September 22, 1983.
31. *Congressional Quarterly Weekly Report,* September 24, 1983, p. 1964.
32. Reagan's remarks are quoted in the *Wall Street Journal,* February 8, 1984; for Shultz's criticisms of Congress see the *New York Times,* February 6, 1984.
33. *Congressional Quarterly Weekly Report,* October 8, 1983, p. 2097.
34. U.S. Congress, Senate Foreign Relations Committee, *Hearings on the War Powers Resolution,* 95th Cong., 1st sess., 1977, p. 172.
35. Elizabeth Drew, "A Political Journal," *The New Yorker,* September 26, 1983, pp. 143-144.
36. U.S. Congress, Senate Committee on Foreign Relations, Subcommittee on Security Agreements and Commitments Abroad, *Security Agreements and Commitments Abroad,* 91st Cong., 2d sess., 1970, pp. 1, 19.
37. *Security Agreements and Commitments Abroad,* pp. 20-21.
38. U.S. Congress, House, 93d Cong., 1st sess., H. Rept. 93-287.
39. The question of whether Congress should have declared war in the Vietnam conflict is discussed more fully in Sen. Jacob K. Javits, "The Congressional Presence in Foreign Relations," *Foreign Affairs* 48 (January 1970): 221-235.

The Intelligence Community

In its fundamentals, the relationship of Congress to the intelligence community is, or should be, no different from its relationship to other parts of the executive branch. The role of Congress is to provide basic legislative authority and to oversee how that authority is used. Legislative oversight is a duty that Congress has imposed on itself. The law [2 U.S.C. 190d(a)] requires each standing committee of the House and Senate to "review and study, on a continuing basis, the application, administration, and execution of those laws, or parts of laws, the subject matter of which is within the jurisdiction of that committee."

But several factors make Congress's relationship to the intelligence community unique. One is the necessity for secrecy in an otherwise open government. Another is the failure of Congress to provide basic comprehensive legislation on intelligence activities. A third is the failure of Congress, until 1976 in the Senate and 1977 in the House, to exercise any true oversight. All of these factors combined to create both in the intelligence community and in Congress mental attitudes that made it a traumatic experience for both parties when Congress finally began to assert itself. The intelligence community had been conditioned by more than a quarter century of experience not to tell Congress what it was doing. And Congress had been conditioned not to ask.

For more than 25 years following the passage of the National Security Act, which created the Central Intelligence Agency in 1947, Congress largely ignored the intelligence community. It allowed the National Security Agency and the Defense Intelligence Agency to be created by executive order. It voted for untold billions of dollars in hidden appropriations for intelligence activities with very few, if any, of its members knowledgeable as to either the amounts or the purposes of the funds. Members of Congress who were actively concerned about the activities of the intelligence community were rebuffed by large majorities on the few occasions they tried to ask questions or to establish procedures for doing so.

During this period Congress interested itself in the intelligence community only when something went so horribly wrong that it came to public view, as when the U-2 was shot down over the Soviet Union in 1960 or when the Bay of Pigs invasion of Cuba failed in 1961. These crises contributed to what was then still a minority view that Congress ought to do something to keep such things from happening. The emphasis in this view was on preventing mistakes.

Further momentum developed in Congress in the early and mid-1970s with the revelations of CIA activities in Chile and of abuses by the CIA and the FBI of constitutional rights of American citizens. The first serious, broad-scale congressional investigation of the intelligence community (the Church committee in 1975-1976) was directed almost wholly to the question of "illegal, improper or unethical activities." [1]

Sen. Frank Church's investigation and a more raucous investigation of the intelligence community in the House laid the groundwork for the creation (in 1976 in the Senate and in 1977 in the House) of the permanent intelligence committees. These committees were given legislative jurisdiction as well as broad powers of oversight. As it turned out, exercising these powers entailed a good deal more than simply preventing mistakes and abuses.

Definitions

The intelligence community is knee-deep in glossaries, technical definitions, and acronyms. The House Intelligence Committee noted in 1978 that it had been "waging a steady campaign against the unnecessary use of acronyms," but added that "victories tend to be few and short-lived." [2]

Because the technical definition of *intelligence* is much more complicated, it is clearer for our purposes to think of *intelligence* as meaning simply "information"—the definition, by the way, that the army used to give it. Intelligence can be acquired in such mundane ways as reading a newspaper or in such exotic ways as taking a picture from space or planting a listening device in an official's office or by bribery or blackmail.

The American intelligence community consists of the governmental agencies engaged in collecting intelligence, either overtly or covertly; in analyzing it; and in countering the activities of foreign intelligence agents (such as the Soviet secret police) who might jeopardize American security. (The names and responsibilities of the specific agencies in the intelligence community were identified in Chapter 1.)

Intelligence is quite separate from covert action—although the United States government is so organized that a single agency, the CIA, engages in both. Whereas intelligence is simply the collection of information, overtly or covertly, by fair means or foul, covert action has to do with sub rosa and theoretically nontraceable efforts to influence (sometimes to overthrow or subvert) foreign governments, groups, or economies. Covert action may involve the surreptitious dissemination of information, either true or false, but any collection of information is coincidental.

Whatever technique is used, covert action is done secretly because public identification of the United States government with the particular activity would be either counterproductive or embarrassing or both. Some examples of covert action that have become public are the secret subsidies of anti-Communist labor unions in Western Europe in the late 1940s and early 1950s, the overthrow of the Mossadegh regime and the restoration to power of the Shah in Iran in 1953, the overthrow of the Arbenz government in Guatemala in 1954, the abortive Bay of Pigs invasion of Cuba in 1961, the attempts to destabilize the Allende government in Chile in 1970-1973, and most recently the operations against Nicaragua that began in 1982.

We are mainly concerned here with Congress's relationship to the CIA and the National Security Agency (NSA), the two most important members of the intelligence community from the point of view of foreign policy. These agencies not only provide most of the intelligence to the community and to policymakers; they also take most of the risks in collecting it. In addition, of course, the CIA is the covert action agency.

The Era of Neglect

Of the agencies whose sole concern is intelligence and covert action, only the CIA was created by Congress. (The principal purpose of the National Security Act of 1947 that created the CIA was to provide for the Department of Defense.) The act made the CIA responsible to the president and put the agency under the general supervision of the National Security Council. The act also gave the director of the CIA the responsibility for coordinating the activities of the intelligence community as a whole, as well as managing the CIA.

National Security Act Provisions

Four other provisions regarding the CIA in the National Security Act should be noted.[3] First, the CIA "shall have no police, subpena, law-enforcement powers, or internal security functions." This restriction has generally been interpreted (perhaps too broadly) as meaning that the CIA is to have no domestic operations other than the administrative and analytical work that goes on in its headquarters. One of the factors that finally prompted Congress to begin investigating the activities of intelligence agencies was the revelation that the CIA had collaborated with local police departments in the United States and had investigated dissenters to America's involvement in the Vietnam War.

The second relevant provision of the National Security Act provides that the director of Central Intelligence "shall be responsible for protecting intelligence sources and methods from unauthorized disclosure."

Successive directors fell back on this as authority for refusing to respond to questions from Congress. It has also been used as the excuse for some of the CIA's domestic activities.

Third, the CIA is "to perform, for the benefit of the existing intelligence agencies, such additional services of common concern as the National Security Council determines can be more efficiently accomplished centrally." The National Security Council, as we noted in Chapter 1, is the highest-level executive agency for advising the president on national security problems.

Fourth, the CIA is to "perform such other functions and duties related to intelligence affecting the national security as the National Security Council may from time to time direct."

Since 1947, these catch-all provisions have been invoked as authority for numerous intelligence operations, some of which have subsequently aroused public and legislative opposition. They form the basis of the legislative authority for the CIA's intelligence gathering and covert action.

Because the act establishing the Department of Defense was also used as the legislative vehicle for creating the CIA, an anomaly was created. Jurisdiction over the CIA in Congress, as to both legislation and oversight, was lodged in the armed services committees, many of whose members were sympathetic to CIA activities. Yet the way the CIA does its job has at least as many political ramifications in the field of foreign policy as military ramifications in the field of defense. And the foreign policy committees in Congress for many years were effectively excluded from contact with the CIA.

The same situation prevailed with respect to the National Security Agency, which was established in the Defense Department by President Truman in 1952 and whose existence was scarcely acknowledged for years. NSA deals with signals intelligence—that is, intelligence derived from monitoring communications, radar activity, and other electronic emissions by foreign countries. It affects foreign policy not only through the intelligence it collects, but also through its methods of collection. For example, NSA needs listening posts in foreign countries, and these usually involve a quid pro quo. The American ship *Pueblo* was on an intelligence-gathering mission for NSA when it was seized by the North Koreans in 1968.

Following the passage of the National Security Act of 1947, subcommittees on the CIA, or on intelligence (they were variously named), were created in the armed services committees of each house. Meetings were not announced, and they were infrequent. A subcommittee sometimes went a whole year without meeting. Similar subcommittees were created in the two appropriations committees to provide funds for the CIA and, later, the NSA. These funds were concealed in appropriations for other agencies, mainly the Defense Department.

During a number of years in the 1960s, when Sen. Richard Russell, D-Ga., was chairman of both the Armed Services Committee and the

Defense Appropriations Subcommittee, membership on the two intelligence subcommittees overlapped so much that the two were, for practical purposes, merged. Only one staff member—the much overworked staff director of the Senate Armed Services Committee—was permitted to be present at meetings, and he was forbidden to brief any other senators on what transpired.

CIA officials have maintained that all of the agency's significant actions were reported to these oversight committees. The members of the committees, however, were clearly not prepared to ask questions and usually accepted whatever they were told about intelligence operations. Leverett Saltonstall, R-Mass., one of the senators concerned with intelligence activities for many years, once said flatly that there were some things about these activities that he did not want to know. Most legislators agreed with Saltonstall or, at the very least, were content to accept existing arrangements. So was the CIA, which operated only under the restraints imposed by the National Security Council; in the 1950s, even the nature of these restraints was a tightly held secret.

Early Efforts by Mansfield

Some members of Congress, however, were uncomfortable about existing procedures for monitoring intelligence operations. The unease stemmed from a feeling that the CIA was inadequately supervised, that Congress was shirking its responsibilities, and that sooner or later this state of affairs would cause trouble for the United States abroad.

One of the most deeply concerned about this possibility was Sen. Mike Mansfield, D-Mont., who later became majority leader and later still ambassador to Japan, in which position he had the responsibility of overseeing intelligence operations in that country. For a number of years after he came to the Senate in 1953, Mansfield introduced resolutions to create a CIA oversight committee modeled after the Joint Committee on Atomic Energy. The analogy was a good one.

The joint committee was created by the Atomic Energy Act of 1946, a landmark piece of legislation that not only established the principle of civilian control of the atom, but also provided for congressional oversight. The act required the Atomic Energy Commission to keep the joint committee "fully and currently informed" of its activities. A similar provision with respect to the CIA would have overridden, as far as Congress was concerned, the director's statutory duty to protect intelligence sources and methods. For 30 years, until it was abolished in a congressional reorganization in 1977, the joint committee was widely regarded as a model of how Congress could responsibly and securely handle highly classified information.

The only time Mansfield was ever able to get a Senate vote on his resolution was in 1956, when it was rejected 27-59. Ten years later, the Senate effectively killed a somewhat different resolution with the same purpose by voting 61-28 to refer it to the armed services committee. On the face of it, things had not changed very much in a decade.

An important factor at work throughout this period was trenchantly described in 1971 by Francis Wilcox, former chief of staff of the Senate Foreign Relations Committee and a former assistant secretary of state:

> What is basically involved is something it pains the Senate to talk about—personality differences and bureaucratic jealousies. To be blunt about it, and perhaps to overstate it, neither the CIA nor the people who now watch over it fully trust the people who want to watch over it; and the people who want to watch over it do not fully trust either the agency or its present watchers.[4]

Although the two votes in 1956 and 1966 were almost identical, the underlying concerns in the Senate had changed. By 1966 evidence had accumulated that intelligence operations or covert actions could have adverse foreign policy repercussions. Two particularly sensitive situations deserve special mention.

The U-2 Incident

The program of U-2 flights over the Soviet Union was developed in the 1950s to give the United States an aerial reconnaissance capability by flying above the range of Soviet antiaircraft weapons and using what were then sophisticated cameras. The intelligence it produced was remarkable and valuable. In May 1960, on the eve of a scheduled summit conference, it turned out that the U-2 was no longer beyond the Soviet reach: the plane was shot down inside the Soviet Union, and its pilot was captured. After an initial period of confusion and contradiction, President Eisenhower admitted that the plane's real purpose was espionage, and Soviet Premier Nikita Khrushchev angrily canceled the summit.

The Senate Foreign Relations Committee held extensive hearings in closed session and published a censored version. In 1982 the committee published the most significant deletions that had been made in 1960, as well as the full transcript of its seven closed-door debates.[5] Administration witnesses refused to answer the key question: What was the plane looking for the day it was shot down? The answer was crucial to a determination of whether the intelligence that it hoped to acquire was sufficiently important to justify the political risk of failure on the eve of a summit. It was also crucial to a determination of what would have been lost if the flight had been postponed until after the summit.

Nevertheless, the administration was more forthcoming in responding to the committee's interest than it had previously been. Throughout most of the 1950s, CIA directors had even resisted requests to brief the Senate Foreign Relations Committee on intelligence analysis, let alone on intelligence itself. This reluctance was somewhat diminished after Secretary of State John Foster Dulles reminded his brother, CIA Director Allen Dulles, that he, Allen, could not give public speeches around the country and then refuse to appear before the Foreign Relations Committee. But the CIA, supported by the White House, generally took the position that it would deal only with the armed services and appropriations committees. The U-2 incident made the first notable breach in this position.

It was the political consequences of the U-2 affair that first aroused the interest of the Senate Foreign Relations Committee. The committee's review raised disturbing questions about the extent to which foreign policy consequences were taken—or not taken—into account in the process of approving intelligence operations. A program consisting of several U-2 flights over a period of months had been personally approved by the president, but he had not concerned himself with individual flights within the overall program. The flight that was shot down was scheduled on technical considerations of the weather without regard to the political considerations of the approaching summit conference. The success of previous flights had bred complacency about assuming the success of this one.

The Bay of Pigs

By 1960 the Eisenhower administration became convinced that if the Castro regime survived much longer in Cuba, it would so consolidate itself that it could never be dislodged and that Soviet power would be established in the Caribbean. At that time such a prospect seemed totally unacceptable. Accordingly, plans were made for a covert action in which the CIA would secretly train and support a group of Cuban exiles to overthrow Castro.

The plans and training were well advanced when the Kennedy administration took office in January 1961. After some hesitation, Kennedy gave the go-ahead. The invasion was launched in April 1961 and promptly ended in disaster, with the American involvement clearly revealed.

Again the consequences were primarily political—acute embarrassment for the United States—and again it was the Foreign Relations Committee, not Armed Services, that investigated. The closed hearings, in which the executive branch cooperated, went on for weeks. They proved mainly that President Kennedy had received and acted on the basis of some very bad advice. The hearings did serve, however, to increase senatorial skepticism of the intelligence community and of the methods by which it was supervised. (The Bay of Pigs also increased Kennedy's skepticism along the same lines; he shortly moved to improve White House control over intelligence activities.)

It also developed that the only good advice Kennedy received about the Bay of Pigs undertaking had come from Congress, but not through any established channel for congressional-executive communication. Because of a combination of circumstances—the most important being the personal relationship between Kennedy and Sen. J. William Fulbright—the president invited Fulbright to join him in a meeting with his advisers to discuss the projected invasion of Cuba before the decision was made to proceed. Fulbright was the only person present to speak out against the plan.

A further incident is also worth reporting here as an indication of congressional inconsistency in approaching oversight. The Foreign Relations Committee, as noted, spent weeks rehashing the failure of the Bay of Pigs mission. After the success of American policy in the Cuban missile crisis the following year, Secretary of State Dean Rusk all but begged the committee to investigate the performance of the intelligence community and of the administration in crisis management. The committee was not interested. The point is that Congress as a general rule tends to be more interested in investigating failures than successes.

The Beginning of Real Oversight

After these false starts, what prodded Congress out of its lethargy about overseeing the intelligence community was a series of events in the early and mid-1970s. One impetus was provided by revelations stemming from the Watergate affair. Other reasons were more directly related to developments in foreign policy.

Chile

In 1972 columnist Jack Anderson published internal documents of the International Telephone and Telegraph Company indicating that ITT had tried to persuade the CIA to intervene in Chilean politics in 1970 to prevent Socialist Salvador Allende from becoming president. The Senate Foreign Relations Committee responded by creating the Subcommittee on Multinational Corporations to investigate this report and also to conduct an in-depth study of multinational corporations in general.

A year later, in March 1973, the subcommittee held lengthy hearings which revealed that ITT had indeed sounded the alarm all over Washington at the time of Allende's election in September 1970. The company had even offered to furnish as much as $1 million for the expenses of clandestine American intervention but had found no takers. Past and present CIA officials testified that the agency had a policy of not accepting contributions from private businesses. John McCone, a director of ITT and a former director of the CIA, was one of the officials who testified to this effect. (In 1980 Congress passed legislation specifically authorizing the director of Central Intelligence to accept gifts, bequests, and property on behalf of the CIA.)

Notwithstanding ITT's efforts, Allende had taken office in 1970. He soon encountered a sea of troubles, most of them of his own making but some of them complicated by a cutoff of American credits, both private and public. The Nixon administration never made any secret of its dislike of Allende but maintained that the policies it was following to impede his regime were all open and aboveboard.

In September 1973, six months after the ITT hearings, Allende was overthrown in a bloody coup d'état. The unseen hand of the CIA was again suspected and again denied. The Subcommittee on Western Hemisphere Affairs of the Senate Foreign Relations Committee held closed hearings. At the hearings CIA Director William Colby reported in greater detail than had ever been done before (but still incompletely) about CIA activities in Chile. In this version, the agency's principal activity was the covert funneling of subsidies to certain political parties, newspapers, and groups opposing Allende. The objective was to enable the opposition to survive until the next regularly scheduled Chilean presidential election in 1976, at which time it was hoped that a non-Socialist candidate could be elected (since Allende was constitutionally unable to succeed himself). This satisfied the subcommittee, or at least its chairman, Senator McGee of Wyoming, that the anti-Allende coup had been the work of local Chilean forces.

The following spring, of 1974, Colby testified again and in somewhat greater detail before the CIA subcommittee of the House Armed Services Committee. The transcript of that testimony was read in June by Rep. Michael Harrington, a Boston Democrat and outspoken liberal. Harrington was not a member of the Armed Services Committee, but he was taking advantage of a law that gives any member of the House or Senate access to any records of a committee of the house in which he serves.

Harrington was outraged by the Colby testimony. In July he sent letters demanding investigations of CIA activities in Chile to Rep. Thomas Morgan, chairman of the House Foreign Affairs Committee, and to Senator Fulbright, chairman of the Senate Foreign Relations Committee. Neither took any action. Fulbright replied that CIA activities in Chile were not so different from CIA activities in other countries and that the remedy lay in an effective joint committee of Congress "with full authority to examine the CIA and control it." Fulbright conceded that he could not get the votes to establish such a committee.

In September Harrington's letter, containing the substance of Colby's hitherto secret testimony, leaked to the press, and an uproar ensued. Sen. Frank Church, who had presided over the ITT hearings but who had not been present for the later Colby testimony, felt that he had been deceived and that information had been withheld from him.

The Hughes-Ryan Amendment

Partly inspired by the Chile affair, Congress used the 1974 foreign aid bill as the vehicle to require that covert actions (as distinguished from purely intelligence operations) conducted "by or on behalf of" the CIA be reported to "the appropriate committees of the Congress." The amendment by which this was accomplished was the handiwork of Sen. Harold E. Hughes, D-Iowa (a member of the Armed Services Committee), and Rep. Leo J. Ryan, D-Calif.

The Hughes-Ryan amendment named the Senate Foreign Relations and the House Foreign Affairs committees as two of the committees to receive the reports; the other "appropriate committees" were not specified in the amendment. By general agreement, they were defined to be the appropriations and armed services committees in each house and later—after they were established in 1976 and 1977—the two permanent intelligence committees as well. In 1980 Congress provided that only the intelligence committees would receive the reports, and in especially sensitive cases only the chairmen, the ranking minority members, the Speaker and minority leader of the House, and the majority and minority leaders of the Senate.

In addition, the Hughes-Ryan amendment tightened administrative control of covert action by requiring, as a precondition, that the president find "that each such operation is important to the national security of the United States." The report to the committees was to be made "in a timely fashion" and was to include "a description and scope" of the activity.[6] The CIA had long maintained that it already reported covert actions to its oversight subcommittees in the appropriations and armed services committees; but given the infrequency of the meetings of those subcommittees, the timeliness of the reports could be questioned.

The foreign policy committees in the House and Senate then had to figure out the mechanics of how they would receive the information required from the executive branch. They also had to decide what, if anything, they would do with the information after they received it.

The House Foreign Affairs Committee (or International Relations Committee, as it was known from 1975 through 1978) has not revealed its procedures. In the Senate Foreign Relations Committee, it was agreed that the reports would be received orally from the director of the CIA by the chairman and ranking minority member, with the committee's chief of staff present and authorized to brief any other committee member who asked. Not many did.

The calendars of the Foreign Relations Committee reflect five meetings of the chairman and ranking minority member with the director of the CIA in 1975, six in 1976, three in 1977, and one in 1978. In 1979, with Church (of ITT and CIA investigating fame) now chairman of the committee, the procedure was changed and indications that a report was received no longer appeared in the calendar. The number of meetings and the number of covert actions undertaken by the CIA are not necessarily related, however. Some meetings were simply to review all covert actions then being carried out. And some covert actions required more than one meeting.

In practice, the question of what to do about the reports came up only if a member disagreed with a particular covert action. The member's recourse, in this case, was to present any objections, not to the CIA, but to higher political authority—namely, the State Department or the president. The few members who were really interested in CIA activities found this procedure frustrating.

Covert action (technically called special activities since President Carter's 1978 executive order) is a means to achieving a policy objective. In 1975 and 1976 three covert actions aroused the apprehensions of one or more members of the Senate Foreign Relations Committee. In two of these, the concerned senators had no particular quarrel with the policy objective, but they believed that over the long term the United States and the two foreign countries involved would be better off if the situations were allowed to work themselves out without intervention by American intelligence agencies. The senators also felt that the risks of possible disclosure were too great to justify the activity in question. In one of these cases, a senator felt so strongly the action in question was mistaken that he wrote a letter about it to President Ford—and never got an answer. As it turned out, one of the actions was successful, the other partially so.

Angola

The third case involved the African country of Angola, which at the end of 1974 found itself on the verge of achieving independence from Portugal after 14 years of guerrilla warfare. Differing tribal loyalties and ideological disputes sharply divided the political factions in Angola. Agreements among them concerning the government that was to replace Portuguese authority proved to be short-lived.

United States covert involvement in Angola began in a very small way, mainly through the payment of a cash subsidy to one of the non-Marxist leaders and his group. By July 1975 this initially limited involvement was rapidly escalating, as was the fighting in Angola where one faction was receiving support from the Soviet Union (later from Cuba as well) and another from South Africa. Ultimately, America's intervention entailed a budget of millions of dollars and consisted of supplies as well as money. As involvement grew, the African Affairs Subcommittee of Foreign Relations, headed by Sen. Dick Clark, D-Iowa, expressed its concern directly to Deputy Secretary of State Robert Ingersoll in an inconclusive meeting.

By November congressional concern had reached the point that the full Foreign Relations Committee summoned CIA Director Colby and Under Secretary of State Joseph Sisco for a session on Angola; in December the Subcommittee on Foreign Assistance received more detailed briefings from executive officials on the American role in Angola. To the embarrassment of the committee and the irritation of the CIA, substantial portions of both meetings were leaked to the press. As a result, Colby fired off a letter to the committee that implicitly threatened to stop cooperating with it. As Colby's letter put it, "publicity of this sort obviously casts serious doubts on my ability to provide sensitive information to the Foreign Relations Committee, its subcommittees, and its staff."

As all of this was happening, the Defense Department appropriations bill, with its hidden funds for the CIA, was making its way through

Congress. Sen. John Tunney, who had not been privy to any of the secret briefings on the CIA, but who read the newspapers, offered an amendment in the Senate prohibiting use of any funds in the bill "for any activities involving Angola directly or indirectly." It was agreed to by a vote of 54-22 on December 19, and the House concurred, 323-99, on January 27, over the strenuous objections of the Ford administration.

The Tunney amendment applied only to the funds in a particular appropriation bill. In 1976 Congress approved an amendment offered by Senator Clark to a foreign aid bill prohibiting as a matter of general law any kind of assistance for any kind of military or paramilitary operation in Angola. In a modified, but not substantially different, form, that remains the law today.

Congressional Investigations

The creation of the intelligence committees followed separate investigations of the intelligence community in both the House and the Senate. In each instance, the focus was on past misdeeds, and thus the committees evolved from a background in which there was a heavy emphasis on preventing mistakes, principally in covert action.

The Church Committee in the Senate

Early in 1975, by a vote of 82-4, the Senate established the Select Committee to Study Governmental Operations with Respect to Intelligence Activities (a name that the resolution creating it said was given "for convenience of expression"!).[7] It was headed by Senator Church, who had presided over the original investigation of CIA-ITT activities in Chile. In the space of 16 months, between January 1975 and April 1976, the Church committee published 17 volumes of reports and hearings dealing with everything from domestic intelligence activities of questionable legality to assassination plots targeted against foreign leaders.

The Church committee soon discovered how extraordinarily difficult it is, even with full access to files and records, to learn the full truth about covert actions in the past. This applies to both executive management and legislative oversight of the intelligence community. Intelligence is a highly compartmentalized business. In order to enhance security and to preserve plausible deniability, intelligence officials are given to speaking, and especially to writing, in ambiguous circumlocutions. And generally they write very little, so as not to leave a paper trail.

It was not until after the Church committee had completed its work that the facts about CIA involvement in Chile came out—and even then no one could be sure it was the full story. The State Department, the American Embassy in Santiago, and eventually the Congress knew about CIA subsidies for Allende's opponents; they did not know that President Nixon had directly instructed CIA Director Richard Helms to "destabilize," as it was put, the situation in Chile so much that Allende could not continue in office. For denying the existence of these activities before the Foreign Relations Committee, Helms was subsequently fined $2,000 when he pleaded nolo contendere to Justice Department charges of failing to testify "fully . . . and accurately." What emerged from the Church investigation was that although in a technical sense the CIA might not have been involved in the coup which overthrew Allende, its whole course of action in Chile for three years had been designed to create a situation in which such a coup would occur.

The principal result of the Church committee was twofold: the creation of a standing committee on intelligence, oriented more to continuing oversight than to investigations of past misdeeds; and a recommendation for legislative charters for all intelligence agencies, spelling out permissible and impermissible behavior. Drafting these charters has proven to be more difficult than it once appeared. By 1983, seven years after the Church report, the charters had still not been written.

The Pike Committee in the House

The work of the Church committee in the Senate had been quiet but ultimately sensational. In contrast, the House was kept in turmoil for a year and a half over how to go about substantially the same job.

On February 19, 1975, the House voted 286-120 to create the Select Committee on Intelligence. Lucien Nedzi of Michigan, the chairman of the Armed Services Committee's Special Subcommittee on Intelligence, was named chairman of the new committee. Its members included Harrington (who had earlier made such a fuss about Chile) and Ronald Dellums of California, another acerbic critic of the CIA. The members fell to quarreling among themselves almost at once. It took three months to hire a staff director. In June Nedzi resigned as chairman and the House rejected his resignation by a vote of 64-290.

Then in July the House took the extraordinary action of abolishing the committee and creating another one with the same name and terms of reference but without Nedzi and Harrington. This committee was headed by Otis Pike of New York. The Pike committee spent the fall of 1975 brawling with the administration over access to classified documents. Ostensibly, the issue was the committee's insistence on its right to declassify them, but, in fact, personalities were at the bottom of the dispute.

In the first place, the administration suspected the committee of leaking confidential information. In the second place, it was edgy over the law giving any member of the House access to any records of a House committee. Harrington had already acknowledged leaking some of the information in press reports about the CIA's activities in Chile and had been reprimanded by the Armed Services Committee, but he was unrepentant.

The matter was brought to the House Committee on Standards of Official Conduct, known as the ethics committee. The Armed Services Committee voted 16-13 to deny Harrington access to confidential information, notwithstanding the law, pending a ruling by the ethics committee. That committee voted 7-3 to do nothing, on the grounds that the Armed Services transcript that Harrington leaked had not been taken at a legal meeting. (There had been no notice, no vote to go into executive session, and no quorum.)

Congress, with reason, thinks the executive branch overclassifies information. The executive branch, also with reason, thinks that Congress is careless in handling classified information. Although members of Congress have frequently felt frustrated by executive insistence on maintaining classifications on information, most of the time they have been willing to accept, however reluctantly, the executive point of view, or at least to negotiate about it. Not so the Pike committee, which in September 1975 released some documents pertaining to the Yom Kippur War that included phrases the administration wanted deleted.

President Ford then angrily demanded that the committee return all the classified documents that it had been furnished and vowed that no more would be produced "until the committee satisfactorily alters its position." The committee refused to return the documents it had and requested more. The administration offered to supply some of them, but only on the condition that their confidentiality would be respected. Pike initially refused to accept them on this basis, but he eventually backed down.

On January 23, 1976, the Pike committee voted 9-4 to release its final report, despite administration objections that it contained material that should remain classified. Three days later, before it was released, a summary of the report appeared in the *New York Times.* On January 29 the House took the extraordinary action of voting 246-124 to prohibit the committee from releasing a report containing classified material until it had been "certified by the President as not containing information which would adversely affect the intelligence activities of the Central Intelligence Agency" or other agencies.[8] Then on February 11 the *Village Voice* in New York published a 24-page supplement containing lengthy excerpts from the report. Two days later CBS correspondent Daniel Schorr confirmed that it was he who gave a copy of the report to the *Voice.*

Schorr's refusal to say where he got the copy set off yet another acrimonious investigation, which delayed for more than a year House action to create a permanent intelligence committee. The House Committee on Standards of Official Conduct tried, and predictably failed, to determine Schorr's source. In the meantime, the Pike committee published its recommendations:

> That the House create a permanent intelligence committee
> That the president put an overall figure for the intelligence community in his budget

That transfers and reprogramming of intelligence funds be subject to the approval of the intelligence and other committees

That the General Accounting Office be empowered to investigate and audit intelligence agencies on the same basis as other agencies

That a Foreign Operations Subcommittee be created by statute in the National Security Council to deal with covert action and hazardous collection of intelligence

That the intelligence community be reorganized to separate the director of central intelligence from the CIA and the National Security Agency from the Defense Department, as well as to abolish the Defense Intelligence Agency

That there be no recruitment by the intelligence community of American citizens associated with religious, educational, or communications organizations

The Permanent Oversight Committees

The Church committee issued its final recommendations April 26, 1976. On May 19, by a vote of 72-22, the Senate created the successor Select Committee on Intelligence. In the House, the Permanent Select Committee on Intelligence was established in July 1977 by a vote of 247-171.

Although the resolutions creating these two committees (S. Res. 400 and H. Res. 658) are basically similar, there are a few important differences. One of these concerns the partisan political makeup of the committees. The Senate resolution assures the minority party of 7 of the 15 seats on the committee, regardless of its strength in the Senate. The House resolution is silent on the subject of minority representation, which largely accounts for the number of votes against it. In the 98th Congress (1983-1984), the 14-member House committee had nine Democrats and five Republicans, a ratio that roughly reflected party strength in the full House.

Both resolutions provide for overlapping memberships with the Appropriations, Armed Services, Foreign Relations (Foreign Affairs in the House), and Judiciary committees, the last being included because of its jurisdiction over the FBI. In the Senate, two members from each of these committees (one Democrat and one Republican) are to be assigned to intelligence; in the House, only one. In the Senate, the vice chairman is elected by the minority members of the committee; no provision is made for a vice chairman in the House. In both House and Senate the majority and minority leaders are ex officio members without votes.

Another difference is in the jurisdiction of the two committees. The resolution creating the Senate committee specifically excluded from its definition of intelligence activities "tactical foreign military intelligence serving no national policymaking function." The resolution creating the House committee, on the other hand, specifically included "intelligence-related activities." This is a technical term that in general means tactical military intelligence.

Continuous service of a member is limited on both committees—to eight years in the Senate, to six years in the House. This limitation is designed as a safeguard against co-option, the subtle process by which the overseen persuade their overseers to become their handmaidens. Co-option is particularly noticeable among the regulatory agencies of the government, and it has existed, at one time or another and to one degree or another, in the relations between most other congressional committees and the executive agencies for whose legislation they are responsible. Prior to 1975, it certainly existed with respect to the appropriations and armed services committees, on the one hand, and the CIA on the other.

Sen. Daniel Inouye, D-Hawaii, the first chairman of the Senate Select Committee on Intelligence, resigned as chairman (while continuing on the committee) at the end of 1977. In a report to the Senate he stated:

> I believe rotation of Chairmanship is the best way to assure that the combination of close detailed work with the agencies and a vigilant attitude toward their activities can be maintained. I am resigning because I believe it is important for the Senate and for the intelligence agencies who are under the charge of the Select Committee to have overseers who come to the issues as I have come to them—with an open, fresh and relatively objective point of view, so necessary for the important task of oversight.[9]

Inouye was succeeded by Sen. Birch Bayh, D-Ind., who served as chairman for three years. Bayh was defeated in the 1980 election, and Sen. Barry Goldwater, R-Ariz., became chairman in 1981 when the Republicans took control of the Senate in the 97th Congress. Goldwater continued as chairman in the 98th Congress. In the House, Rep. Edward P. Boland, D-Mass., has been chairman since the creation of the Intelligence Committee in 1977. (The six-year limitation on service on the committee did not begin to run until 1979.)

With the advent of Goldwater, there were several signs that the Senate committee had indeed been co-opted. Goldwater himself said in a television interview that he did not believe the committee should exist. And in the Senate he said he would have preferred no congressional oversight of intelligence agencies. "The Russians have a very fine system. . . . No part of their government has any idea of what is going on [in the KGB]. That is the way . . . I wish it were here in our country, but it is not." [10] As staff director, Goldwater brought in John Blake who had previously worked for the CIA for 32 years, rising as high as acting deputy director. Blake in turn was succeeded by Robert R. Simmons, who had worked for the CIA for 10 years before moving to Capitol Hill to be legislative assistant to Sen. John H. Chafee, R-R.I. In 1982 Dan Childs, the committee's senior budget officer, left to become comptroller of the CIA. (This sort of staff movement back and forth does not necessarily mean co-option or even an undesirably close relationship. There are abundant examples where committee staff members drawn from executive agencies are extremely valuable because they know what questions to ask and where to look in the bureaucratic maze. In the case of both intelligence committees, however, even a former CIA Director, Stansfield Turner, concluded that "the Congress is now co-opted.") [11]

It seems anomalous that the Senate would make Goldwater chairman of the Intelligence Committee. Why have the committee if the chairman does not think it should even be there? The answer lies partly in the traditions and folkways of the Senate and partly in the 1980 election returns. Goldwater had been the ranking Republican member of the committee before Republicans took control of the Senate in 1981. Although the Senate now has a procedure for voting on committee chairmen individually, it has never been used. The unbroken practice is to follow seniority. (Another question is why, if he opposed oversight, Goldwater wanted to be a member of the committee in the first place. The answer may be that this would permit him to use what influence he had to minimize oversight.) Second, the 1980 election revealed a marked conservative shift in the country and resulted in a much more conservative Senate, one that was more willing to give the executive branch free rein. Notwithstanding all of this, the members of Goldwater's committee have not been willing to go as far as the chairman might have liked in loosening controls on the intelligence community.

Finally, it is interesting to note that in 1977 consideration was given to establishing the principle of rotating members and chairmen in all Senate committees. In this respect, the practice of the Intelligence Committee (and of the Budget Committee as well) may be a harbinger of broader changes in congressional organization.

Intelligence Appropriations

Both the House and the Senate intelligence committees get their real power from their legislative jurisdiction over authorizations for appropriations for the intelligence agencies, and from congressional rules that specifically prohibit appropriating funds that have not first been authorized. This means that the committees not only have access to information about the secret intelligence budget, but they also can approve or disapprove it, in whole or in part.

Subcommittees of the appropriations committees have always been in this position, of course, but the intelligence committees are taking the job more seriously. They consider the budget on a line-item basis— they vote separately on each major category of expenditure, including each covert action project. The authorization bill resulting from this process is unique in that it says "funds are hereby authorized to be appropriated," but it does not contain any figures. These are included in the committees' classified reports, which are made available to the appropriations and armed services committees and to the executive branch.

The published portions of the bill contain only the authorizations for the counterterrorism activities of the FBI, for the intelligence community staff, and for the CIA Retirement and Disability Fund. For fiscal year 1983, these amounted to approximately $12,125,000, $15,400,000, and $91,300,000, respectively.

The appropriations made pursuant to the authorizing legislation are still concealed in the Defense Department appropriation bill. There has been much discussion of whether at least an overall figure for the intelligence budget should be published, and both the House and the Senate have specifically directed their intelligence committees to study the question.

One of the recommendations of the Pike committee in the House was that the president include an overall intelligence figure in his budget. The Church committee in the Senate voted 6-5 to let the Senate decide whether the figure should be made public, a decision that the Senate has shown no inclination to make. The House committee in 1979 voted specifically not to reveal the overall figure. This congressional reluctance is curious in light of the fact that former CIA director Stansfield Turner repeatedly said that he had no objection to releasing a single, inclusive figure.[12] (It is even more curious why, then, Turner did not release it himself.)

In 1982 the House Intelligence Committee again considered the question and again decided not to publish even a total figure. "By itself," the committee said in its report on the fiscal 1983 intelligence authorization bill, "a single intelligence budget total would probably not harm intelligence activities or capabilities. Such a number, however, would be meaningless in a vacuum.... Budget disclosure might well mean more to this country's adversaries than to any of its citizens." [13] It reached the same conclusion with respect to fiscal 1984.

There is clearly an anomaly in the existence of a secret law in a country governed on the basis of public laws. On the other hand, the disclosure even of an aggregate total would give other countries an indication of the level of the American intelligence effort. Variations in the total from year to year have sometimes been substantial as large new projects are undertaken or old ones are phased out (for example, the war in Laos) or as expensive new technology is developed. Such information would provide a basis at least for guessing what American intelligence is up to and would give foreign intelligence services an indication of where to look. A further, less persuasive, objection to publishing an overall figure is that pressures would then mount for publication of a more detailed breakdown.

It may fairly be said that since the establishment of the two intelligence committees, the intelligence budget has been subject to a more searching congressional review than ever before. The committees' ultimate power, of course, lies in withholding money or in prescribing the purposes for which it is to be spent. But the committees—like those operating in public—have gone further and have used their classified reports on the authorizing legislation to give policy guidance to the intelligence community. In its report on the 1980 bill, for example, the

Senate committee stated: "The committee expects that the classified report, although not available to the public, will have the full force of any Senate report, and that the intelligence community will comply with the guidelines and directions contained therein." [14]

Congressional committees generally think of their reports as having more force than is actually the case. They certainly do not have the force of law. The influence of the reports varies from time to time and from agency to agency, an important factor being whether the agency wishes to comply and whether it thinks it can get away with noncompliance. Secrecy makes it impossible to measure this influence in the intelligence community.

On the face of it, Congress has delegated extraordinary powers to its intelligence committees. Yet it is no more power than the appropriations and armed services committees once had and failed to exercise. (The appropriations committees still have it; they actually provide the money which the intelligence committees authorize.)

Furthermore, any member can read the intelligence committees' classified reports, although few legislators actually do. If the member does not like them, he or she can precipitate a debate in closed session; if enough legislators are persuaded to agree, the committees can be overridden. This has never happened. Except for the fact that the debate would take place in closed session, the procedure is not significantly different from that followed with respect to any other issues considered by a House or Senate committee.

Nicaragua

When Congress limited the reporting of covert actions to the House and Senate intelligence committees, it went some distance toward shutting out the foreign policy and armed services committees. (The appropriations committees could not be shut out because of their hands on the purse strings.) The interests of the foreign policy and armed services committees were protected in two ways. First, they each had members who also served on the intelligence committees and could be expected to report significant matters of mutual interest. Second, the 1980 law specifically directed the intelligence committees to call to the attention of any appropriate committee any matter the committee should know about.

These provisions were not effective, however, in the case of a major covert action directed against Nicaragua. The chairman of the House Foreign Affairs Subcommittee on Western Hemisphere Affairs, Rep. Michael Barnes, D-Md., said in the spring of 1983 that he had purposely avoided asking the House Intelligence Committee about Nicaragua because of the constraints he would then have had to accept on his public discussion of the matter.

The roots of the Nicaraguan problem run deep into the history of that country and of its relations with the United States, but for our purposes we may begin with the revolution that culminated in the overthrow of the dictatorial regime of Anastasio Somoza in the summer of 1979. Somoza was the last of a family dynasty which had greatly enriched itself while ruling Nicaragua with an iron hand for more than 40 years. All the Somozas were pro-American, and the youngest was even a graduate of the United States Military Academy in West Point. Significantly, the principal faction in the ultimately successful revolutionary movement took its name after César Augusto Sandino, who was the leader of a rebel group against the U.S. Marine occupation of Nicaragua in the 1920s and early 1930s.

As the revolution gathered momentum in 1978 and 1979, the United States distanced itself from Somoza and sought, with only partial success, to encourage the broadening of the revolutionary leadership so as to dilute radical Sandinista influence. In the summer of 1979 the administration was also worried about getting the Panama Canal implementing legislation through the House and was reluctant to offend Somoza's friends in that body, of whom the most prominent and influential was Rep. John M. Murphy, D-N.Y. (see Chapter 3). With the triumph of the revolution, the Carter administration adopted a policy of cooperative, friendly relations and of trying to help, in a modest way, in the recovery of the war-damaged Nicaraguan economy. Congress, on the other hand, delayed for nine months in passing a $75 million aid bill and then hedged it with restrictions. Many members were apprehensive of growing Cuban influence in Nicaragua (the fall of Somoza was followed by an influx of Cuban teachers, doctors, and other technicians), and the leftist rhetoric of the Sandinistas caused some nervousness on Capitol Hill. U.S.-Nicaraguan relations began a long slide downhill.

The slide picked up momentum in January 1981 with the advent of the Reagan administration, which was less inclined than Carter's to be cooperative; with growing evidence of Nicaraguan support for the rebels in El Salvador; and with the continued drift of the Sandinistas to the left. As early as March 1981, William J. Casey, the Reagan administration's CIA director, reported to the intelligence committees on a covert action aimed at protecting Nicaragua's neighbors, Honduras and Costa Rica, against the spread of revolution; more specifically, the action was intended to stop the flow of arms from Nicaragua through Honduras to the guerrilla movement in El Salvador.[15] By December Casey's plan had evolved into a $19 million program to train and support a 500-man force of anti-Sandinista Nicaraguans based in Honduras with the objective of disrupting the flow of Cuban support through Nicaragua to the Salvadoran guerrillas.

By early 1982 some of this began to leak to the press. One of the unlearned lessons of the Bay of Pigs was the difficulty of maintaining the secrecy of operations involving large numbers of people. Further, the training of the Honduran-based anti-Sandinistas was being done by Argentines whose distinctive accents immediately called attention to their presence in the Honduran capital of Tegucigalpa. (The Argentines left after the United States incurred their displeasure by siding with Great Britain in the Falkland Islands war in the spring of 1982.) Finally, as shown by both the Bay of Pigs and Angola, these operations tend to grow beyond what was intended. The Nicaraguan action started with 500 men and mushroomed by the summer of 1983 to 10,000.

The House Intelligence Committee became concerned enough to put a secret amendment in the fiscal 1983 intelligence authorization bill. As it became law later in 1982, that amendment prohibited any support for military activities "to any group or individual, not part of a country's armed forces, for the purpose of overthrowing the government of Nicaragua or provoking a military exchange between Nicaragua and Honduras." When the House considered the Defense Department appropriation bill in December 1982, Rep. Tom Harkin, D-Iowa, offered an amendment that would also have banned assistance to nongovernmental groups "for the purpose of ... carrying out military activities in or against Nicaragua." [16] Chairman Boland of the Intelligence Committee then offered as a substitute the text of the amendment that was already secretly in the intelligence authorization bill. The Boland amendment passed 411-0.

By the spring of 1983 it became apparent that whatever the purposes of the Reagan administration and Congress, the anti-Sandinistas who were receiving the no longer covert U.S. assistance fully intended to overthrow the Nicaraguan government. A group of them even invited some American correspondents to accompany them for a week in northern Nicaragua and talked frankly about what they were doing.

The Reagan administration took the disingenuous position that it was complying with the Boland amendment because its purpose in aiding the rebels was to interdict supplies to the guerrillas in El Salvador, not to overthrow the Nicaraguan government, and that the purposes or ambitions of the Nicaraguan rebels did not matter. This position was endorsed by Senator Goldwater, the chairman of the Senate Intelligence Committee, but the House Intelligence Committee would have none of it. By a party-line vote of nine Democrats to five Republicans, the House committee reported a bill prohibiting the direct or indirect support of military or paramilitary operations in Nicaragua. Instead, the committee authorized $30 million for 1983 and $50 million for 1984 for overt assistance to "friendly" Central American countries to prevent the use of their territory for the transfer of military equipment to any group trying to overthrow the government of a Central American country. Countries receiving this assistance would have to agree that they themselves would not contribute to destabilizing or overthrowing any Central American government. The main purpose of this assistance was to help Honduras stop the flow of Cuban/Nicaraguan arms through its territory to the Salvadoran guerrillas (which is what the Reagan administration maintained it really wanted to do), but the intelligence committee bill would also have had the effect of cutting off both U.S. and Honduran help for the Nicaraguan rebels.

Because the bill authorized this overt assistance, it had to be referred also to the Foreign Affairs Committee, which has jurisdiction over foreign aid generally. That committee also approved the bill. It passed the House in July by a vote of 228-195 after debate in a rare secret session. The Intelligence Committee also included the provisions of the bill in the fiscal 1984 intelligence authorization bill.

Meanwhile, the Senate Intelligence Committee voted to allow the covert action to continue through September but provided that before then the president would have to submit a new plan. The new plan made no mention either of overthrowing the Sandinistas or of interdicting supplies to El Salvador; instead, it was to bring pressure on the Sandinistas to abandon their policy of promoting "revolution without frontiers," as they put it, throughout the area.

The Senate committee found this sufficiently persuasive to authorize, by a vote of 13-2, $19 million for the first six months of fiscal 1984. The House committee was more skeptical and stuck to its position of ending the whole program. In this, it had the support of former CIA director Turner. In October the full House voted 227-194 (almost identically how it had voted earlier on the same issue) to keep the provision in the bill. In November, the full Senate likewise endorsed the position of its Intelligence Committee. The matter was resolved in an agreement to allow $24 million for the covert action, an amount that it was estimated would support the program until June.

Conclusion

No more dramatic example of the new congressional assertiveness with respect to foreign policy is to be found than that of the changed relationship between Congress and the intelligence community. The change was slow in coming and was more the result of an evolutionary process than a single event, although the Watergate crisis accelerated the trend.

Congress investigated, but did nothing about, such earlier misadventures as the U-2 flight and the Bay of Pigs invasion. Then in the immediate aftermath of Vietnam the atmosphere changed. Controversial policies in Chile and Angola and abuses of constitutional rights in the United States combined to effect this change. Underlying the congressional concern was the implicit notion that if Congress had known about these and other questionable activities, it would have prevented them. This belief was reinforced by the example of Senator Fulbright's advice to the Kennedy administration not to undertake the Bay of Pigs venture. In some of these cases also, there was congressional resentment over having been hoodwinked by executive officials.

One of the weaknesses of the old system of intelligence oversight lay within Congress itself. In most instances, some legislators were knowledgeable of misdeeds or questionable behavior by intelligence agencies, but they did nothing about it—nothing, at any rate, that appears on the public record. There is, of course, no guarantee that such lapses will not happen again. Members of Congress are no less fallible than officials in the executive branch. But the more formalized structure of the legislative oversight mechanism, and the fact that more people are now involved in it, make the prospect of oversight failure less likely than in the past.

The basis of congressional concern about the intelligence community has nearly always been the political effect on foreign policy—that is, the consequences of failures. This concern has been directed mainly to covert action, less so to intelligence collection and analysis. With the two intelligence committees now voting on line-item authorizations for covert actions, Congress—or at least the members of the committees—will share the burden of future failures. In the past Congress has generally been reluctant to assume this kind of responsibility, and it may be questioned whether legislative attitudes have changed fundamentally.

Effective legislative oversight involves a great deal more than simply keeping intelligence operations and related policy decisions from going awry, however. Legislative oversight is also concerned with making things go right, or at least making them go better. In the attention the intelligence committees have given to the quality of the intelligence product and analysis in recent years, they have demonstrated their awareness of broader concerns.

The committees have publicly considered a number of problems regarding the quality or adequacy of intelligence. Some of these were the failure to detect for a period of several years the presence of a brigade of Soviet troops in Cuba, intelligence in Central America, and intelligence in Iran before the fall of the Shah. The law now requires the community to report any "significant intelligence failure" to the committee.

There remains a long agenda. A checklist would include such difficult and complex questions as the following.

• The long-awaited statutory charters and guidelines for intelligence operations. (In 1978 Congress did pass the Foreign Intelligence Surveillance Act, but this had more to do with constitutional process in the United States than with foreign policy. And in 1982 Congress passed the Intelligence Identities Protection Act, but again this had more to do with domestic affairs—that is, with punishing certain disclosures—than with foreign policy.) How detailed should the law governing intelligence activities be? The more detailed the law is, the less operational flexibility is left for the intelligence community. Yet the more flexibility left to its members, the greater the possibility for abuse or bad judgment in intelligence activities.

• What kinds of intelligence ought to be collected? What are the political risks involved in collecting it? What information is vital to maintaining national security and to assessing long-range trends in the international system? And what information is of marginal interest, focusing too much on current (and perhaps relatively unimportant) events?

• What can be done, or needs to be done, to insulate agencies that belong to the intelligence community from executive pressures to shape their activities and reports according to what the president and his principal subordinates want to hear? The best safeguard perhaps is the existence of the two intelligence committees in Congress, with memberships broadly spanning the political spectrum. Yet even this change is likely to provide only minimum protection against biased intelligence analysis if Congress fails to use the committees effectively.

• Are there feasible alternatives to covert action, particularly on a scale so large that it is impossible to keep it secret? If the United States drastically reduces the number of covert actions but does not dismantle its capability for undertaking them, how does the national government keep its covert action operatives occupied, trained, and ready when they are needed?

• Should there be statutory criteria for undertaking covert action—for example, that the action is consistent with publicly stated policy, that the anticipated benefits outweigh the consequences of disclosure, or that less sensitive alternatives would not work?

• Should certain intelligence activities be excluded regardless of circumstances because they offend American ideological values and ethical concepts? It is generally agreed that peacetime assassination attempts should be ruled out. Nevertheless, the Nicaraguan government, as late as June 1983, said it had discovered a CIA plot to poison Foreign Minister Miguel d'Escoto. Other activities raise more difficult questions. Is it acceptable for the CIA to use scholars, clergymen, or media correspondents to achieve its objectives? If it does so, and this fact becomes known (as has occurred in the past), then legitimate scholars, clergymen, and correspondents fall under suspicion that they are really CIA agents—a suspicion they encounter routinely in many foreign countries anyway. But if the CIA does not do so, then the forms of cover available to intelligence agents are significantly reduced.

• What should be the relationship of the CIA to American business firms and activities abroad? Many Americans with experience overseas can provide important information to the intelligence community. Yet, again, for intelligence agencies to utilize this resource places all American business activities abroad under suspicion.

• What sorts of trade-offs can reasonably be made for allowing American intelligence agencies (such as the National Security Agency) to collect information in foreign countries? To gain this concession, should the United States routinely exchange intelligence data and reports with foreign intelligence agencies? Should the United States allow foreign governments cooperating with it to carry on intelligence operations within its borders?

Today the intelligence committees of Congress are well staffed, and thus far there has been no serious leak of classified information. Members of the committees take their jobs seriously. The House committee, under Chairman Edward P. Boland, has proceeded soberly and responsibly.

The Senate Intelligence Committee, under a succession of chairmen, has played a useful role in the treaty-making process. Its thorough investigation squelched charges that the Panama Canal treaties had been tainted by the compromise of intelligence operations, and it helped clarify the issue of verification in connection with the SALT II arms control agreements. Some proposed intelligence activities have been abandoned because of questions raised by the committees.

With the intelligence process necessarily shrouded in secrecy, an outside observer cannot be wholly confident of judgments based on evidence from the public record. But at least Congress now has an institutional structure and an adequate staff to meet the challenge of supervising American intelligence operations. All the returns are not yet in, but a hopeful and helpful start has been made in solving an extremely difficult problem for the American democracy.

Notes

1. U.S. Congress, Senate, S. Res. 21, 94th Cong., 1st sess., 1975, establishing the Select Committee to Study Governmental Operations with Respect to Intelligence Activities.
2. U.S. Congress, House Permanent Select Committee on Intelligence, 95th Cong., 1st sess., 1977, H. Rept. 1795, p. 16.
3. National Security Act of 1947, 50 U.S.C. 403(d).
4. Francis O. Wilcox, *Congress, the Executive, and Foreign Policy* (New York: Harper and Row, 1971), p. 86.
5. *Executive Sessions of the Senate Foreign Relations Committee* (Historical Series), 86th Cong., 2d sess., 1960, 12: 251-404 (released November 1982).
6. Sec. 662 of the Foreign Assistance Act of 1961 as amended, 22 U.S.C. 2422.
7. U.S. Congress, Senate, 94th Cong., 1st sess., 1975, S. Res. 21.
8. U.S. Congress, House, 94th Cong., 2d sess., 1976, H. Res. 982.
9. U.S. Congress, Senate Select Committee on Intelligence, *Report to the Senate on the Work of the Senate Select Committee on Intelligence,* n.d., p. 15.
10. *Congressional Record,* 96th Cong., 2d sess., p. S6147 (daily ed. June 3, 1980).
11. George Lardner, Jr., "Ex-CIA Director Faults New Intelligence Order," *Washington Post,* December 9, 1981.
12. U.S. Congress, House Permanent Select Committee on Intelligence, *Intelligence and Intelligence-Related Activities Act, Fiscal Year 1980.* For the additional views of Rep. Romano L. Mazzoli, see H. Rept. 96-127, pt. 1, p. 10.
13. H. Rept. 97-486, pt. 1.
14. U.S. Congress, Senate, 96th Cong., 1st sess., 1979, S. Rept. 71, p. 2.
15. A good account of the development of the covert action program against Nicaragua is given in Don Oberdorfer and Patrick E. Tyler, "U.S.-Backed Nicaraguan Rebel Army Swells to 7,000 Men," *Washington Post,* May 8, 1983. See also House Permanent Select Committee on Intelligence, *Amendment to the Intelligence Authorization Act for Fiscal Year 1983,* 98th Cong., 1st sess., 1983, H. Rept. 98-122, pt. 1 (to accompany H.R. 2760).
16. *Congressional Record,* 97th Cong., 2d sess., p. H9148 (daily ed. December 8, 1982).

The Human Rights Issue

The issue of how much weight should be given to human rights in American foreign policy originated in Congress and has been pressed on a succession of presidents from Nixon to Reagan. The issue first arose as a simple argument over American support of dictators and nondemocratic governments. It has become possibly the most tangled web in American foreign policy, full of confusion, contradiction, and inconsistency—and not without a measure of moral posturing, bordering at times on hypocrisy. Nevertheless, it is a peculiarly American issue, and it has brought into focus many of the dilemmas of post-World War II foreign policy.

Congressional interest in the human rights issue has been notable, among other reasons, for the attention given to bilateral relations with other countries and the relative neglect shown for multilateral agreements to promote human rights. Initially, congressional efforts to influence human rights policy were fundamentally directed to putting a certain distance between the United States and oppressive regimes. This is different from actively promoting, as the multilateral agreements seek to do, the improvement and extension of human rights. As the issue developed, this distinction became blurred, and Congress eventually adopted the broader and more positive goal for bilateral policies; but Congress did not always follow through, nor did it become any more supportive of multilateral agreements.

In many respects, human rights has become more an argument over unrelated questions than a substantive issue. Members of Congress who are opposed to a policy of détente with the Soviet Union cite the Soviet record on human rights. (Yet the same members tend to overlook the equally abysmal human rights record of the Chinese.) Similarly, members of Congress who disliked the Somoza regime in Nicaragua emphasized its flouting of human rights. But those who feared Cuban involvement in Nicaragua talked instead about Castro's human rights violations and those of the Nicaraguan government that succeeded Somoza.

Despite the complexities and subtleties of the human rights question, the trend in Congress in the 1970s and early 1980s was to give greater weight to human rights issues in formulating and administering American foreign policy. Congress was well ahead of the Nixon and Ford administrations in this respect, and at times it even outran Jimmy Carter, who proclaimed in his January 20, 1977, inaugural address, "[O]ur commitment to human rights must be absolute.... The powerful must not persecute the weak, and human dignity must be enhanced." The Reagan administration, which took office in 1981, deemphasized human rights somewhat compared to Carter and also shifted the focus of its concern toward violations by leftist governments (for example, the Soviet Union, Cuba, Nicaragua) and away from violations by rightist governments (for example, Argentina, Chile). Congress kept the pressure on Reagan, especially with respect to Central America, as it did on his three immediate predecessors.

The Origins of Congressional Concern

Concern over the kinds of foreign governments the United States became closely identified with began to manifest itself in Congress during the late 1950s, particularly with respect to Latin America, where dictatorships were being ousted by democratic governments. The United States had long been criticized by liberals, both at home and throughout Latin America, for having supported the dictators. (The degree and nature of support varied; what some of the critics meant was that Washington had not actively aided groups seeking a dictator's overthrow, and this was quite a different matter.)

The criticism reached its most dramatic point in May 1958, when Vice President Richard Nixon, on a tour of South America, was set upon by anti-U.S. rioters in Caracas, Venezuela. Later Nixon set forth what remains the most sensible policy: "A formal handshake for dictators; an *embraso* [he probably intended *abrazo,* meaning embrace] for leaders in freedom." [1]

Congressional involvement in human rights questions, however, was largely rhetorical until the late 1960s. By that time, the wheel of Latin American political history had taken another turn, moving away from democratic governments and back toward the old pattern of dictatorships.

The human rights issue was first posed with painful clarity with respect to Brazil in the aftermath of a military takeover of the government in April 1964. The previous government had led Brazil into a chaotic situation, with inflation running 100 percent a year or more. The new government adopted economic policies that started Brazil on the road to what was widely described as a miracle of economic development. Using draconian measures of repression, it also energetically set about a transformation of Brazilian political institutions.

Predictably, these two policies led to opposite reactions in the United States. The business community and the Johnson administration hailed the sound economic policies and the favorable treatment of foreign investment evident in Brazil under the new regime. Others deplored the disregard for civil liberties and the growing reports of torture by Brazilian authorities. The reaction of the State Department was to downplay the reports of human rights violations and to continue its warm embrace of the new government.

The situation in Brazil focused attention on one of the minor activities of the Agency for International Development—its public safety program. This program had been started a few years before to help selected developing countries deal with growing problems of public order, ranging all the way from street demonstrations to terrorist activities. The purpose of AID's public safety program was to provide equipment (tear gas and radios were two of the most popular items) and training for foreign police and paramilitary forces in techniques of crowd control and investigative work. One of the countries that received this kind of foreign aid was Brazil.

As reports of police torture in Brazil increased, charges were made that the AID public safety team was somehow involved in these abuses. Given the difficulty during this period of distinguishing between the Brazilian police and military, the American military mission in the country was also implicated in these charges. Some of the accusations were quite specific—that torture techniques were part of AID's program of instruction and that torture devices were among the equipment supplied Brazil by the United States.

No reliable evidence was ever found to substantiate these charges. Indeed, the object of AID's public safety program was precisely the opposite: to teach the techniques and to supply the equipment needed for effective law enforcement *without* the use of torture. But the accusations of American complicity in Brazilian violations of human rights persisted. They were made in connection with other countries as well. In Uruguay, for example, an American public safety adviser was kidnapped and murdered by terrorists who accused him of complicity in police brutality.

By 1971, Sen. Frank Church, D-Idaho, chairman of the Latin American Subcommittee of the Foreign Relations Committee, was sufficiently exercised about such complaints to hold comprehensive hearings on United States policy toward Brazil. These hearings, augmented by subsequent staff reports on Guatemala and the Dominican Republic, demonstrated, at least to the satisfaction of Church and some of his colleagues, that the basic problem of the American public safety program was one of public relations. Police forces in Brazil, Guatemala, and the Dominican Republic were undoubtedly guilty of using excessive force against citizens—to put the most charitable interpretation on the evidence. Through its public safety program, the United States was identified with these excesses.

Because of this unfortunate association, a movement began in the Senate to abolish the public safety program. It eventually succeeded in 1974, after overcoming stiff bureaucratic opposition and some resistance in the House.

Congress Acts on Human Rights

Chile

Just as events in Chile brought a turning point in congressional relations with the intelligence community, so did they alter Congress's response to the problem of international human rights. The overthrow of President Salvador Allende's regime in September 1973 ushered in a period of mass arrests; prisoners were commonly held incommunicado without charges for long periods. These actions were accompanied by the inevitable allegations of mistreatment and torture. Some of the allegations were impressively documented.

The Nixon administration reacted to the overthrow of Allende and the emergence of the new military government in Chile much as the Johnson administration had reacted to the new government in Brazil in 1964. Although the Nixon embrace was perhaps a trifle less fervent, the administration made no secret of its approval of the downfall of the Allende government (while deploring the fact that the president had been killed in the process), and it loosened the strings on American loans and grants to Chile.

The initial congressional action (as distinguished from oratory) toward those developments was quite mild. The Foreign Assistance Act of 1973, approved December 17, contained two provisions that did no more than express the sense of Congress. Expressions of the sense of Congress are intended as guidance to the executive branch and do not have the force of law. They are frequently the result of legislative compromise over stronger proposals, which, if cast in mandatory language, would provoke debate and opposition. They are, in short, a means of avoiding a test of strength in Congress while getting some kind of a policy on record. They may also indicate that majority support does not exist in Congress for stronger measures; the administration can usually expect not to be called to account if it does not take the sense of Congress seriously. That was not, however, the case in this instance.

The two human rights provisions in the Foreign Assistance Act of 1973 dealt with the question of political prisoners in general and with the problem of human rights in Chile in particular. With respect to political prisoners in all countries, it was the sense of Congress that the president should deny foreign aid to any government "which practices the internment or imprisonment of that country's citizens for political purposes." [2]

With respect to Chile, Congress had more to say. It was the sense of Congress that the president should:

"Request the Government of Chile to protect the human rights of all individuals, Chilean and foreign," with respect to "the granting of asylum, safe conduct, and the humane treatment or release of prisoners"

"Support international humanitarian initiatives by the United Nations High Commissioner of Refugees and the International Committee of the Red Cross to insure the protection and safe conduct and resettlement of political refugees, the humane treatment of political prisoners, and the full inspection of detention facilities under international auspices"

"Request the Inter-American Commission on Human Rights to undertake an immediate inquiry into recent events . . . in Chile" [3]

After the passage of the Foreign Assistance Act of 1973, Congress became steadily more assertive about Chile and enacted a series of specific limits on aid that could be given that country. In 1974 it placed a limit of $25 million on military assistance. In 1975 it put a ceiling of $90 million on economic assistance, including housing guarantees and sales of surplus agricultural commodities. (During the 1960s American assistance to Chile had sometimes been twice that amount.)

In 1976 Congress prohibited any kind of military assistance, sales, exports, or training; economic assistance was limited to $27.5 million (not including grants of surplus agricultural commodities distributed by charitable organizations). American aid could be doubled if the president made certain certifications to Congress in writing, certifications Congress did not expect the president to be able to make. They were that the Government of Chile:

"Does not engage in a consistent pattern of gross violations of internationally recognized human rights, including torture or cruel, inhuman, or degrading treatment or punishment, prolonged detention without charges or trial, or other flagrant denials of the right to life, liberty, or the security of person"

"Has permitted the unimpeded investigation, by internationally recognized commissions on human rights (including the United Nations Commission on Human Rights and the Inter-American Commission on Human Rights of the Organization of American States) of alleged violations of internationally recognized human rights"

"Has taken steps to inform the families of prisoners of the condition of and charges against such prisoners" [4]

In 1981 Congress loosened the restrictions a bit. Instead of prohibiting assistance unless the government of Chile was *not* engaging in consistent and gross human rights violations, Congress now would permit assistance if certain positive findings were made. The most important of these were that the government of Chile had made "significant" progress in human rights, that it was not encouraging international terrorism, and that it had cooperated in prosecuting Chileans indicted in connection with the murders of Orlando Letelier and Ronni Moffitt.*

In 1983 the House Foreign Affairs Committee amended the 1984 foreign aid authorization bill to add a further and much tougher precondition: that an elected civilian government be in power. The committee applied this to Argentina as well, and a similar requirement was applied to Paraguay and Uruguay. However, the bill was not considered by the House, and for the third year foreign aid was financed through stopgap spending authority.

The Ford administration's foreign policy (1974-1976) was dominated by Secretary of State Henry Kissinger, who greeted each new congressional initiative on human rights with resistance that varied in proportion to the specificity and stringency of the initiative. In this, Kissinger was reacting in a typically bureaucratic fashion. Regardless of who has been secretary, the State Department has never liked binding policy directives or limitations from Congress. (There are rare exceptions to this in cases when the department is seeking to bolster its negotiating position with a foreign country and wants to be able to say, in effect, "Look, we understand your position, but Congress has tied our hands." Even in these cases, the department does not like to have its hands tied too tightly.)

In the case of human rights, Kissinger made the usual bureaucratic plea for diplomatic flexibility. He argued that public protests of human rights violations were likely to be counterproductive and that more could be achieved through quiet diplomacy. In the abstract, there is much to be said for this argument. Sovereign governments ordinarily do not respond well to public criticism, let alone preaching, from other governments, particularly when it is directed at something they regard as a domestic matter.

The trouble with the argument in this case was a widespread disbelief that Kissinger was really conducting any quiet diplomacy aimed at improving the human rights of Chileans or anybody else. When Sen. Claiborne Pell, D-R.I., who had been particularly outraged by the Johnson and Nixon administrations' embrace of a repressive government in Greece, asked Kissinger to cite some examples of quiet diplomacy, the secretary demurred that it would be inappropriate to do so in public. Pell accepted that objection and invited the secretary to submit a classified memorandum. It took the State Department eight months to find a handful of examples worldwide.

It must also be remembered that these exchanges took place as the full story of the CIA's maneuvers in Chile was beginning to unfold. If

---

* Letelier was Allende's foreign minister and had earlier been ambassador to the United States. After Allende's overthrow Letelier was imprisoned in Chile for a time and then went into exile in the United States. In September 1976 the car in which he was riding with Moffitt, his research assistant, was blown up on a Washington street by a remote-controlled bomb. An American working for the Chilean intelligence service was convicted of the murder, and three Chilean officials were indicted for their roles in the conspiracy. The Chilean government refused to extradite them.

Kissinger had had any credibility left in the human rights area, Congress (or at least the Senate) might well have accepted his argument for quiet diplomacy. But he did not, and Congress took the bit in its teeth on the human rights question. In doing so, it subsequently complicated life for the Carter administration, which ironically had promised to put more emphasis on human rights in American foreign policy. Still later, Congress complicated life even more for the Reagan administration, which did not share the congressional enthusiasm for human rights in the first place.

A General Human Rights Policy

The concern over human rights that led to the enactment of limitations on aid to Chile paralleled a congressional attempt to formulate a general policy relating foreign aid to a recipient government's human rights practices. This attempt was complicated by the variety of kinds and purposes of foreign aid.

It is one thing to cut off aid to a repressive government for economic infrastructure projects (such as road building or harbor construction) or for balance of payments support; in that case the government is hurt first and most. It is something else to cut off shipments of food; then the people oppressed by the government suffer most.

Congress attempted to deal with this problem by distinguishing between security assistance, on the one hand, and food and development assistance on the other. (In the jargon of foreign aid, *security assistance* is military aid, including military credit sales, military training, and economic assistance directly related to military or political purposes. *Development assistance* is aid directly related to economic progress.)

Security Assistance. The Foreign Assistance Act of 1974 expressed the sense of Congress that

> except in extraordinary circumstances, the President shall substantially reduce or terminate security assistance to any government which engages in a consistent pattern of gross violations of internationally recognized human rights, including torture or cruel, inhuman or degrading treatment or punishment; prolonged detention without charges; or other flagrant denials of the right to life, liberty, and the security of the person.[5]

In cases in which assistance was proposed or furnished to such governments, the president was to inform Congress of the extraordinary circumstances necessitating the assistance. In determining whether a government consistently violated human rights, consideration was to be given to the extent of its cooperation in permitting unimpeded investigations "by appropriate international organizations." This left the president considerable leeway in determining what circumstances were "extraordinary." The requirement for these to be reported to Congress gave Congress the chance to second-guess him and tended to ensure that presidential definitions of *extraordinary* would not be whimsical.

In 1976 Congress rewrote this section of the Foreign Assistance Act of 1974, tightening the standards and procedures. Now, for the first time, Congress did more than withhold aid from human rights violators. It declared that "a principal goal of the foreign policy of the United States shall be to promote the increased observance of internationally recognized human rights by all countries." Previously, security assistance to human rights violators had been prohibited except in "extraordinary circumstances," as determined by the president; now it was prohibited except in specified circumstances. This change ensured a larger foreign policy role for Congress.

In the first place, security assistance programs generally were to be formulated and conducted "in a manner which will promote and advance human rights and avoid identification of the United States, through such programs, with governments which deny to their people internationally recognized human rights and fundamental freedoms."

In the second place, the materials presented to Congress by the executive branch justifying the request for security assistance programs were to include "a full and complete report" on the human rights practices of each country for which such assistance was proposed. In preparing the report, consideration was to be given to "the relevant findings of appropriate international organizations" and the extent to which proposed recipient governments cooperated in permitting unimpeded investigations by such organizations.

In the third place, on request from Congress with respect to any country, the secretary of state was to submit an additional, more detailed statement responding to seven specific areas of concern set forth in the law. If the statement from the secretary was not forthcoming in 30 days, all security assistance to the country was to be cut off until the statement was transmitted or Congress specifically authorized assistance to be resumed.[6]

Congress tinkered with the law again in the International Security Assistance Act of 1978. For governments consistently and grossly violating human rights, security assistance could not be provided to the police, domestic intelligence agencies, or similar law enforcement agencies, nor could licenses be issued for the export of crime control and detection equipment. Neither could members of the armed forces of such a country receive American military education or training. In each case, exceptions were made if the president certified to Congress that extraordinary circumstances existed. Although Congress had ordered the demise of the AID public safety program in 1974, the 1978 revisions went one step further in preventing the export of crime control and detection equipment (even through commercial channels) to governments with bad human rights records.

In 1979 Congress added the carrot to the stick in its approach to human rights. It directed that in allocating security assistance funds, "the President shall take into account significant improvements in the human rights records of recipient countries, except that such allocations may not contravene any other provision of law." [7] This made explicit what had long been implicit in the legislative requirements for withholding aid from governments that violate human rights. The withholding implied that if human rights performance improved, the aid would be restored. Now Congress as much as said that explicitly. But it left unanswered the weight that should be given to this consideration in the totality of American interests presumably served by security assistance programs.

Finally, in 1980 Congress added the clause "causing the disappearance of persons by the abduction and clandestine detention of those persons" to the acts included as "gross violations of internationally recognized human rights." This was a slap at Argentina, where the military government had been the object of particular complaints over its alleged complicity in the disappearance of some thousands of persons, although the practice is not confined to Argentina.

Development Assistance. In 1974 Congress had attempted to shift the thrust of foreign aid programs from large infrastructure projects (for example, hydroelectric dams) to activities that more directly and immediately affected the lives of the poor (for example, food production, health, education). The following year, when Congress considered the matter of development assistance to governments violating human rights, it faced the problem of how to punish those governments without at the same time punishing the people they were mistreating, among whom needy people were presumably suffering the most. The answer it came up with was to cut off aid to the governments unless the aid was directly benefiting the needy.

This answer at best proved only partially satisfactory. To the degree that the United States helps the needy in a country, it relieves the government of that country of its own obligations to do so. More to the point, it relieves the government of having to face the consequences of not doing so—consequences that are likely to take the form of internal political pressures, social unrest, and possible economic collapse. All of these would be likely to hasten the replacement of the offending government, perhaps by a less oppressive one.

Furthermore, it is next to impossible to operate an aid program, even one limited to helping the needy, without dealing with the country's government. The worse a government's record is with respect to human rights (especially in the Third World), the worse it is also likely to be with respect to honesty and efficiency in public administration.

A case in point is Haiti, which has been chronically misgoverned. During the oppressive regime (1957-1971) of President François Duvalier it was impossible for the United States even to carry out free food distribution programs without becoming entangled in red tape and demands for payoffs by government officials. This is why the Kennedy administration stopped trying to operate an aid program in Haiti.

In the International Development and Food Assistance Act of 1975, Congress stated that no development assistance could be provided to any government consistently engaging in gross human rights violations "unless such assistance will directly benefit the needy people in such country." [8] Congress had just said the year before that development assistance was supposed to be aimed at helping the needy in any event. But the new provision did serve to give another dimension to human rights legislation, and it required the president to report annually on what he had done about it.

In 1977 Congress broadened the scope of the report required and made the secretary of state, rather than the president, responsible for submitting it. The annual report must deal with the status of human rights in each country receiving development assistance, and it is to include steps that have been taken "to alter United States programs ... in any country because of human rights considerations." In 1979 Congress further broadened the reporting requirement and made it applicable to all countries that were members of the United Nations, regardless of whether they were receiving foreign aid.[9] The reason for this was to include such countries as the Soviet Union, the People's Republic of China, Cuba, and Vietnam. The 1982 report, received in February 1983, covers 160 countries and runs 1,323 pages.

Food.   In 1977, pursuant to the Agricultural Trade Development and Assistance Act (popularly known as P.L. 480), Congress linked human rights and the sale of surplus agricultural commodities:

> No agreement may be entered into to finance the sale of agricultural commodities to the government of any country which engages in a consistent pattern of gross violations of internationally recognized human rights ... unless such agreement will directly benefit the needy people in such country.

Congress also produced guidelines as to what would, or would not, benefit the needy:

> An agreement will not directly benefit the needy people unless either the commodities themselves or the proceeds from their sale will be used for specific projects or programs which the President determines would directly benefit the needy people of that country. The agreement shall specify how the projects or programs will be used to benefit the needy people and shall require a report to the President on such use within six months after the commodities are delivered.[10]

These guidelines are lacking in specificity, but they serve to underline the point that regardless of the indirect benefits to governments and others from P.L. 480 sales, the direct benefits must go to the needy. This is perhaps easier to require in legislation than it is to carry out in administrative practice.

Multilateral Aid Programs.   It was in connection with multilateral aid programs that the chickens hatched by congressional distrust of the Nixon-Kissinger policy in Chile came home to roost in the Carter administration.

In 1976, Kissinger's last year as secretary of state, the United States' executive directors of the Inter-American Development Bank and the African Development Fund were directed, by law, "to vote against any loan, any extension of financial assistance, or any technical assistance to any country which engages in a consistent pattern of gross violations of internationally recognized human rights ... unless such assistance will directly benefit the needy people in such country." The United States governor of the bank (that is, the secretary of the treasury) could be required to explain how proposed assistance would benefit the needy. In the case of the African Development Fund, the ban applied also to countries "providing refuge to individuals committing acts of international terrorism such as the hijacking of an aircraft." [11]

Limiting aid to what directly benefits the needy is a tougher standard for multilateral lending agencies than for the bilateral aid program. The multilaterals are more likely to finance large capital projects such as port improvements or industrial development programs, in which it is more difficult to show direct benefits to the needy.

In 1977, in one of its first major battles with Congress, the Carter administration tried unsuccessfully to get these provisions out of the law and to keep them from being applied to other multilateral agencies: the International Bank for Reconstruction and Development (World Bank), the International Development Association, the International Finance Corporation, and the Asian Development Bank. The administration had come to power in 1977 with a program of its own to emphasize human rights, not only in connection with aid but throughout the whole broad sweep of foreign policy. Faced with making day-to-day operating decisions, it now adopted the traditional executive branch posture of seeking as much diplomatic flexibility as possible, relying on its oft-repeated commitment to human rights as evidence of its good faith.

The Carter administration argued that such flexibility would strengthen its negotiating position and would result in more, rather than less, global progress toward respect for human rights. In effect, this was the same argument that Kissinger had made for quiet diplomacy. The Senate, which had always been more sympathetic to this argument than the House, was now willing to accept it; so was the House Committee on Banking, Finance and Urban Affairs. But the House as a whole would have none of it.

In the end, the House prevailed. As enacted, the law required the United States to oppose any assistance to countries consistently engaging in gross violations of human rights or providing refuge to aircraft hijackers, unless the assistance was "directed specifically to programs which serve the basic human needs of the citizens of such country."

The 1977 law also introduced a positive emphasis on human rights, as distinguished from the approach of denying benefits to countries violating rights. The United States was called upon to use "its voice and vote" in the international financial institutions to advance the cause of human rights, and it was encouraged to channel assistance toward countries other than those with bad human rights records. In addition, the secretary of state and the secretary of the treasury were directed to:

> initiate a wide consultation designed to develop a viable standard for the meeting of basic human needs and the protection of human rights and a mechanism for acting together to insure that the rewards of international economic cooperation are especially available to those who subscribe to such standards and are seen to be moving toward making them effective in their own systems of governance.[12]

This law covered all international financial institutions in which the United States participates except the International Monetary Fund (IMF). With respect to that institution, a 1978 law simply directs the secretary of the treasury to report annually to Congress on the status of human rights in each country that draws on funds made available under the IMF's Supplementary Financing Facility. In 1983, when Congress authorized an increase of $8.4 billion in the American contribution to the IMF, it also required the U.S. executive director of the fund to vote against loans to any country that practices apartheid, or racial segregation. This provision was aimed at South Africa. The law also required a U.S. vote against loans to any country with a Communist dictatorship. Both requirements could be waived if the secretary of the treasury gave Congress 30 days' notice and certified that the loan was in the best interests of a majority of the people of the borrowing nation.

Summary.   In order to fine tune aid programs to achieve the goal of promoting human rights, Congress has applied the tightest standards to security assistance and multilateral programs, the loosest to development assistance and food aid.

A valid distinction can be made in the case of security assistance, because it is directly related to military or political objectives and therefore more closely identifies the United States with the recipient government. But Congress has also directed that security assistance programs be formulated and conducted to promote human rights. This is different from simply withholding assistance because of human rights violations, and it represented a particular change of direction in the case of security assistance, which by definition had hitherto been primarily concerned with more narrow questions of security. Congress has not decreed such an emphasis on human rights with respect to development assistance and food aid, although it has with respect to multilateral programs.

Development assistance programs are more easily designed to promote human rights than are security assistance programs. Development assistance programs could, for example, provide help through programs designed to improve judicial systems or legal education—although such assistance would scarcely qualify as directly benefiting the needy. Congress has, in fact, authorized development assistance money to help countries develop programs to promote human rights, but Congress has not said how this might be done.

Country-Specific Enactments

Besides the provisions that have been mentioned with respect to Chile, Congress at one time or another has enacted human rights provisions of varying strictness with respect to Argentina, Cambodia (Kampuchea), El Salvador, Guatemala, Haiti, Korea, Mexico, Nicaragua, South Africa, and Uganda. For Cambodia, with which the United States does not even have diplomatic relations, and for Korea, with which the United States has an important military relationship, the provision was purely hortatory. For Uganda, it consisted of a prohibition on imports (since repealed when a new government mended the ways of its predecessor). For South Africa, it consisted of restrictions on Export-Import Bank loans. For Mexico, it was limited to concern over the treatment of Americans imprisoned in that country, most of them on drug charges.

Haiti.   Here Congress contradicted itself in one of the inconsistencies that are so abundant in the problem of fitting a concern for human rights into an overall foreign policy. This also illustrates the point that Congress's approach to its role in foreign policy is influenced by its view of the substance of a policy. The International Security and Development Cooperation Act of 1981 authorized aid to Haiti, but only if the president determined, among other things, that Haiti was cooperating in halting illegal emigration, that it was not otherwise encouraging illegal emigration, and that it was not consistently and grossly violating internationally recognized human rights. Furthermore, the act authorized the use of foreign aid funds to assist Haiti in halting significant illegal emigration to the United States—not to other countries, only to the United States.

These provisions came about because both Congress and the executive branch were perplexed over what to do about the wave of illegal Haitian immigrants arriving in the United States, most of them in small boats on the Atlantic beaches of Florida and most of them having left Haiti in violation of Haitian law. The rub was that in other contexts Congress had maintained that the freedom to emigrate was a basic human right, implying that there should not be any such thing as illegal emigration. A particularly notable example was the treatment of the Soviet Union in the Trade Act of 1974 (described later in this chapter).

Nicaragua.   After the fall of Somoza in Nicaragua in July 1979 (see Chapter 6), the Carter administration waited almost four months and in November sent to Congress a request for $75 million for an aid program in Central America, most of it in Nicaragua. This delay was partly attributable to bureaucratic difficulties and inertia. But it was also partly attributable to the desire of the Carter administration to see the implementing legislation for the Panama Canal treaties (see Chapter 3) through the House before irritating Somoza's friends in Congress, some of whom did not like the treaty anyway. There was opposition to Nicaraguan aid, especially in the House. Some of it came from Somoza's friends; some came from conservatives who were nervous about the Sandinistas' leftist rhetoric and ties with Cuba. In any event, Congress did not complete action on the aid authorization bill until May 1980, and on the appropriation bill until July.

As finally passed, the bill was loaded with human rights require-ments. This represented something of a switch. Previously, such require-ments with respect to specific countries had been directed mainly against those with rightist governments. Now, they were applied, in unaccus-tomed detail, to a country with a leftist government. (It should be noted that the Nicaraguan aid bill provided one of the few legislative vehicles available to Congress for enacting restrictions applying to leftist gov-ernments, not many of which receive aid.) Before furnishing aid to Nicaragua, the president had to certify that the Nicaraguan government had not encouraged terrorism. He had to terminate aid if the govern-ment consistently and grossly violated internationally recognized human rights, if it consistently violated the right to organize and operate labor unions, and if it systematically violated freedom of speech and of the press.

After Congress passed the appropriation bill in July, a bureaucratic argument broke out in the executive branch over whether the president could fairly certify that Nicaragua was not helping terrorists. The argu-ment was occasioned by reports that Cuban and Soviet arms were flowing through Nicaragua to the Salvadoran guerrillas. Finally, on September 12 Carter made the required certification and was accused by some conser-vative members of the House of acting illegally. The same charge would be heard later from liberals about Reagan's certifications with respect to human rights in El Salvador.

With the steady deterioration of United States relations with Nicara-gua and with the advent of the Reagan administration, the question of aid became moot. Congressional attention focused rather on the question of covert action (see Chapter 6).

El Salvador.　The congressional nervousness about El Salvador stemmed partly from a reluctance for the United States to become identified with the government there. President Carter had taken steps to put some distance between the United States and the Salvadoran govern-ment, but he reinstated a modest aid program shortly before leaving office in January 1981. President Reagan asked Congress for more aid.

This posed a painful dilemma for Congress. It tried to bridge the dilemma by tying continued aid to improved human rights performance. The International Security and Development Cooperation Act of 1981, approved December 29 of that year, contains two long sections (727 and 728), covering almost three closely printed pages, on human rights in El Salvador. The first, and shorter, is a policy statement setting forth the goals of the American aid program in El Salvador. These include not only full observance of fundamental human rights, but also economic and political reforms; investigation of the deaths of all Americans killed in El Salvador since October 1979; free, fair, and open elections (which were in fact held in March 1982); an end to extremist violence; and establishment of a unified command and control of all government security forces.

The other section makes military assistance contingent on a certification to Congress by the president that the government of El Salvador:

(1) is making a concerted and significant effort to comply with internationally recognized human rights; (2) is achieving substantial control over all elements of its own armed forces, so as to bring to an end the indiscriminate torture and murder of Salvadoran citizens by these forces; (3) is making continued progress in implementing essential economic and political reforms, including the land reform program; (4) is committed to the holding of free elections at an early date.

In connection with the last point, the Salvadoran government was also required to demonstrate good-faith efforts to reach a political solution of its internal strife which would include a renouncement of further military or paramilitary activity.

The first such certification by the president was required within 30 days of enactment of the act (that is, by January 28, 1982), and others were required at intervals of 180 days thereafter through fiscal years 1982 and 1983 (that is, through September 30, 1983). Each certification was to discuss fully the justifications for each of the four findings required, and the first two certifications could be made only if they included findings that the Salvadoran government had made good-faith efforts to bring to justice those responsible for the murders of six American citizens in December 1980 and January 1981. In the summer of 1983 a separate bill was passed, requiring a report on prosecutions in these cases to be included also in the certification due in July of that year.

President Reagan made each of the four certifications required by this act, and they became increasingly weak in their findings. In January 1983 he said that "the situation is not perfect and the progress was not as great as desired, but it is progress nonetheless." This provoked Sen. Christopher Dodd, D-Conn., to say that certification was "unwarranted" and showed the administration was "going to certify regardless of the circumstances." [13]

The July 1983 certification noted the rise in civilian deaths, the continuing inability of the government to identify and punish those in the military who abuse human rights, and "uneven and disappointing" progress toward solving the murders of four American churchwomen. But it said that those shortcomings were counterbalanced by the establishment of a Peace Commission to persuade all factions to participate in elections, an amnesty program that had resulted in the release of 500 political prisoners, and extension of land reform. In an accompanying letter, Secretary of State George P. Shultz wrote, "It is evident that the record falls short of the broad and sustained progress which both the Congress and the administration believe is necessary for the evolution of a just and democratic society in El Salvador."

All of this led Sen. Patrick J. Leahy, D-Vt., to say, "There has been no progress in the nuns' case and civilian deaths have gone up. If we can have certification under these circumstances, I cannot imagine how bad things would have to get before this administration would not certify that the conditions of the law had been met." [14]

Just before adjourning in November 1983, Congress passed a bill to keep the certification requirement alive, but Reagan vetoed it. Because Congress was not in session, there was no opportunity to try to override the veto. In January 1984 a number of House Democrats, led by Rep. Michael D. Barnes, D-Md., and Rep. Barney Frank, D-Mass., went to court seeking to have the veto declared invalid on procedural grounds. Still later in January, the State Department sent to Congress a report on El Salvador covering the same points as the vetoed bill, but without a formal certification of progress. In February the House, beginning the legislative process anew, passed another bill requiring certification.

Organization of the State Department

In 1975 the State Department established by administrative action the position of coordinator for humanitarian affairs (with a total staff of two) in the office of the deputy secretary of state. As one result of the congressional suspicion that Henry Kissinger's quiet diplomacy on human rights was really no diplomacy at all, the new position was provided for by law in 1976 and was made a presidential appointment subject to confirmation by the Senate. The coordinator was to be responsible to the secretary of state for matters pertaining to human rights and humanitarian affairs in the conduct of foreign policy, including those relating to refugees, prisoners of war, and members of the armed services missing in action. Finally, the human rights reports to Congress with respect to security assistance were to be the responsibility of the coordinator.[15]

In 1977 Congress upgraded the position of coordinator to the status of assistant secretary. The expanded duties of the assistant secretary for human rights and humanitarian affairs included:

Gathering "detailed information regarding humanitarian affairs and the observance of and respect for internationally recognized human rights" in countries affected by foreign assistance requirements

Preparing the statements and reports to Congress required in connection with security assistance

Making recommendations to the secretary and to the administrator of AID regarding compliance with human rights requirements of the foreign aid legislation

Performing "other responsibilities which serve to promote increased observance of internationally recognized human rights by all countries" [16]

The statutory creation of this office and its subsequent upgrading to the level of assistant secretary were acts of more than ordinary bureaucratic significance. Congress spelled out the duties and responsibilities of the office to a greater extent than is normal with respect to assistant secretaries of state. These congressional actions provided a focal point for human rights concerns in the executive branch. Congress gave the new assistant secretary a legislative mandate. More particularly, it created a vested bureaucratic interest in human rights. The assistant secretary for human rights and humanitarian affairs has a constituency in Congress, and members of Congress interested in human rights have a constituency in the assistant secretary's office.

The arrangement centralizes, in terms of organization, concern for human rights in the State Department; it gives the assistant secretary a measure of bureaucratic independence; and it ensures that a voice advocating consideration of human rights is going to be heard in the department's policymaking process. As this worked in practice during the Carter administration, the role of the assistant secretary for human rights and humanitarian affairs in policy decisions was the source of irritation to the State Department's geographic bureaus.

The Reagan administration's first nominee for the position—Ernest W. Lefever—so unfavorably impressed the Senate Foreign Relations Committee that it recommended against his confirmation by a vote of 13-4. The nomination was then withdrawn. It is highly unusual for the Senate to refuse to confirm a nomination by a new president in the first six months of his term. In the Lefever case, the Foreign Relations Committee doubted the nominee's commitment to human rights. It was also troubled by evidence of conflicts of interest involving Lefever as director of the Ethics and Public Policy Center, the center's corporate contributors, and some of its consultants. There was particular difficulty over a contribution by Nestlé to finance a report on infant formula sales in developing countries.

The president next nominated Elliott Abrams, who had been serving as assistant secretary for international organization affairs. Abrams was a Washington lawyer who had worked for Democratic senators from 1975 to 1979; he was confirmed without difficulty. He brought a low-key approach to the job, and the turmoil subsided. But the position remained vacant from Reagan's inauguration January 20 to Abrams's confirmation November 20.

Communist Countries

The Trade Act of 1974

The main purpose of the Trade Act of 1974 was to provide the president with authority to engage in a new round of international trade negotiations aimed at stimulating world commerce through mutual reductions both in tariffs and in nontariff barriers to trade. One of the additional purposes was to authorize the extension of most-favored-nation treatment to Communist countries, most of which had been excluded from it by earlier legislation.

Under most-favored-nation treatment, a country is guaranteed that, with respect to tariffs on any particular item, it will be treated like the nation that receives the best treatment. Inasmuch as the United States extends most-favored-nation treatment to most countries, the term is a misnomer. It suggests special treatment that does not exist. Instead, the *absence* of most-favored-nation treatment is discriminatory.

Implementation of the trade agreement negotiated in October 1972 between the United States and the Soviet Union was dependent on the extension to the Soviet Union of most-favored-nation status. An earlier U.S.-Soviet agreement settling the Soviet lend-lease debt from World War II, in turn, was dependent on implementation of the trade agreement.

The trade bill was designed, among other things, to make it possible to put these two agreements into effect. The bill was considered in 1973 and 1974 in the context of a larger debate over the Kissinger policy of détente with the Soviet Union. The issue of human rights was injected into this debate by an argument over linking most-favored-nation treatment with Soviet emigration practices. At issue was the desire of many Soviet Jews to resettle in Israel.

In 1972 the Soviets began levying steep exit taxes on emigrants holding advanced academic degrees, a group that included many Jews. The Soviet rationale was that the taxes would repay the cost of the free education that such persons had received and from which Soviet society would no longer benefit if the persons emigrated. The Soviets also denied exit visas on national security grounds to persons who had had access to classified information. There were other obstacles to emigration, the most common being the de facto one of simple inaction on applications for emigrant visas.

The two issues of détente and emigration came together in a confusing way. Americans opposed to détente were also generally opposed to closer trade relations with the Soviet Union and were skeptical that such relations would result in net economic or political benefits to the United States. This school of thought held that, on the contrary, the trade bill, on balance, would benefit the Soviet Union. Such a benefit, it was further argued, provided leverage to the United States in forcing Soviet concessions on emigration.

The Jackson-Vanik Amendment

"To assure the continued dedication of the United States to fundamental human rights," Sen. Henry M. Jackson, D-Wash., and Rep. Charles A. Vanik, D-Ohio, offered an amendment to the Trade Act of 1974.[17] After this rhetorical beginning, the Jackson-Vanik amendment proceeds to outline specific provisions. Products from "any nonmarket country" shall not be eligible for most-favored-nation treatment. Nor shall any such country participate in any United States government program "which extends credits or credit guarantees or investment guarantees directly or indirectly."

The amendment also states that the president shall not conclude "any commercial agreement" with any such nonmarket economy country if the president determines that the country: (1) "denies its citizens the right or opportunity to emigrate"; (2) "imposes more than a nominal tax on emigration or on visas or other documents required for emigration, for any purpose or cause whatsoever"; or (3) "imposes more than a nominal tax, levy, fine, fee or other charge on any citizen as a consequence of the desire of such citizen to emigrate to the country of his choice."

Once the president makes the determination that a country engages in the emigration restrictions cited, there are two ways it can be removed from the ban on credits and most-favored-nation treatment. One is a presidential finding and report to Congress that the country is no longer restricting emigration. The report has to include "information as to the nature and implementation of emigration laws and policies and restrictions or discrimination applied to or against persons wishing to emigrate," and it has to be updated semiannually.

The other way is through a presidential waiver of the ban with respect to a particular country. The waiver has to be based on a presidential determination that it will "substantially promote" the objective of free emigration and on assurances that the emigration practices of the country in question "will henceforth lead substantially" to the same objective. The waiver was to be good only for the 18-month period immediately following enactment of the act (that is, January 3, 1975, to July 3, 1976). Thereafter, it could be renewed for no more than a year at a time, and each renewal was subject to a legislative veto. This procedure has now been found by the Supreme Court to be unconstitutional.

A separate provision of the Trade Act deals in a similar way with any Communist country that "denies its citizens the right or opportunity to join permanently through emigration, a very close relative in the United States, such as a spouse, parent, child, brother, or sister." [18]

The Jackson-Vanik amendment posed a complex set of issues. There was general sympathy for the plight of Soviet Jews, and members of Congress were reluctant to oppose anything that looked like it would ease that plight. Yet real doubts existed that the amendment, in fact, would do so. As Secretary of State William P. Rogers put it to the Ways and Means Committee in May 1973, the best hope for a satisfactory resolution of Soviet emigration practices "will come not from the confrontation formal legislation would bring about, but from a steady improvement in our over-all relations." [19] This was essentially the same quiet diplomacy argument that Kissinger was to make later with respect to human rights legislation in connection with foreign aid.

Throughout the debate, the Soviet Union repeatedly made it clear that it regarded its emigration practices as an internal matter and not an appropriate subject for international negotiation. Yet once the issue had been raised in Congress, it was taken as a political imperative that some provision on the subject go in the trade bill. The problem for the administration and its supporters thus became one of finding language that would satisfy a majority in Congress without driving the Soviets to scuttle the trade agreement and perhaps to clamp down on emigration even more. The task was complicated by the fact that some members of Congress no doubt wanted to use an emigration amendment as a device to kill most-favored-nation treatment for the Soviets, or at least would not care if that proved to be the result.

During most of 1973 and 1974 two sets of negotiations were in progress: negotiations between Kissinger and the Soviet Union and negotiations between Kissinger and the Jackson-Vanik forces on Capitol Hill. By October 1974 it appeared that an agreement had been reached. It was formalized in an exchange of letters between Secretary Kissinger and Senator Jackson.

"[O]n the basis of discussions that have been conducted with Soviet representatives," Kissinger wrote to Jackson, "I should like on behalf of the Administration to inform you that we have been assured that the following criteria and practices will henceforth govern emigration from the USSR." There followed six understandings, the most important of which were that there would be no discrimination in issuing exit visas, that no punitive measures would be taken against applicants for emigration, and that the exit visa tax that had been suspended would remain suspended.[20]

Jackson went further. He said the agreement assumed that the annual rate of Soviet emigration would rise from the 1973 level of about 35,000 and in the future would correspond to the number of applicants. (The rate in 1974 was about two-thirds that of 1973.) He also said that 60,000 emigrants a year would be the "minimum standard" of compliance in order for the president to certify to Congress that Soviet practices were leading to substantially free emigration. He added that this was based on assurances from Soviet leaders.

In testimony before the Senate Finance Committee on December 3, Kissinger said, in effect, that Jackson was overstating the matter. According to Kissinger, his own letter to Jackson had been based on "clarifications" given to him and President Ford by Soviet officials. No commitments "either in form or substance" had been made by the Soviet Union. Jackson's letter, Kissinger said, contained interpretations and elaborations "which were never stated to us by Soviet officials," and there was no Soviet "commitment as to numbers."[21]

The Senate passed the Jackson amendment by a vote of 88-0 on December 13. Five days later, the Soviet Union denied it had given any specific assurance, as Senator Jackson had indicated. To the contrary, Moscow asserted that the number of emigrants was declining. It released the text of an October 26 letter to Kissinger from Foreign Minister Andrei A. Gromyko, calling the Jackson-Kissinger exchange a "distorted picture of our position as well as what we told the American side on that matter." Gromyko restated the longstanding Soviet position that the emigration issue was a wholly domestic one.[22]

Both houses agreed to the conference report on the trade bill December 20, and Ford signed it January 3, 1975. On January 14, Kissinger announced that the Soviets had rejected the conditions of the Jackson-Vanik amendment and consequently would not implement the 1972 trade agreement.

There the matter stood. Jewish emigration from the Soviet Union decreased in 1975 and in ensuing years, but it increased markedly in 1979 to more than 50,000. It then decreased sharply to a total of only 2,700 in 1982. In 1983 it was down to 1,315. This roller coaster performance was possibly related to broader Soviet foreign policy objectives. In 1979 the Kremlin wanted to improve the climate for Senate consideration of the SALT II agreement. It also wanted to be sure that the Soviet Union received most-favored-nation treatment if China did. Neither of these motives existed thereafter. After the Soviet invasion of Afghanistan in December 1979, President Carter asked the Senate to lay aside SALT II. And China got most-favored-nation treatment in early 1980.

International Human Rights Agreements

Although Congress has made human rights in foreign policy a major concern, the Senate has consistently refused to approve multilateral human rights treaties. June 1983 marked the thirty-fourth anniversary of the Genocide Convention on the Senate Foreign Relations Committee calendar. No other treaty has been pending for so long. (Pending bills and resolutions die at the end of a Congress every two years; treaties stay before the Senate until they are either acted on or returned to the president.)

Genocide emerged as one of the crimes against humanity for which leaders of the Axis Powers were tried during and after World War II.[23] The word *genocide*, which was coined in the aftermath of the Nazi campaign against the Jews, means the murder of a whole race. The Convention on the Prevention and Punishment of the Crime of Genocide was adopted unanimously by the United Nations General Assembly on December 9, 1948, and formally signed by the United States. President Harry S Truman sent it to the Senate with a request for advice and consent to ratification on June 16, 1949. A subcommittee of the Foreign Relations Committee held hearings in 1950 and recommended that the convention be approved, but no action was taken by the full committee.

There the matter stood for 20 years. Then, in response to a renewed push by the Nixon administration, further hearings were held. This time the Foreign Relations Committee reported the convention favorably to the Senate with the recommendation that it be approved with understandings and a declaration, but the Senate did not consider it. The convention was reported again in 1971. The Senate actually debated it in 1972 but did not vote.

The major effort to secure Senate action on the convention came in 1973-1974 and succumbed to a filibuster. Two motions to end the debate failed by almost identical votes of 55-36 and 55-38. (It takes 60 votes to invoke cloture against a filibuster.) The votes indicated that, even without a filibuster, the convention was well short of the two-thirds majority needed for approval. The Foreign Relations Committee again reported the convention favorably in 1976 and held further hearings on it in 1977 and 1981. There the matter rests.

Seldom has there been such a large tempest in such a small teapot. The Genocide Convention seems innocuous enough. All it does is outlaw the crime of genocide. Yet there is intense opposition to this simple proposal to outlaw a crime that nobody defends. Certainly there is no more basic human right than the right not to be killed because of one's race.

Senatorial opposition to the Genocide Convention has many sources, most of them stemming from apprehension that it would injure the federal system in the United States. Genocide, this argument runs, is mass murder. Murder is already a crime in every state in the union. Further action on the subject is not part of the federal government's business. In addition, opponents of the convention have never been at a loss to find technical provisions in it that form the basis for legalistic quibbles.

Yet none of these considerations seems sufficient to explain the public's emotional response to the genocide debate. The reaction has very little to do with the language of the convention itself. On one side, there is the deep feeling that the United States ought to join most of the rest of the world in a solemn statement of international law repudiating Hitler's holocaust. On the other side, there is the fear that the convention is somehow part of a plot to bring about world government, and that it could be used to pillory the United States for its treatment of Indians, blacks, or other minorities.

Another consideration has been the reluctance of the Senate to advise and consent to human rights treaties generally: most of the rights that are dealt with by these treaties are already protected in the United States either by the Constitution or by federal statute. Certain other rights specified in the treaties are viewed by senators more as economic or social goals—for example, the right to health and education. Out of approximately 40 international treaties in force with respect to human rights, the United States is a party to only 10. Most of the others have not even been submitted to the Senate, and some have not been signed by the United States.

In keeping with his inaugural promises, President Carter submitted four international human rights treaties to the Senate in 1978: the International Convention on the Elimination of All Forms of Racial Discrimination; the International Covenant on Economic, Social and

Cultural Rights; the International Covenant on Civil and Political Rights; and the American Convention on Human Rights. Hearings were held in 1979, but no further action has been taken.

Conclusion

The multifaceted practice of diplomacy involves balancing frequently contradictory national interests, such as military security, access to essential raw materials, the protection of American business abroad, the growth of foreign trade—and the protection and promotion of human rights. The line between standing up for human decency and meddling in another country's internal affairs is exceedingly fine. Violations of human rights can range from the occasional roughing up of a prisoner by police to systematic torture and mass murder. At what point in this spectrum does international concern become appropriate?

And what is a human right anyway? Congressional attention has focused on the right not to be physically abused; but the Jackson-Vanik amendment involves the right to emigrate, and the American government through both the president and the Congress has spoken out on the treatment of Soviet dissidents—an issue that essentially involves free speech.

To much of the Third World, however, human rights encompass what many Americans regard not as rights so much as desirable social or economic goals, such as education, housing, and medical care. The inclusion of these subjects in international agreements is one reason for the Senate's reluctance to approve them. In its human rights reports to Congress, the Carter administration adopted the broader definition; in this respect the executive branch has gone further than Congress.[24] The Reagan administration defined rights more narrowly, as those included in "the right to be free from governmental violations of the integrity of the person" and those included in "the right to enjoy civil and political liberties." [25]

A further difficulty comes in avoiding the appearance of self-righteousness or hypocrisy. The record of the United States with respect to human rights, particularly with respect to racial discrimination, is far from flawless. The history of Soviet Jewry is scarcely sadder than the history of American Indians.

Nevertheless, the record is clear that the United States generally enjoys better relations with countries where there is a decent respect for the individual than with those where there is not. The most prominent example, of course, is America's relations with its European allies and with countries like Canada and Australia, but the point applies to other countries as well.

The emphasis that human rights issues began to receive in the 1970s was in part a reaction to the neglect these issues had suffered during the cold war period, when considerations of national security were paramount. But the change entailed more than that. It followed the flowering of the civil rights movement in the 1960s and the national disillusionment over Vietnam.

Exactly how to implement a human rights policy remains a question on which Congress and the White House do not always see eye to eye. Short of military intervention, the options available to the United States (from the less to the more drastic) include:

Private diplomatic representations
Public criticism
Reduction or termination of foreign aid or credits
Call for action by an international organization (actions ranging from a condemnatory resolution to international sanctions)
Recall of the American ambassador
Severance of diplomatic relations
Embargo of trade

All of these options are available to the executive branch, but only some of them (public criticism, reduction of aid, trade restrictions) are available to Congress. Taking any of these actions on behalf of human rights may mean a sacrifice of some other foreign policy objective. Nor is there any guarantee that the observance of human rights by other countries actually will be improved.

The trade-offs are sometimes agonizing, and it is rarely easy to strike an acceptable balance. The decision to sacrifice one foreign policy objective for another has led to charges of inconsistency or even hypocrisy. The Carter administration, for example, bore down hard on human rights abuses in Argentina, to the consternation of the American business community there, but not in China, where the abuses were equally egregious. Larger reasons of global geopolitics dictated a policy of rapprochement with China; no such considerations prevailed with respect to Argentina. The Reagan administration made a distinction, of which Ambassador Jeane Kirkpatrick was the principal architect, between what were labeled totalitarian and authoritarian governments. The former (for example, Cuba) sought to control every facet of a country's life according to a particular ideology. The latter (for example, the Philippines) merely ruled with an iron hand, frequently corruptly, but ordinarily ignored actions not perceived as threatening to the regime in question. The Reagan administration's rhetoric against totalitarian governments matched anything heard from the Carter administration; with respect to authoritarian governments, the Reagan administration was more muted.

The results of administration policies are difficult to assess and impossible to quantify. One of the few certainties is that some political dissidents themselves, notably in Brazil and Uruguay, said they felt less threatened because of Carter administration pressure on their governments. In connection with its policy in Central America, the Reagan administration pressured the government of El Salvador to control the death squads, but the government was unable to do so; nonetheless, the administration continued to support the Salvadoran government. Such are the dilemmas that confront U.S. policymakers in balancing human rights and foreign policy.

Notes

1. Richard M. Nixon, *Six Crises* (Garden City, N.Y.: Doubleday and Co., 1962), p. 192.
2. Foreign Assistance Act of 1973, sec. 32, P.L. 93-189, approved December 17, 1973.
3. Ibid., sec. 35.
4. International Security Assistance and Arms Export Control Act of 1976, sec. 406, P.L. 94-329, approved June 30, 1976.
5. Foreign Assistance Act of 1974, sec. 46, P.L. 93-559, approved December 30, 1974.
6. International Security Assistance and Arms Export Control Act of 1976, sec. 301(a). This section in its present form is sec. 502B of the Foreign Assistance Act of 1961, as amended.
7. International Security Assistance Act and Arms Export Control Act of 1979, sec. 4, P.L. 96-92, approved October 29, 1979.
8. International Development and Food Assistance Act of 1975, sec. 116, P.L. 94-161, approved December 20, 1975.
9. International Development Cooperation Act of 1979, P.L. 96-53, approved August 14, 1979.
10. Agricultural Trade Development and Assistance Act of 1954, as amended, sec. 112, added by the International Development and Food Assistance Act of 1977.
11. P.L. 94-302, approved May 31, 1976, secs. 103 (a) and 211.
12. P.L. 95-118, approved October 3, 1977, sec. 701.
13. *Congressional Quarterly Weekly Report,* January 29, 1983, pp. 217-219.
14. Lou Cannon and Charles Fishman, "Reagan to Seek Additional Aid for Region," *Washington Post,* July 21, 1983.
15. International Security Assistance and Arms Export Control Act of 1976, sec. 301(b), P.L. 94-329, approved June 30, 1976.
16. Foreign Assistance Act of 1961, as amended, sec. 624(f)(1), added by the Foreign Relations Authorization Act, Fiscal Year 1978, 91 Stat. 846.
17. Trade Act of 1974, sec. 402, P.L. 93-618, approved January 3, 1975.
18. Ibid., sec. 409.
19. U.S. Congress, House Ways and Means Committee, *Hearings on H.R. 6767, Trade Reform Act of 1973,* 93d Cong., 1st sess., May 9, 1973, p. 165.
20. *New York Times,* October 19, 1974, p. 10.
21. U.S. Congress, Senate Finance Committee, *Hearing on Emigration Amendment to the Trade Reform Act of 1974,* 93d Cong., 2d sess., December 3, 1974, pp. 53-54.
22. *New York Times,* December 19, 1974, pp. 1, 18.

23. See Gerhard von Glahn, *Law Among Nations: An Introduction to Public International Law,* 3d ed. (New York: Macmillan Publishing Co., 1976), pp. 713-715.
24. *Report on Human Rights Practices in Countries Receiving U.S. Aid,* pp. 2-3.
25. U.S. State Department, *Country Reports on Human Rights Practices for 1982,* submitted to the Senate Foreign Relations and House Foreign Affairs committees, February 1983, pp. 1-2.

PART III

Conclusion

Part I (Chapters 1 and 2) provided a general discussion of the respective roles of the executive branch—focusing upon the powers of the president—and of Congress in the foreign policy process. In Part II (Chapters 3-7) five specific issues from recent American diplomatic experience were selected to illustrate the role of Congress in foreign policy since the Vietnam War. These case studies had two common elements: they addressed significant questions confronting the United States in foreign relations, and they identified one or more important prerogatives of Congress and the president in the foreign policy field.

In the final chapter of this study, which comprises Part III, our purpose is twofold. First, it is to identify congressional behavior patterns in the recent era of legislative activism in foreign relations. What approaches has Congress taken to a series of diverse external problems? In what respects has Congress's approach in recent years marked a change from the long preceding period of legislative acquiescence in presidential diplomatic leadership?

Second, what are the more noteworthy long-term implications of an active and independent role by Congress in foreign affairs? To answer that question, we must consider the factors that have sustained congressional assertiveness in confronting foreign policy questions. How durable are these factors? Are they likely to provide momentum for forceful legislative initiatives in foreign relations in the years ahead? Or can they be expected to diminish as memories of the Vietnam conflict recede and as the United States confronts new and difficult problems in the international system? On balance, what has been the impact of an assertive Congress upon American diplomacy?

The era of congressional dynamism in foreign policy was to no inconsiderable degree an inevitable outgrowth of the Vietnam War. That traumatic experience brought about a reappraisal of the whole process of reaching foreign policy decisions. In Southeast Asia, the United States found itself embroiled in a massive military conflict because of a series of separate, unrelated, and often modest steps—an approach to foreign policy sometimes called *incrementalism.*

In effect, the war "just happened" as the result of no conscious or deliberate design by policymakers or American citizens. (In fact, officials in Washington frequently denied their intention of expanding America's responsibility for the defense of South Vietnam, even while they were in the process of doing so!) In time, however, the United States found itself saddled with the dominant responsibility for the Vietnam War effort—primarily because officials in Washington and informed citizens failed at each stage to perceive the cumulative effect of a series of isolated steps that collectively produced America's involvement in that conflict.

From the end of the Vietnam War until the late 1970s, American diplomatic behavior was massively influenced by what was sometimes called the post-Vietnam syndrome. Its principal elements were a pervasive feeling of guilt and disillusionment with the results of America's massive involvement in Southeast Asia, an evident reluctance to become embroiled in "another Vietnam" abroad, and preoccupation with internal problems (many of which had been neglected during the Vietnam conflict). By the end of the decade, however, Americans had become genuinely concerned about such developments as the deterioration of America's influence abroad; potential or actual Soviet gains in regions like the Persian Gulf area, East Africa, and Latin America; and the "indecisiveness" of national leadership, as epitomized by the Carter presidency. While domestic economic factors were perhaps the crucial element in the outcome, these foreign policy issues unquestionably contributed to the election of a Republican administration under Ronald Reagan in 1980. Moreover, such changes in the public opinion context of foreign policy decisionmaking fundamentally affected congressional attitudes and behavior toward foreign policy questions.

What are the principal implications of congressional activism in foreign affairs for the remainder of the 1980s? What specific forms does this diplomatic activism take? How has congressional assertiveness in foreign relations affected the ability of the United States to respond effectively to diverse challenges abroad? What kind of new balance may be emerging in executive-legislative relations in the years ahead? Such questions are fundamental in any attempt to understand the American foreign policy process. Our answers to them must be tentative; they are perhaps inescapably conditioned by underlying value judgments; and they cannot anticipate the conditions that will confront the United States in its relations with more than 150 independent nations. With due recognition of these uncertainties, Chapter 8 presents an assessment of the overall impact of Congress upon the foreign policy process in the United States.

Congressional Assertiveness and Foreign Affairs: A Balance Sheet

8

A recent British ambassador to the United States was asked what surprised him most about the conduct of American diplomacy. He replied, "The extraordinary power of your Congress over foreign policy." [1]

Executive policymakers have increasingly acknowledged the crucial role that Congress plays in the foreign relations of the United States. Although before entering government service Henry Kissinger was dubious about undue legislative influence in foreign affairs, as secretary of state he called for "a new national partnership" between the president and Congress in dealing with international issues.[2] During the early 1980s the chairman of the Senate Foreign Relations Committee, Sen. Charles H. Percy, R-Ill., observed that unless there were "a joint approach to U.S. foreign policy, which both branches of government backed by substantial elements of both parties must work to forge," the United States would be unlikely to achieve its foreign policy goals.[3] Early in his administration President Ronald Reagan revived the concept of bipartisanship in foreign affairs that had characterized executive-legislative relations under the Truman and Eisenhower administrations. Reagan and his White House aides acknowledged that successful dialogue between executive and legislative leaders was indispensable for unified efforts in the foreign policy field.[4]

Although executive officials and informed students of American foreign policy are becoming increasingly aware of the expanding role of Congress in foreign policy, they are often far from enthusiastic about the disturbing implications of congressional diplomatic assertiveness. Presidents Johnson, Nixon, Ford, Carter, and Reagan vocally opposed legislative efforts to limit their powers abroad and to exercise constitutional and historical prerogatives they believed belonged to the executive branch. From the perspective of the White House, former Michigan Rep. Gerald R. Ford lamented that congressional activities not infrequently impeded America's ability to achieve its foreign policy objectives: "The pendulum has swung so far that you could almost say we have moved from an imperial Presidency to an imperiled Presidency. Now we have a Congress that is broadening its powers in foreign relations too greatly." [5]

Comparable judgments were expressed by informed students of the American governmental system under the Reagan administration. An experienced State Department official, for example, feared that legislative activism in foreign affairs had brought about a reversal in the traditional contributions of the president and Congress to the foreign policy process—to the detriment of American diplomatic undertakings. Sen. Alan K. Simpson, R-Wyo., complained that Congress was so internally "fragmented" that it was perhaps incapable of providing leadership in foreign and domestic affairs. Another experienced observer of the American political scene asked: "How does a nation live with a Congress that counts more brilliant men than ever before but cannot lead, and will follow no leadership?" Since the Watergate crisis of the Nixon administration, Congress had been "in revolt" against the presidency. Yet Congress itself "can offer no solutions" to urgent internal and external problems. [6]

What have been the principal causes of recent congressional activism in the foreign policy field? What can be identified as the most significant consequences of forceful legislative influence upon American foreign relations? And what will be the future balance between executive and legislative influence in the foreign policy process? These three important and interrelated questions provide the framework for discussion in the concluding chapter of our study.

Congressional Assertiveness: Background and Causes

According to the provisions of the Constitution, as we saw in Part I, Congress possesses a number of prerogatives that allow it to influence foreign relations. Congress must appropriate funds needed for innumerable programs in foreign affairs. It has the power to declare war; and it must raise and support the armed forces. The Senate has two unique constitutional functions not shared with the House of Representatives: the requirement that treaties receive the advice and consent of the Senate; and the provision that most of the president's major appointments be confirmed by the Senate. From the foundation of the American republic, therefore, it was envisioned that Congress would be involved in the solution of diplomatic problems, although in many important respects the exact scope and nature of its involvement was left to be determined by experience.

The powers of the chief executive in foreign relations expanded significantly over the course of time—leading by the mid-1960s to a condition of virtually unchecked presidential authority in diplomacy. The steady accretion in the president's diplomatic influence became particularly pronounced after the United States emerged as a superpower at the end of World War II. Perhaps the most remarkable fact about this growth in presidential authority in foreign relations was how seldom it was challenged by Congress. In fact, during several eras the enhancement of presidential power could have occurred only with the explicit or tacit *concurrence* of Congress. The Roosevelt administration's conduct of World War II and the escalation of the Vietnam War under Presidents Kennedy and Johnson are two examples.

Today the era of congressional passivity or acquiescence in presidential decisions in the foreign policy field has ended. As a former official of the Johnson administration has expressed it: "In the present world situation, far greater congressional and public involvement in formulating our foreign policy seems to me not only right but nearly inevitable." [7] One reason for greater congressional involvement in foreign policymaking is the interrelationship between foreign affairs and domestic issues. According to a former member of the House of Representatives, "foreign and domestic policy have merged into a seamless web of interlocking concerns." [8]

Since the New Deal program of the 1930s, the American society has also witnessed what might be called a legislative explosion of vast dimensions. Untold thousands of new laws have been enacted by Congress during the past half-century. An increasing proportion of Congress's time is devoted to adding to this list, to making needed changes in existing legislation, and to overseeing the administration of the laws already enacted. Much of this activity is based upon the premise that the solution to pressing national problems lies in the enactment of legislation. [9]

In America's approach to problems beyond its own borders since World War II, basically the same tendency can be discerned. The Truman administration's adoption of the containment strategy for resisting Communist expansionism in 1947 committed the United States to a new diplomatic role, inescapably enhancing the powers of Congress in foreign affairs. For over a generation thereafter, the continuity of American foreign policy—from ongoing economic and military assistance programs, to the defense of NATO, to the creation and maintenance of an adequate defense establishment—has depended upon favorable action by Congress. Moreover, congressional behavior in confronting closely related domestic issues, such as the level of taxation, overall governmental spending, and the development of natural resources, has directly affected America's relations with other countries.

Internal Changes in Congress

A number of identifiable changes have occurred within Congress in the past ten years; these have contributed to legislative activism in foreign affairs. We will examine three of the changes.

Diffusion of Power on Capitol Hill. Partly as a result of efforts to reform Congress since World War II, the problem of dispersed power within the House and Senate has become increasingly acute in recent years. As we noted in Chapter 2, most congressional committees are involved in some aspect of foreign affairs, and their jurisdictions over foreign policy issues frequently overlap. Congressional deliberations today seem more disunified than at any other stage in American history. According to an experienced observer of the Washington scene, "Never since the Senate defied Woodrow Wilson on the importance of creating a League of Nations . . . has the Congress . . . seemed as parochial, personal or divided as it does now." [10]

The problem of internal disunity within the legislative branch did not improve perceptibly under the Reagan administration. Thus in 1982 one study of how legislators themselves perceive Congress found widespread complaints about the lack of effective leadership in the House and Senate; about the independence enjoyed by the principal committees of Congress; and about the degree to which overlapping committee jurisdictions and responsibilities inhibited a unified legislative approach to major policy issues. Despite several efforts since World War II, the need for far-reaching reforms within Congress remained compelling. Under the chairmanship of Senator Percy, the Senate Foreign Relations Committee was often highly factionalized by personal and policy disagreements, such as that between Percy and Sen. Jesse A. Helms, R-N.C.; Helms was a spokesman for ultraconservative groups, which often sought fundamental changes in American diplomacy from the course recommended by President Reagan.[11]

Expansion of Staff. A second change that has affected the ability of Congress to play a more assertive role in foreign policymaking is the expansion of legislative staff. In mid-1979 Sen. William Proxmire, D-Wis., confounded his colleagues by conferring the "Golden Fleece Award" for questionable expenditures of taxpayers' money on none other than Congress itself. In Proxmire's view, Congress had earned this distinction; the House and Senate staff had grown during the past decade from 10,700 to 18,400 people, an increase of some 70 percent. The cost of maintaining this legislative bureaucracy had climbed from $150 million to $550 million annually. Ten years earlier, the average number of staff employees for each senator had been 34. By 1979, 68 employees was the average.[12]

Today members of the House and Senate can no longer legitimately complain about staff shortages on Capitol Hill. One study of Congress has asserted that "Congress, in the last five years, has developed a virtual counter-State Department composed of predominantly young, experienced and aggressive experts who are out to make their own marks on the foreign policy map." [13] A greatly expanded staff has had a twofold impact upon Congress's role in foreign affairs. A larger staff provides Congress the *means* to assert its own independent position vis-à-vis the executive branch with regard to major international questions. It also supplies national legislators with a new *incentive* to become active in a field where, during an earlier period, they often had neither the interest nor the expertise to become deeply involved.

Staff expansion has also added momentum to centrifugal tendencies within Congress itself. Hardly a committee or individual member of Congress lacks (or is unable to acquire) adequate staff assistance in dealing with international issues. As one commentator has observed, now each member of the House and Senate is better equipped than ever "to go his separate way and establish his own domain of power and prestige." [14]

Increased Participation by the House. Until the period of the Vietnam War, the House of Representatives usually played a subordinate role in the foreign policy process. Although members of the House sometimes chafed at their inferior position vis-à-vis the Senate in external policymaking, they were normally content to accept understandings worked out between executive officials and influential senators and Senate committees with jurisdiction over foreign policy questions. [15] In recent years, however, the era of passivity by the House in foreign relations has ended. As we saw in the case study on the Panama Canal treaties in Chapter 3, the House strenuously objected to being excluded from the treaty-making process. Under the Reagan administration, committees and subcommittees of the House of Representatives played an active role in attempting to influence national defense policy and American diplomacy toward Latin America.

Increased participation by the House in foreign affairs can be explained on several grounds other than mere jealousy of the Senate's constitutional prerogatives. The growing interrelationship between domestic and external problems, for example, dictates a more dynamic role by the House in diplomatic decisionmaking. As never before, Congress is called upon to enact legislation and to appropriate funds for implementing foreign policy proposals and programs. Advocates of greater House influence are convinced that the House can make a vital and distinctive contribution in Congress's deliberations on international questions. Since its members must stand for election every two years, the House provides the kind of "recurrent plebiscite on the foreign policy of the United States" that no other institution of the American government can contribute. [16]

External Influences on Congress

Legislative activism in foreign affairs has been influenced not only by changes *within* Congress. Several new forms of external pressure have also contributed significantly to this tendency. Congressional activism has been given considerable momentum by the nature and dynamics of American public opinion, by increased lobbying efforts by interest groups, and by lobbying on the part of executive agencies. Let us examine each of these external influences on Congress in turn.

Public Opinion. Since the Wilsonian era, public opinion has emerged as an influential force affecting the course of American diplomacy. Mounting public opposition to Soviet expansionism, for example, was a potent factor inducing the Truman administration to adopt the policy of containment against the Soviet Union. Conversely, a generation later, growing public disenchantment with the nation's role in Southeast Asia was crucial in the Nixon administration's decision to terminate the war in Vietnam. In the late 1970s congressional opinion and public opinion were significant factors in inducing the Carter and, after 1980, the Reagan administrations to stiffen their positions toward Soviet interventionism and toward strengthening the American defense establishment. In both instances, legislators were instrumental in communicating the nature and force of public sentiment to executive officials.

In keeping with the idea that Congress is the most representative branch of the American government, legislators believe that viewpoints expressed in the House and Senate provide the most authoritative expression of public thinking available to the president and his advisers. The House International Relations Committee (now the Foreign Affairs Committee) emphasized this point in a 1977 report on Congress and foreign policy:

> Congressmen, by being in continuous contact with the people and representing their disparate interests and concerns, have served not only to insure democratic control over the foreign policymaking process, but have also been the conveyors of sometimes ambivalent and occasionally vociferous public opinion.
>
> Recent events have demonstrated that without a genuine public consensus of support, the executive branch cannot legitimately and effectively pursue any foreign policy.[17]

Congress's perception of its relationship to public opinion as it bears upon foreign relations has several specific implications. Many legislators believe it is uniquely incumbent upon Congress to foster public awareness and better understanding of foreign policy issues. As the chairman of the Senate Foreign Relations Committee defined its responsibilities in 1979, the committee had an obligation to "stimulate public debate"; it was the "main forum" for promoting public discussion of external policy questions.[18]

Alternatively, some legislators believe it is the responsibility of Congress to confront executive policymakers with public sentiment concerning a particular course of action in foreign affairs. This contribution by Congress to the American foreign policy process was well illustrated in the early 1980s by legislative insistence that President Ronald Reagan and his military advisers rethink the proposed MX missile system. As a result of legislative opposition, the president appointed a bipartisan commission to study the question; its recommendations (which clearly reflected a number of public and congressional apprehensions about the MX missile system) went far toward providing a basis of legitimacy for the administration's nuclear strategy.[19]

On most foreign policy questions, however, the American people seldom speak with a unified voice. Particularly since the Vietnam War, popular attitudes toward foreign affairs have been marked by confusion, ambiguities, and contradictions. On the one hand, as the election of Ronald Reagan in 1980 indicated, by the end of the 1970s the American people had once again become apprehensive about Communist gains and the deterioration of American power abroad. Reflecting public sentiment, Congress clearly supported the Reagan administration's effort to strengthen the defense establishment and to bolster American power in regions like the Persian Gulf area. On the other hand (as was illustrated by the continuing controversy over American diplomacy in Central America), Americans were alarmed by the prospect that they would become involved in another Vietnam; and they were plainly reluctant to support interventionist policies in Latin America and other regions. In another sphere, Soviet-American relations, American opinion showed the same ambivalence: the people and their representatives in Congress remained apprehensive about the Kremlin's diplomatic goals and behavior, but they also called for the Reagan administration to undertake serious negotiations with Moscow to reduce the level of global armaments and to resolve other outstanding issues between the superpowers.[20]

During the 1980s, as in earlier eras of American diplomatic experience, calls for diplomatic caution and restraint often alternate with calls for decisive initiatives abroad to counterbalance, for example, growing Soviet influence in Africa or pervasive disregard for the nation's diplomatic interests in the Third World. Even toward a single important issue such as détente with the Soviet Union, American attitudes oscillated between approbation and fear of many of its consequences and implications.[21] As one commentator has pointed out:

> We may simply have to learn to conduct foreign policy for a very long time without a single unifying theme on which to base a broad national consensus. Both the nature of the problems abroad and their diverse impact on American public opinion at home now point strongly to such a conclusion.[22]

A national consensus is also lacking on such issues as the operations of the intelligence community and human rights practices abroad. As we noted in Chapter 6, Congress responded to the American people's apprehensions about certain questionable activities of the CIA and other members of the intelligence community. Yet as demonstrated by developments like the Iranian revolution and the discovery of a large Soviet military presence in Cuba during the late 1970s, the American people questioned the adequacy of American intelligence operations and called for their improvement. Under the Reagan administration, many legislators and segments of American public opinion were apprehensive about certain intelligence activities directed against Marxist governments and political movements in Latin America. Yet Congress was also concerned about Communist gains in the region and was, therefore, reluctant to prohibit or substantially curb American intelligence operations there. As in other spheres of American diplomacy, congressional attitudes with regard to Latin America have reflected the underlying ambivalence in the public mind between continued opposition to Communist expansionism and apprehension about another Vietnam-style conflict abroad. Similarly, on international human rights issues, Congress has actively sought to protect and promote human rights in other countries. At the same time, evidence of human rights violations has not deterred Congress from providing economic and military aid to such countries as the Philippines, South Korea, and El Salvador.[23]

Toward these and other issues, the public has approached major international questions since Vietnam eclectically, pragmatically, and with a good measure of common sense. As one commentator explained:

> Faced with some different ideas and a changing world, Americans chose eclectically what they thought made sense and rejected what they thought didn't. . . . Such, then, has been the pattern of accommodation, eclecticism and shameless synthesis that the American public has demonstrated in recent years. . . . Exposed to new doctrines [in foreign policy], the public made careful choices. . . . They put their choice to one essential test: *Did it make common sense?* If it did—fine. If not—back on the shelf.[24]

Inevitably, Congress's approach to foreign policy issues is heavily colored by these dominant characteristics of American public opinion.

Lobbying by Interest Groups and Foreign Governments. While lobbying is not a new phenomenon in the nation's history, some members and former members of Congress believe that legislators have become increasingly responsive to the campaigns of well-funded and highly organized pressure groups.[25]

A number of factors have produced a favorable environment for pressure group activity in recent years: the expanding role of government in all spheres of American life; the lack of a public consensus in the United States on foreign policy issues; the decline of party identification by citizens and the weakening of party discipline on Capitol Hill; the emergence of single issue politics (in which one issue, such as gun control or abortion, can dominate a political campaign); and the growing diffusion of power within the House and Senate. One recent study called attention to the "385 standing committees and subcommittees [of Congress] being pursued by more than 1,300 registered lobby groups." Instead of America's traditional two-party system, there now appeared to exist on Capitol Hill "a 385-party system."[26]

Lobbying by foreign governments, whose efforts are frequently supported by internal pressure groups, has also had momentous consequences for recent American foreign policy. In many cases, foreign governments appeal White House decisions in foreign affairs to the more sympathetic legislative branch. Governments abroad now routinely ignore the once firmly established principle that the president is "the sole organ" of the nation in its relations with other countries.[27]

Many foreign governments today have a direct stake in supporting a more active and independent foreign policy role by Congress.[28] As we saw in Chapter 4, the pro-Israeli lobby has repeatedly mounted intensive campaigns to have Congress block or reverse White House decisions thought inimical to Israel. Early in the 1980s one report on lobbying by foreign interests referred to "multimillion dollar lobbying campaigns aimed at swaying U.S. policies" abroad. It is estimated that overall spending by lobbyists representing governments and political groups overseas exceeds $100 million annually. Justice Department records show that in 1982, 701 persons were registered as agents of foreign governments (versus 452 in 1970). Among this group were a number of former senators and representatives.[29]

Lobbying by the Executive Branch. Lobbying activities by executive agencies in behalf of the president's programs and policies can be another crucial factor in determining Congress's role in the foreign policy process. Most executive agencies have one office that is primarily responsible for communicating to Congress the views of the executive branch. For example, within the State Department the legislative liaison function is performed by the Bureau of Congressional Relations. And sometimes executive agencies also form alliances with private citizens' organizations to influence attitudes both within Congress and throughout American society.[30]

A correlation exists between effective lobbying activities by the executive branch and the level of congressional activism in foreign affairs, as illustrated by the record of the Carter administration. On numerous occasions President Carter and his advisers complained about congressionally imposed restraints upon executive management of foreign affairs. Yet no administration in modern history appeared to be less interested in generating support for White House measures on Capitol Hill, and in promoting executive-legislative cooperation in external affairs, than President Carter's. President Carter's aides were not only inexperienced in legislative relations; in some instances, their tactics in dealing with legislators generated real resentment and irritation on Capitol Hill.[31]

By contrast, the legislative liaison efforts of the Reagan White House appeared to be considerably more effective. In mid-1983, for example, President Reagan and his aides had revived the concept of bipartisanship in foreign affairs—a synonym for more collaborative executive-legislative relations. Toward that end, the president and his subordinates adopted such measures as appointing a bipartisan commission to study the controversial MX missile system; by engaging in dialogue with committees of the House and Senate interested in particular foreign policy questions; and by providing reassurances to legislators that the United States would not become militarily overcommitted in Central America. For their part, legislators were reported to be gratified by the willingness of executive officials to consider their viewpoints on diplomatic issues.[32]

The failure of a president and his subordinates to engage in effective legislative liaison activities produces a condition tailor-made for legislative diplomatic activism. Not only does it ensure that Congress will exert its viewpoints and prerogatives forcefully in the foreign policy process; it also contributes to making congressional efforts episodic, uncoordinated, and inconsistent.

Leadership Failure in the White House

By the late 1970s a deep-seated anxiety existed on Capitol Hill and among many segments of American public opinion that the influence of the United States abroad had declined in recent years.[33] In the years that followed, the fear that the United States would find itself involved in another Vietnam was at the forefront of legislative and popular sentiment toward foreign policy issues.

Advocates of a more forceful congressional role in external affairs have brought two somewhat contradictory indictments against recent chief executives. Presidents Johnson, Nixon, and Reagan were criticized for *using* (or threatening to use) the vast powers of the presidency in behalf of ill-conceived foreign policy ventures, such as the Vietnam conflict and military intervention in Latin America. By contrast, Presidents Ford and Carter were criticized widely for *failing to use* the powers at their command to respond forcefully and successfully to external challenges, such as the discovery of Soviet troops in Cuba and the invasion of Afghanistan. In both cases, critics believe that a precipitous decline in American power and influence abroad has resulted. During the late 1970s Senate Minority Leader Howard Baker of Tennessee expressed a typical American opinion when he complained that Americans were tired of being "pushed around" by other countries. They wanted President Carter "to be firmer, more consistent, a little less smiling, and Mr. Nice Guy." Baker and other Republicans accused the Carter administration of "presiding over the decay of American influence and the decline of American military power."[34] Mounting Senate opposition to the SALT II arms limitation agreement with the Soviet Union (ultimately withdrawn by President Carter from Senate deliberations) reflected this pervasive anxiety on Capitol Hill.[35] In the same period legislators also expressed apprehension about a substantial Soviet military presence in Cuba.[36] Then by the early 1980s (as the American society confronted a serious domestic recession and a mounting federal deficit), the opposite viewpoint was widely expressed. Critics charged that President Reagan and his advisers had become preoccupied with a massive defense buildup, that they were neglecting the nation's internal well-being, and that they were engaging in diplomatic adventurism that entailed unwanted foreign commitments and burdens.

Divisions within the executive branch have also invited strong legislative initiatives in foreign affairs. As one American political commentator lamented: "The misconduct of foreign affairs in the United States has lately become something of an international scandal. You can seldom pick up a newspaper these days without reading about some self-appointed Secretary of State who is embarrassing the country." [37]

President Carter's secretary of state, his chief national security adviser, and his special envoy to the Middle East all held different views on the appropriate steps to be taken in resolving the Arab-Israeli conflict. During the Reagan administration the problem of intra-executive conflicts on major foreign policy issues showed no signs of disappearing. Secretary of State Alexander Haig's resignation less than 18 months after he took office called attention to ongoing conflict among Reagan's advisers on external problems. A fundamental unresolved question—the precise role of the president's national security adviser vis-à-vis the secretary of state in the foreign policy process—continued to engender divisiveness within the administration in dealing with diplomatic issues. Confusion within the executive branch was also produced by the diplomatic activities of other officials (such as Secretary of Defense Caspar Weinberger) whose viewpoints did not always appear to coincide with those of the State Department.

Insofar as fundamental policy disagreements and bureaucratic infighting among executive officials weaken the president's leadership position, Congress is irresistibly tempted to fill the ensuing vacuum. Moreover, disunity within the executive branch is bound to exacerbate the problem of disunity within Congress itself in approaching diplomatic questions.

Late in 1979 one of President John F. Kennedy's former White House aides, Theodore C. Sorensen, made an earnest appeal to President Carter to "regain control" over the foreign policy machinery. Sorensen said, "Effective control over the conduct of foreign affairs is slipping away from Jimmy Carter, and that is sad to see ... because a coherent and effective American foreign policy requires Presidential leadership." [38]

Recent experience has shown that unless and until a unified foreign policy approach is supplied by the chief executive, the diplomacy of the United States will be marked by drift, ineffectualness, and the decline of national power abroad.

Congressional Assertiveness: Consequences and Implications

What impact has a more assertive and independent diplomatic role by Congress had upon American foreign policy? What have been its consequences—both positive and negative—upon the conduct of foreign relations by the United States? These questions merit more detailed examination in the light of our case studies and of other examples of Congress's recent dynamism in the foreign policy field.

Independent Legislative Initiatives

Until the period of the Vietnam War it was a clearly established principle that negotiations with foreign governments were an executive prerogative. For example, longstanding precedent supports the view that the president or his designated agent makes or negotiates treaties with other governments. One of the earliest enactments of Congress was the Logan Act, which prohibits unauthorized contacts or negotiations between Americans and foreign officials. Although such contacts today have become frequent—and no citizen has ever been prosecuted for violating its terms—the Logan Act remains the law of the land.[39]

In practice, from World War II until the 1970s legislators were frequently involved in the conduct of diplomatic negotiations—but nearly always at the invitation of the president. Today the appointment of legislators as members of American negotiating teams is an accepted technique for creating bipartisan support for the nation's foreign policy. The Carter administration attempted to win widespread congressional support for the proposed SALT II strategic arms limitations agreements with the Soviet Union by allowing "26 Senators, 14 Republicans and 12 Democrats, including opponents and critics, and 46 members of the House of Representatives, to sit in on the arms negotiations in Geneva" at one time or another. President Ronald Reagan utilized legislators as "observers" of national elections in El Salvador in 1982; and in 1983, he appointed a former senator, Richard Stone, to serve as his special envoy in an effort to promote political stability in Central America.[40]

The novel feature of Congress's involvement in diplomatic negotiations today is the tendency of legislators to engage in them *independently*—without White House approval, and sometimes in the face of presidential opposition. In 1979 Sen. Jesse Helms, a member of the Senate Foreign Relations Committee, sent two staff members to London to observe at first hand diplomatic discussions (to which the United States was not even a party) designed to end the longstanding civil conflict in Zimbabwe (Rhodesia). Senator Helms's justification was candid: "I don't trust the State Department on this issue."[41]

Another newsworthy example of Congress's direct intervention in foreign relations occurred after Iranian students seized the American embassy in Tehran on November 4, 1979, and held some 50 Americans hostage. After early White House efforts to gain the release of the hostages failed, Rep. George Hansen, R-Idaho, undertook his own self-appointed peace mission to Iran, where he visited the hostages and sought to obtain their release. Hansen's efforts also failed, and his unauthorized negotiations during the crisis were criticized by executive and legislative officials alike, who feared his initiatives would undermine the president's authority and would provide evidence of disunity within the American government during the crisis.[42]

Independent diplomatic efforts by Helms, Hansen, and other members of Congress appear to have established the precedent that legislators may now engage in the negotiating process freely. Perhaps legislators do so on the theory that, in the absence of overt White House objections, they have the president's tacit approval. In any case, the practice is bound to raise questions abroad about who is ultimately in charge of American foreign policy and about how durable agreements reached with a variety of American officials are likely to be.

The recognition of other governments is another area—long regarded as an executive province—into which Congress has intruded during the past decade. Early in 1979 several senators attempted to make President Carter's decision to recognize the People's Republic of China (PRC) contingent upon Peking's pledge not to use force in exerting its long-standing claim to sovereignty over Taiwan. In effect, these legislators wanted to threaten the PRC with withdrawal of American recognition if it attempted to seize Taiwan by force.[43] While the president and his advisers were mindful of congressional concern about the future of Taiwan, they were unwilling to condition American recognition upon the PRC's behavior in the matter.

Another recent example of this congressional behavior pattern involves Zimbabwe. Several members of the Senate Foreign Relations Committee proposed sending a team of private citizens, chosen by the committee, to observe the forthcoming 1980 elections in that country—an unusual step designed to compel the White House to recognize a new, politically moderate regime that might supersede the incumbent white-dominated government. Executive officials opposed this congressional initiative because it encroached upon the president's traditional diplomatic prerogatives and because it was an evident attempt by some legislators to divert American foreign policy in Africa away from closer identification with revolutionary political movements.[44]

Expansion of Treaty-Making Role

As we noted in Chapter 2, the Senate has relied upon its constitutional prerogatives in the treaty-making process to assert its influence in the diplomatic field, and the House has sought to use other prerogatives (for example, its dominant role in the appropriations process) to compensate for the Senate's constitutionally unique position. Several significant aspects of Congress's involvement in the negotiation and ratification of treaties have come to the fore in recent years. In contrast to earlier years, since World War II the Senate has shown that it is determined to construe its role in the treaty process actively and to leave its imprint on major international agreements entered into by the United States.

Three recent examples—the new Panama Canal treaties, the SALT II arms limitation accord, and demands on Capitol Hill that the Reagan administration negotiate a nuclear freeze with the Soviet Union—are cases in point. In the instances of the Panama Canal treaties and SALT II, Senate deliberations were prolonged, thorough, and in the end extremely influential. (Mounting Senate opposition to SALT II was one factor motivating President Carter to withdraw the treaty from further Senate deliberation.) The issue of the nuclear freeze presented an essentially different question: Could legislators compel an obviously reluctant chief executive to *undertake negotiations* with another government in behalf of a nuclear freeze or some other goal favored by Congress? Legally and on the basis of precedents, the answer was not really in doubt: as was explained in Chapter 1, under the Constitution the president makes treaties, or enters into negotiations with other governments; and the Senate considers treaties submitted to it by the executive branch. Yet realistically, President Reagan and other modern chief executives knew that such forceful expressions of legislative sentiment unquestionably reflected deep public concern about the threat of nuclear devastation; and they were no less aware that, even if Congress could not force a president to negotiate a Soviet-American arms freeze, legislators *could* demonstrate their discontent about American diplomacy in other ways (such as by cutting defense expenditures).

During the late 1970s another interesting aspect of the Senate's prerogative in treaty making was raised when 25 senators contended in federal court that the existing defense treaty with Taiwan could be terminated only with congressional approval. In a decision by a United States court of appeals—sustained by the Supreme Court—the judiciary ruled that the termination of the treaty in this case was a presidential prerogative.[45]

The Pattern of Overseas Commitments

Since World War II Congress has been determined to play a more influential role in the assumption and maintenance of the overseas commitments of the United States. Has there been a consistent pattern of legislative activity concerning these overseas obligations? For the most part, the answer is no. Congress has curtailed some of them; it has expanded others; and it has maintained still other international commitments largely intact. Most important, Congress has insisted far more adamantly than ever before that the nation's international obligations be made a matter of public record.

First, let us examine overseas commitments that have been cut or curtailed by Congress since the late 1960s. The Vietnam War was terminated by act of Congress (although in the Nixon administration's view, that process had already begun before Congress directed it). In the ensuing years, adverse congressional sentiment was a potent factor in preventing possible consideration of foreign aid to North Vietnam.

By enacting the War Powers Resolution in 1973, Congress imposed several new limitations upon the authority of the chief executive to use the armed forces; yet, as we saw in Chapter 5, congressional insistence upon strict compliance with the terms of the War Powers Resolution has been less than stringent. Toward Angola, Congress denied the White House authority to use military force and to carry on covert intelligence operations. And in several foreign countries with repressive governments that jeopardized the rights of their citizens, Congress has—or has threatened to—cut off American aid and trade.

The limitations imposed by Congress upon the president's management of foreign affairs operate both ways, however. Beginning with the Johnson administration, every chief executive has complained about congressionally imposed restrictions upon presidential freedom of action in foreign relations. President Nixon and his national security adviser, Henry Kissinger, were persuaded that—except for congressional interference in the conduct of the Vietnam War—executive policymakers could have obtained a much more advantageous settlement of the conflict.[46] President Ronald Reagan believed that congressionally imposed restrictions upon executive activities in Central America seriously impeded his efforts to contain Communist expansionism in the Western Hemisphere.

On other occasions, however, executive policymakers have found actual or potential congressional restraints upon their freedom of action diplomatically useful. Former Secretary of State Kissinger has recounted several instances in which the president and his advisers used the threat of a severe congressional reduction in America's overseas commitments as a diplomatic gambit in negotiating with foreign governments. And the Nixon administration repeatedly informed the NATO allies that unless they increased their contribution to the defense of the Western Hemisphere, Congress would almost certainly reduce America's troop contribution to the NATO area.[47] Similarly, the Reagan administration unquestionably relied upon actual or potential congressional reductions in economic and military aid to El Salvador in order to induce internal reforms in that country.

Since the Vietnam War congressional activism in foreign affairs has not infrequently taken the opposite course: expansion of the nation's overseas obligations. Congress has at least tacitly approved most military base agreements negotiated by executive officials with foreign countries. It did not block efforts by the White House to augment American military power in the Indian Ocean area. Nor were there significant congressional objections to several naval "demonstrations" during the late 1970s and early 1980s in the Persian Gulf area; and the Reagan administration's determination to engage in naval exercises off the coast of Libya, even at the cost of a minor armed clash with Libyan aircraft, elicited no noteworthy congressional disapproval.

Even before the Carter administration left office—and the impetus continued under the Reagan administration—support was evident on Capitol Hill for the acquisition of new naval bases in the Persian Gulf area, along with the creation of a powerful military strike force (the Rapid Deployment Force, RDF) capable of protecting American defense and security interests in the Middle East and other foreign settings. Moreover, although the funds provided for the purpose vary from year to year, Congress continues to support foreign economic and military aid programs. Despite periodic efforts to reduce America's contribution, Congress also continues to support a substantial American military presence in Western Europe. It is perhaps most significant that, despite disagreements on Capitol Hill about the precise allocations for new weapons, manpower needs, research and development, and other budgetary components, most legislators approved major increases in the defense budget, as recommended by the White House.

Congressional insistence that the formal and informal overseas obligations of the United States be reported to Congress must be reckoned among the more notable results of legislative activism in foreign affairs. Prolonged legislative deliberations on the new Panama Canal treaties, for example, raised public consciousness and helped produce favorable public sentiment in behalf of the agreements. Under the Reagan administration, Congress was insistent that the nature and goals of American military and intelligence activities toward the government of Nicaragua be clarified and justified by the White House.

Congress has also insisted that intelligence agencies now report more fully than in the past to committees of Congress on their operations. Owing in no small measure to congressional initiatives, contemporary American foreign policy is governed now, more than in any previous era of history, by the Wilsonian principle of "open convenants, openly arrived at." Henry Kissinger's visit to the Chinese mainland in 1971 on behalf of the Nixon administration was remarkable not only because it inaugurated the new era of rapprochement in Sino-American relations, but also because it was a diplomatic initiative by the executive branch that was kept secret for some time from Congress.[48]

To the degree that a better informed Congress and citizenry provide a more secure foundation for effective diplomacy, legislative insistence upon maximum publicity for international commitments has clearly been a gain. The Vietnam War experience demonstrated convincingly that public support is indispensable for military and diplomatic success abroad.

Problems with Congressional Policymaking

Although Congress has adopted a more assertive role in foreign affairs, it may be doubted that the nature of congressional decisionmaking lends itself to effective foreign policy management. A former State Department official has called legislative power in foreign policy a "blunt instrument," which not infrequently has resulted in "a series of uncoordinated actions that annoyed the Secretary of State more than it advanced coherent policy." On some occasions, legislators have threatened to paralyze American foreign policy unless the White House abandoned or changed a proposed course of action.[49] According to one of President Carter's aides,

"Congress ties the President's hands on foreign policy, scrutinizing and criticizing every move he makes, sometimes jeopardizing relations with our allies and unpredictable foes." [50]

Even individuals with legislative experience have expressed concern about Congress's intrusion into the foreign policy field. Former Senate Foreign Relations Committee chairman J. William Fulbright said:

> I confess to increasingly serious misgivings about the ability of the Congress to play a constructive role in our foreign relations. . . . those of us who prodded what seemed to be a hopelessly immobile herd of cattle [Congress] a decade ago, now stand back in awe in the face of a stampede. [51]

Basically the same complaints—not infrequently from legislators themselves—were expressed about Congress's foreign policy role in the 1980s. Thus, one legislator acknowledged that cabinet members and other officials of the executive branch could justifiably complain about the "repetitious testimony" they were required to give the House and Senate, and about the lack of identifiable and effective leadership on Capitol Hill. Another legislator has lamented the Senate's apparent inability "to control events," its internal fragmentation, and its growing susceptibility to pressure group campaigns mounted by special interest groups. As legislators considered such complex issues as the proposed MX missile system and Soviet-American arms control negotiations, another senator deplored "the incredible lack of knowledge about the Soviet people and Soviet history" that existed on Capitol Hill. After reviewing the consequences of a number of congressionally imposed restrictions upon the president's diplomatic behavior during the 1970s, another experienced legislator called upon Congress to "reexamine its role in the conduct of foreign policy and repeal or amend, as necessary" most of this legislation, since it clearly posed an obstacle to "a unified, coherent and cohesive foreign policy" for the United States. [52]

In the words of one young, liberal senator, Congress possesses the ability to "foul up foreign policy"—and it has done so from time to time in recent years. [53] The congressional response to the discovery in August 1979 of a large contingent of Soviet troops in Cuba, for example, was confusing and ambiguous. One national news journal concluded that the Kremlin was "notoriously loath to let U.S. Senators beat them with sticks" on the Cuban question. Mishandling of the whole affair in Washington, the article concluded,

> not only casts still more doubt on the leadership of the Carter administration but also raises a longer-term and more disturbing question about whether the Congress—recently so assertive about playing a bigger role in foreign policy—can help solve crises rather than manufacturing and aggravating them. [54]

Congress often approaches external policymaking as an exercise in *lawmaking,* and that may be one reason why its assertive role in foreign affairs has not always been productive. According to a former State

Department official, by the end of the 1970s Congress had imposed "more than 150 statutory limitations on the United States' relations with foreign countries." Commenting on the congressional tendency to envision diplomatic questions in legal terms or as legal contests, he added: "Foreign policy has become almost synonymous with lawmaking. The result is to place a straitjacket of legislation around the manifold complexity of our relations with other nations." [55]

Although he was an advocate of bipartisan executive-legislative collaboration in foreign affairs, Sen. Arthur Vandenberg, R-Mich., was also concerned about some of the implications of Congress's forceful intrusion into the foreign policy field. On one occasion he warned: "I think the Senate is entitled, at any time it pleases, to ... tell the Executive what it thinks concerning foreign affairs. But I think it would be a tragic and unfortunate thing if the habit ever became general or too contagious." [56] Implicit in Vandenberg's admonition is a distinction, although it has become increasingly ill-defined, between an expanded legislative voice in *policy formulation* and in the *conduct or execution* of foreign affairs. The former is a province in which Congress can and should participate. The day-to-day management of foreign relations, however, is another matter. This is not a realm into which Congress should intrude regularly, nor is it really equipped to do so. Nevertheless, as one study pointed out, Congress has appeared "determined to play havoc with policy implementation." [57] Years later, Vandenberg's sage advice remains timely and provocative. From his experience Senator Vandenberg was cognizant—more so than many of his colleagues in Congress—that the House and Senate are poorly equipped to undertake the day-to-day conduct of American foreign relations. If they should attempt to do so, the result will almost certainly be to create a new, and conceivably worse, set of diplomatic problems for the United States.

Foreigners have always found unique and bewildering the American system of separation of powers among three coordinate branches of government. But in no previous era has the foreign policy process in the United States perhaps proved so mystifying and frustrating for outsiders. Recent diplomatic experience has shown that agreement with the administration, even when the president's party controls Congress, often counts for little. After arriving at understandings with executive officials, in many cases foreign negotiators then have "to enter into separate external relations with the American Congress, and renegotiate ... the agreement reached." [58]

Most governments endeavor to arrive at a unified foreign policy position *before* they enter into negotiations with other states; but judging by recent examples of American diplomacy, in the United States a unified position among policymakers was often arrived at only *after* understandings had been reached with foreign governments. This led one Soviet spokesman to ask, "With whom in America can we have dealings?" For foreign officials, it was "still not clear who exactly in the U.S. can speak in international relations on behalf of the United States." [59]

Congressional Assertiveness:
Probabilities and Prospects

What is the future of congressional assertiveness in American foreign relations? Has it become a permanent feature of the foreign policy process in the United States, or is it merely a phase that will be followed in time by a new era of executive dominance in external affairs? A number of diverse and contrary factors will determine the answers to these questions in the years ahead.

Factors Favoring an Expanded Role

A persuasive case can be made for the contention that Congress will continue to exercise a powerful—and in some instances, a decisive—voice in foreign affairs for the indefinite future. Executive officials, foreign governments, and the public must come to terms with this possibility.

Global and Domestic Setting. Among the forces that engender and sustain an energetic role by Congress in foreign affairs, none is perhaps more important than the changing nature of the global agenda. In the second half of the twentieth century, unique and often extremely difficult issues have come to the forefront of international concern: global economic stability, the pressing needs of the less developed societies, the increasingly acute world food shortage, runaway population growth throughout most of the Third World, and worldwide environmental problems. Today the solution to these major international and regional problems requires active participation by Congress.

In the United States and in most other countries since World War II the role of government has expanded to meet these challenges. This trend is both exemplified and sustained by the volume of legislation produced by Congress in the postwar era. One way of looking at the diplomatic activism of Congress, therefore, is to say that the legislative branch is finally taking the same approach in dealing with external affairs that it has taken toward domestic issues since the New Deal: Congress is attempting to solve major public policy questions by enacting legislation and by relying upon other powers incident to lawmaking, such as the oversight function.

The assertiveness of the House and Senate in foreign relations can also be attributed to the American cultural milieu. Since the early 1960s sweeping changes have occurred in American life styles, in traditional modes of thought, and in behavior norms. On all fronts, customs and long-established practices have been challenged.[60] Perhaps more in the political realm than in other sectors of American life, established authority has come under attack. Demands are heard on all sides that political decisionmaking be made more democratic. And American voters today are more independent, refusing to identify themselves with either major political party.

In the post-Vietnam War period, there is a deep-seated feeling of disillusionment and skepticism about the results achieved in domestic and foreign affairs by the nation's leaders. In this milieu, the possibility of a fundamentally different approach to foreign relations—with Congress playing a decisive role in the process—finds many advocates on Capitol Hill and throughout the nation as a whole.

Executive Encouragement.   As much out of necessity as conviction perhaps, executive officials today frequently support a more dynamic and meaningful role by Congress in foreign relations. The president, the secretary of state, and other high-ranking executive officials at times have called upon legislative officials to join them in creating a unified approach to foreign policy issues.[61] Moreover, the attitude of executive officials toward congressional activism in foreign affairs is often highly variable and eclectic. While executive officials routinely complain about congressional restrictions upon the president's authority, in particular instances they have favored forceful legislative intrusion into the diplomatic arena.

Early in 1979 Sen. Frank Church, chairman of the Senate Foreign Relations Committee, bluntly notified officials of Saudi Arabia that the United States expected their diplomatic support in its efforts to resolve the Arab-Israeli conflict. Church informed the Saudi government—apparently with the full encouragement of executive officials—that unless the Saudis supported U.S. efforts, there would be a major congressional review of American foreign policy toward the Middle East. (For several months, State Department officials had been reluctant to convey such a warning directly to Saudi Arabia.) [62]

An even more dramatic example of executive encouragement of congressional activism was provided by former National Security Adviser and Secretary of State Henry Kissinger when he testified before the Senate Foreign Relations Committee in July 1979 on the SALT II strategic armaments agreements. Kissinger encouraged what one commentator called "congressional forays into the foreign-affairs power of the executive" by urging the Senate to make ratification of the accords contingent upon a significant increase in American defense spending—a move not favored by the White House at that time.[63] During the Reagan administration visits by legislators to El Salvador and other Latin American nations, as well as expressions of active congressional interest in developments in Central America, strengthened the hand of the White House in its efforts to encourage internal reforms within these countries. Similarly, outspoken opposition in Congress to Israel's diplomatic behavior encouraged greater Israeli flexibility in efforts to achieve peace in the Middle East.

Congress's Accomplishments.   The positive results Congress has achieved in foreign policy are another factor that has sustained congressional activism in foreign affairs and may continue to do so in the years ahead. Advocates of a more forceful and independent legislative role in foreign affairs believe the track record of Congress is good. Proponents of this view are convinced that it was Congress that extricated the nation from the Vietnam War and, by enacting the War Powers Resolution in 1973, ensured that there will be no more Vietnams to mar the nation's diplomatic record. Similarly, it was the Senate that protected American security interests by insisting upon changes in the Panama Canal treaties as negotiated by the executive branch. Owing in large part to Congress's efforts during the 1970s, American intelligence agencies were placed under tighter control, and the United States became identified with the international promotion of human rights, as symbolized particularly by the diplomacy of the Carter administration.

In more general terms, Congress has helped reverse the trend toward virtually unchecked executive authority in the field of foreign relations since the Vietnam War. Congressional influence has also been a potent factor in changing the direction of American diplomacy. It has reversed America's tendency to become overcommitted abroad, and it has endeavored to ensure that another Vietnam does not mar the nation's diplomatic record. The influence of Congress has also been cast in the direction of broadening the base of American foreign policy by insisting that legislative and public opinion be considered *early* in the stage of policymaking—not merely (as in the Vietnam War) after diplomatic defeats have been sustained and in the allocation of blame for these setbacks. Moreover, as in its frequent review of intelligence activities, Congress has insisted upon the periodic reexamination of American diplomatic activities; and it has demanded *continuing* consultation between the legislative and executive branches in dealing with complex foreign policy issues.

Factors Favoring Restraint

A number of short- and long-term factors, however, point to restraint and possibly a reversal in the pattern of legislative activism witnessed since the Vietnam War. Initially, we need to be reminded that a forceful and independent role in foreign affairs by legislative bodies is a distinctive phenomenon among modern governments, confined almost entirely to the American system. In nearly all other countries, the tide has been running strongly in the contrary direction; other national legislatures have steadily lost the power to act independently, especially in the foreign policy field.

In Great Britain, France, West Germany, Japan, and other democracies today, the responsibility for managing foreign affairs is vested almost solely with executive officials. In the rare cases when the legislative body does successfully challenge the incumbent government's foreign policy, a political crisis (followed by new national elections) normally ensues. The experience of many countries suggests that the successful conduct of foreign relations inherently militates against a high degree of legislative activism and independence.

Cycles in Diplomatic History.   Moreover, the forceful assertion of Congress's powers in foreign relations has been a cyclical occurrence in the nation's diplomatic experience. The "War Hawks of 1812," who demanded and got another war with Great Britain, had many members on Capitol Hill. Following the end of the Mexican War in 1848, Congress once more asserted its influence dynamically in foreign affairs. And the period before and after World War I marked another era of congressional assertiveness.

The cyclical nature of Congress's diplomatic militancy—and of the ensuing struggle between executive and legislative officials for primacy in foreign affairs—may be explained in various ways. No single existing theory adequately accounts for it. To some extent, congressional assertiveness in foreign relations may be related to the oscillating isolationist and interventionist moods of the American people toward international affairs.[64]

Alternatively, it may be a function of the political balance between the executive and legislative branches and of the shifting political tides within the American society. For reasons that are even now difficult to explain satisfactorily, the zenith of bipartisan cooperation in foreign affairs in the postwar era was reached under the Truman and early Eisenhower administrations—when the presidency and Congress were controlled by different political parties. President Truman had much greater success in arriving at a constructive working relationship with a Republican-controlled Congress on foreign policy than President Carter experienced with a House and Senate controlled by his own political party![65] By contrast, under the Reagan administration the Democratic-controlled House of Representatives was the center of intense congressional activism in dealing with such issues as the national defense budget, the proposed new MX missile system, and political developments in Central America.

Problems with Executive-Legislative Consultation.   The nature of consultation between policymakers in the executive and legislative branches of government is a significant factor in determining the outcome of efforts to achieve constructive bipartisan collaboration on major foreign policy issues, as advocated by the Reagan administration during the early 1980s. Yet, as emphasized in Chapter 5, there is the problem of when to consult—before or after the president has decided upon a particular diplomatic course of action? There is the additional question of which members of Congress should be included in such discussion and of deciding who really represents Congress and can arrive at understandings in its name.

Even if the problems of when and whom to consult can be solved, a third serious inhibition upon successful executive-legislative consultation remains. What responsibility do members of Congress incur by participating in consultation on foreign policy issues? Does a policy decision resulting from such consultations become their decision, fully as much as the president's?

More specifically, does concurrence in a particular intelligence mission by selected members of the House and Senate make Congress as a whole responsible for its success or failure? Does a president's consultation with a selected group of legislators, in adherence to the terms of the War Powers Resolution, make Congress equally responsible with the executive branch when American military forces are used for diplomatic objectives?

If the answer to such questions is yes, how can this fact be reconciled with Congress's traditional role as a critic of executive policies, especially when they miscarry? Alternatively, if the answer is no, what inducement does an incumbent president have to consult legislators on particular diplomatic questions, when they refuse to share with executive officials responsibility for the outcome of a proposed policy?

The success or failure of executive-legislative consultation may also be determined by individual personalities. During the late 1940s Secretary of State Dean Acheson and other executive officials worked harmoniously and effectively with influential legislators such as Senators Arthur H. Vandenberg and Tom Connally to formulate diplomatic undertakings (such as the Marshall Plan) acceptable to the White House and Congress. Although these officials often belonged to different political parties, an atmosphere of mutual trust and respect governed their deliberations. Agreements reached between them nearly always were subsequently supported by majorities in the House and Senate.[66]

By contrast, during the Johnson administration legislative and executive officials were often far from agreement on foreign policy issues. Sen. J. William Fulbright outspokenly criticized White House policies toward Vietnam, the Dominican Republic, and other areas. The personal animosity and distrust ultimately existing between Johnson and the Senate Foreign Relations Committee chairman served as a major deterrent to constructive executive-legislative relations in the foreign policy field.

Public Attitudes toward President and Congress. "Capacity in government," one informed student of the American system has said, "depends, in the United States as elsewhere, on leadership."[67] By the beginning of the 1980s, the American people's desire for clear and firm White House leadership in meeting the nation's internal and external problems was unmistakable. President Jimmy Carter's inability, for example, to manage Congress—to create and maintain minimal unity on Capitol Hill in behalf of his programs—was a key element in the widespread perception that he was a weak and indecisive chief executive.[68]

Even congressional voices were heard in the chorus calling upon the chief executive to exhibit forceful and dynamic diplomatic leadership. Sen. Adlai Stevenson III, D-Ill., declared that in recent years Congress had excelled at the game of "kick the President"—perhaps an understandable reaction on Capitol Hill to abuses of presidential power. Yet,

Stevenson informed his colleagues, Congress's "weaknesses will come back to haunt us. I want a strong executive." [69]

A resurgence of executive authority rather than congressional militancy in foreign affairs may be the wave of the future. According to one study of contemporary executive-legislative relations:

> Left and right want a strong Presidency, the left in domestic affairs, the right for foreign policy.... Americans not only prefer Presidential leadership but the scope of foreign and domestic problems and the recurrent emergencies facing a world power simply demand Presidential power— particularly when Congress' foreign policy decisions are so often governed by domestic policies. [70]

Or as another study of public attitudes expressed it, for most Americans the presidency is "everyone's first resort." Realistically or not, the American people expect the chief executive to be forthright and successful in solving national problems; and they complain vocally about the lack of White House leadership when this does not happen. [71]

The celebrated American comedian Will Rogers once told his audiences, "There's good news from Washington. Congress is adjourned." Such humor always strikes a responsive chord with Americans, for whom the denigration of Congress's deeds and misdeeds sometimes seems a national pasttime. [72] Today, as in the past, the American people are aware that Congress's record has been badly tarnished. Influence peddling on Capitol Hill, misuse of campaign contributions, scandalous personal behavior by legislators, recurring disunity within the House and Senate, and the obstructionist moves by Congress in dealing with national policy issues have become public knowledge. Legislators can be energetic and decisive in dealing with executive wrongdoing but dilatory and ineffectual in correcting unethical practices, illegal activities, and organizational problems on Capitol Hill.

Public confidence in Congress's performance has fallen steadily in recent years. One poll showed that in 1974 almost half of the American people approved of the way Congress was doing its job. By mid-1979 this figure had declined to 19 percent. According to another study of public attitudes, twice as many Americans blamed Congress as blamed President Carter for deadlocks between the two branches of the government. Another study, in 1983, found that just over 7 percent of those interviewed believed that Congress was doing a better than adequate job of dealing with urgent internal and external issues; almost half (46.5 percent) thought that Congress's performance was disappointing or poor. According to one experienced observer, Congress still needed to display "more backbone in confronting the president" and to be less concerned with "nitpicking, constituency service and the thousands of small issues" dominating the activities of legislators. A Gallup Poll in 1982 showed that only 29 percent of the public approved of the way Congress was performing its duties, while 54 percent disapproved. Earlier Gallup polls showed that public approval of Congress's performance varied from a low of 19 to a high of 38 percent. Aware of such public attitudes, even legislators have deplored the fact that on some occasions, the behavior of legislators was "demeaning," making Congress the "laughing stock of America." [73]

Popular anxieties about the imperial presidency do not automatically translate into heightened public confidence in Congress's performance or leadership potential. Implicit in public criticism of President Carter's lack of leadership was the twofold demand that the White House take charge of the governmental machinery and that the president exercise more leadership in dealing with Congress to produce unified and effective policies and programs.

Public and Congressional Domestic Concerns. Another factor restraining congressional activism in foreign policy is that the American public exhibits a low level of interest in international questions. This has been true of the American society historically (it was a major force, for example, sustaining the isolationist approach to foreign relations), and it is no less the case in the contemporary period. Almost invariably, on any list of the dominant concerns of the American people, pollsters have found that internal problems are given highest priority by citizens. Only some 15 percent of the people belong to the *attentive public*—or that minority of opinion which is reasonably interested in, and informed about, foreign relations.[74] The behavior of Congress is inescapably affected by this public opinion trait.

This leads to another, closely related factor likely to inhibit a dynamic and sustained role by Congress in the diplomatic field. Constituency-related business ranks as a primary claim upon the time and energies of most legislators. Even with a greatly enlarged staff, most legislators today are hard pressed to meet the diverse demands made upon them by their constituents.[75]

As several of our case studies emphasized, relatively few legislators have the time to acquire expert knowledge of a broad range of complex foreign policy questions. Only a minority of legislators has shown any real desire to receive and to assimilate detailed information about the activities of intelligence agencies—although legislators are legally entitled to it. Similarly, few legislators are inclined to read and digest voluminous reports from executive officials regarding human rights problems in more than 150 independent nations.

The high priority accorded to domestic concerns by the American people and their legislative representatives has two specific consequences. First, perhaps even more today than in the past, Congress's approach to foreign affairs is heavily colored by local and domestic considerations vis-à-vis a commitment to the national interest. Late in 1979 one of the nation's most knowledgeable reporters characterized the foreign policy process in the United States in such terms as "chaos" and "an international scandal." To a considerable degree, he blamed Congress for this state of affairs: "Seldom in memory has it seemed so divided, so concerned with personal, local or state interests and so indifferent to its own Congressional leadership or the disturbing problems of the 1980s." [76]

Second, Congress's involvement in external affairs is likely to be characterized by a short attention span and to be heavily conditioned by the current newsworthiness of a particular foreign policy issue. As our discussion in Chapter 6 illustrated, members of the House and Senate were actively concerned for a time about various misdeeds of the CIA. After a relatively brief period, however, the attention of most legislators had shifted to other issues, leaving only a handful of senators and representatives to monitor intelligence activities on a continuing basis. Summing up a conversation about attempts by Congress to restore its powers, one senator characteristically exclaimed, "I think we've made substantial headlines—I mean headway." [77]

Invitation to Struggle

From the time of George Washington's administration until the present day, the president and Congress have vied for control over foreign relations. And the lively interaction between Congress and the president—the major theme of our study—will continue to be a dominant feature of the American foreign policy process in the future. During some periods (the era from World War II until the closing stage of the Vietnam War), executive authority in the foreign policy sphere has been preeminent. In other periods (during the 1930s and the 1970s), the congressional voice has been louder and more decisive.

Continuation of this institutional rivalry in foreign affairs seems assured by two fundamental conditions: the provisions of the United States Constitution and the obligations inherent in America's role as a superpower in a complex and unstable international system. Although many formal and informal changes have been made in the Constitution since 1789, the basic pattern of divided responsibility and power in foreign affairs remains unaltered. The president still serves as commander in chief of the nation's armed forces; he alone has the power to recognize other governments; and only he and his agents can officially negotiate treaties and agreements with other countries in the name of the United States.

After two centuries, Congress also retains influential prerogatives in national security and foreign affairs. The size and nature of the American military establishment are determined by Congress; funds for current military operations and for the development of new weapons must be provided by the legislative branch. In addition, Congress must authorize and appropriate funds for a host of other programs and governmental activities in the foreign policy field—ranging from the State Department budget, to foreign military and economic aid programs, to the activities of intelligence agencies. Also implicit in Congress's lawmaking function is its power to investigate the operations of executive agencies and the administration of programs it has authorized and funded—a power the House and Senate have used with telling effect on numerous occasions since World War II.

The nature of the contemporary international system also provides incentives for the executive and legislative branches to use their respective powers vigorously in the foreign policy field. Since World War II the United States has been one of the two superpowers in world affairs, and all indications are that it will indefinitely remain so. As a superpower, the United States has certain inescapable and continuing global responsibilities; discharging them nearly always entails policies and programs that involve executive and legislative officials.

Continuing Disunity in the Policy Process. Since the Vietnam conflict, the executive and legislative branches of the American government have faced comparable problems with respect to their role in the foreign policy process. Stated negatively, the efforts of both branches have often been seriously weakened by the schisms, organizational rivalries, and centrifugal forces that impair their internal cohesion and their ability to arrive at unified positions on major diplomatic issues. Stated positively, policymakers at opposite ends of Pennsylvania Avenue have important contributions to make to the American foreign policy process. Better understanding of their significant and distinctive roles may guide officials in both branches in their approach to foreign policy issues in the years ahead.

Our discussion in Chapter 1 called attention to the fact that within the executive branch the traditional authority and premier position of the State Department in the diplomatic field has been steadily diluted by the proliferation of executive agencies that play a major or minor role in contemporary American foreign policy. Since the Nixon administration particularly—with the emergence of the president's national security adviser as a rival to the secretary of state—executive efforts in foreign affairs appear to have become increasingly disunified and uncoordinated.[78] Under the Reagan administration, the dramatic resignation of Secretary of State Alexander Haig focused public attention upon the question: Who really speaks for the administration in foreign affairs? Haig's tribulations provided a newsworthy example of a problem that has become chronic and that has seriously impeded executive efforts in the foreign policy field since World War II.

As our case studies have shown, the role of Congress in contemporary American foreign policy is also beset by comparable difficulties. If the House and Senate have now established—and can be expected to maintain—an influential congressional presence in the foreign policy field, how well are they equipped to continue to play this role? Recent experience indicates that the answer must be: rather poorly and inadequately. To date, in terms of organizational, procedural, and behavioral changes required, few members of Congress have faced up squarely to the necessary implications of their demand for a position of equal partnership with the White House in foreign affairs.

By the early 1980s Congress appeared to be more decentralized, fragmented, and resistant to unifying influences than in any previous period of American history. To date Congress has supplied little evidence to show that it is prepared to adapt its own organizational structure and internal procedures to the demands of the active foreign policy role its members are determined to play. In the long run, this failure could prove decisive in determining the future of congressional activism in foreign affairs.

In judging the respective claims of the presidency and Congress to leadership in the foreign policy process, the American people are likely to apply their customary pragmatic and eclectic tests. Has the active intrusion of Congress into many dimensions of foreign affairs improved, or has it detracted from, the ability of the United States to achieve its diplomatic goals? Has congressional assertiveness on foreign policy questions enhanced the domestic well-being of the American society? Has the influence of Congress upon the course of the nation's diplomacy reversed, or has it contributed to, the tendency toward weakened American power and influence abroad? As much as any other single factor, how the American people perceive the answers to these questions will determine Congress's future foreign policy role.[79]

Shared Goals. Executive and legislative officials alike, we may safely assume, ultimately seek the same goal: a unified, rational, and successful foreign policy for the United States. Moreover, all participants in foreign policy decisionmaking would no doubt subscribe to the theoretical proposition that continuing discord, disunity, and competing efforts within the American government—regardless of whether they arise within the executive branch, within Congress, or from conflicts between the executive and legislative branches—nearly always impair the ability of the United States to achieve its diplomatic objectives.

If broad agreement exists in Washington on these propositions, it follows that officials in each branch need to devote greater attention to defining their respective contributions to the foreign policy process more clearly. By virtue of their differing constitutional responsibilities, their experience, and their resources, executive and legislative policymakers ought to make different contributions to the common effort, reflecting what each group is uniquely prepared to supply.

Presidential Role. What contributions are the president and his executive advisers singularly qualified to make? The president symbolizes and represents the national interest of the United States both to the American people and to foreign countries. The chief executive alone can speak in behalf of the American society to governments, leaders, and political movements abroad. As commander in chief of the armed forces, only the president is in a position to respond promptly and decisively to external threats.

The president and the executive officials under his jurisdiction also play an indispensable role in policy formulation. Relying upon the State Department's communications system with American embassies overseas and upon the intelligence community's resources for collecting and analyzing data, the White House remains in an unrivaled position to consider available options and to devise diplomatic strategies and programs for which it will later seek legislative support. Moreover, the president's position as a leader and educator of public opinion remains dominant. As the presidency of the Great Communicator, Ronald Reagan, illustrated, the chief executive is in a unique position to inform the American people about major diplomatic issues and to elicit their support in behalf of foreign policies and programs advocated by the White House. In the past (and the presidency of Franklin D. Roosevelt provided a graphic example), this has been a potent instrument of presidential influence in foreign relations. In the post-Vietnam War era—when the American people and Congress remained apprehensive about American military commitments abroad—the president's ability to use this instrument effectively depended heavily upon his ability to demonstrate that the security of the United States was at stake in Central America, the Middle East, and other regions in which the United States had major diplomatic interests. Lacking convincing evidence that such security considerations were present (as the Reagan administration discovered in its Latin American diplomacy), the president is likely to find that the legitimacy of his foreign policy ventures is widely questioned at home and abroad.

Contribution of Congress.   Congress also brings certain distinctive powers and perspectives to bear in foreign policymaking. First, there is the legislative power to grant or to withhold funds for foreign policy ventures and programs. Although Congress has possessed this prerogative since 1789, only since the closing stage of the Vietnam War has it relied regularly upon its control over the purse strings to determine the course of American diplomacy. As the internal and external demands upon the financial resources of the American government continue to escalate— and there is no reason to anticipate a reversal of that tendency in the near future—Congress will be challenged as never before to use the power of the purse wisely and effectively in allocating funds to a variety of foreign policy undertakings.

Second, Congress makes an essential contribution in supplying a base of legitimacy to American foreign policy. For a democracy, this vital element—a pervasive public belief that the nation's diplomatic goals are rational, are attainable at reasonable cost, and are consonant with the American society's cherished values—is a prerequisite for diplomatic success. Since the Vietnam War, even executive officials have acknowledged this legislative contribution to the foreign policy process. Thus, as the United States prepared to enter the 1980s, one State Department official said that there was "an important need after Vietnam and Watergate to legitimize American foreign policy." Referring to President Carter's decision to sell arms to certain nations in the Middle East, this spokesman observed, "If the President had made the Middle East arms sales decision on his own, he could have been run out of town on a rail. But the congressional vote legitimized the sale." [80] During the early 1980s the Reagan administration depended upon this same contribution of Congress to create a foundation of legitimacy under its efforts to counter Communist influence in Central America. Conversely, the administration's military intervention in Lebanon steadily lost the necessary public support, and this fact required the president to withdraw American forces from that country.

Third, as our discussion of legislative activities with regard to the intelligence community illustrated (Chapter 6), Congress can make a positive contribution to foreign policy decisionmaking—and to the future of American democracy—by scrutinizing the activities of executive agencies and by imposing more stringent guidelines upon their operations. This contribution of the legislative branch is highlighted by the continuing challenge of imposing effective controls upon the CIA and other members of the intelligence community, especially with regard to covert activities directed against Communist or unfriendly governments abroad. By the early 1980s few informed students of American government believed that this problem had been definitively solved—and perhaps in the American democratic system, it will always pose a dilemma for governmental officials and concerned citizens. Yet continuing oversight of intelligence activities by the House and Senate has gone far toward restoring popular confidence in the intelligence agencies and assuring that their operations promote the national interest. Congress has largely compelled the president and his advisers to impose limits upon such intelligence activities overseas while carrying on those intelligence functions that are essential for national security.

A fourth essential and distinctive contribution of Congress to the foreign policy process was brought into sharp focus by our analysis of Congress's role in the disposition and control of the armed forces (Chapter 5). Relying upon its constitutional prerogatives over the military establishment, Congress can prescribe limits to the president's use of armed force for foreign policy ends. By doing so, Congress creates powerful restraints upon diplomatic adventurism, upon a tendency by the United States to become overextended abroad, and upon the tendency to intervene indiscriminately in the affairs of other countries.

Efforts by the House and Senate to impose more stringent controls over the president's use of the armed forces abroad make another singular contribution to American foreign policy. They serve to remind executive policymakers that, although the United States is a superpower, it is not omnipotent. Even superpowers must base their diplomacy upon a set of priorities. They must define and continually redefine their diplomatic vital interests with care and discrimination. As Walter Lippmann cautioned Americans many years ago, success in foreign policy lies in arriving at and maintaining a balance between what the nation would *like* to accomplish abroad and what it is *able* to accomplish on the basis of the power available to it. Failure to preserve an approximate balance between these elements can result in a kind of "diplomatic bankruptcy." [81]

The executive and legislative branches of government would do well to concentrate upon the unique contributions each is equipped to make in the foreign policy process. Too often in the past each branch has jealously guarded and asserted its own powers in foreign affairs, while endeavoring to exercise or usurp those properly belonging to the other. A clearer sense of a division of labor in the diplomatic field by officials on both ends of Pennsylvania Avenue would go far toward achieving the goal of a more unified, stable, and successful American approach to external problems in the years ahead.

Notes

1. See the views of Ambassador Peter Jay, as quoted in William D. Rogers, "Who's in Charge of Foreign Policy?" *New York Times Magazine,* September 9, 1979, p. 49. The author is a former State Department official, but he is not to be confused with former Secretary of State William P. Rogers.
2. *New York Times,* January 25, 1975, dispatch by Bernard Gwertzman.
3. See Charles E. Percy, "The Partisan Gap," *Foreign Policy* 45 (Winter 1981-1982): 3.
4. *New York Times,* May 16, 1983, dispatch by Francis X. Clines.
5. For President Ford's view on Congress's activities in foreign affairs, see Gerald R. Ford, *A Time to Heal* (New York: Harper and Row and the Reader's Digest Assn., 1979), pp. 138-139, 150; Ford's views are also quoted in Marvin Stone, "Presidency: Imperial or Imperiled?" *U.S. News & World Report,* January 15, 1979, p. 88.
6. See Warren Christopher, "Ceasefire between the Branches: A Compact in Foreign Affairs," *Foreign Affairs* 60 (Summer 1982): 998; *New York Times,* March 21, 1983, dispatch by Steven V. Roberts; and Theodore H. White, "Weinberger on the Ramparts," *New York Times Magazine,* February 6, 1983, p. 77.
7. Nicholas DeB. Katzenbach, "Foreign Policy, Public Opinion and Secrecy," *Foreign Affairs* 52 (October 1973): 18.
8. For the views of John V. Lindsay, former member of Congress and mayor of New York, see "For a New Policy Balance," *Foreign Affairs* 50 (October 1971): 1.
9. For a detailed analysis of the "legislative explosion" witnessed since World War II, see James McClellan, "The State of the American Congress," *Modern Age* 21 (Summer 1977): 227-239.
10. *New York Times,* September 21, 1979, dispatch by James Reston.
11. See "What Congress Really Thinks of Itself," *U.S. News & World Report,* March 15, 1982, pp. 22-24; see the views of Sen. Alan K. Simpson, R-Wyo, on the fragmentation that has seriously impeded the operation of the Senate, in the *New York Times,* March 21, 1983, dispatch by Steven V. Roberts; and Martin Tolchin, "Howard Baker: Trying to Tame an Unruly Senate," *New York Times Magazine,* March 28, 1982.

12. Marvin Stone, "Proxmire's Well-Placed Jab," *U.S. News & World Report,* September 10, 1979, p. 84.

13. See the views of Professors Thomas Franck and Edward Weisband in the *New York Times,* November 29, 1976.

14. McClellan, "The State of the American Congress," p. 237. See also Susan W. Hammond, "Congressional Change and Reform: Staffing the Congress," in Leroy N. Reiselbach, ed., *Legislative Reform: The Policy Impact* (Lexington, Mass.: D. C. Heath and Co., 1978), pp. 183-193.

15. See Dean Acheson, *Sketches from Life of Men I Have Known* (New York: Harper and Row, 1961), pp. 124-125. For historical background, see Holbert N. Carroll, *The House of Representatives and Foreign Affairs* (Boston: Little, Brown and Co., 1966).

16. See the views of Rep. Paul Findley in the *New York Times,* October 6, 1966.

17. U.S. Congress, House Committee on International Relations, *Congress and Foreign Policy,* 94th Cong., 2d sess., 1977, p. 19. See also the dialogue between executive and legislative officials on the role of public opinion in foreign affairs in William O. Chattick, *State Department, Press, and Pressure Groups* (New York: John Wiley and Sons, 1970), pp. 43-45.

18. See the views of Sen. Frank Church in the *New York Times,* January 9, 1979, dispatch by Richard Burt.

19. *New York Times,* May 15, 1983, dispatch by Steven V. Roberts; and *New York Times,* May 26, 1983, dispatch by Steven V. Roberts.

20. The attitudes of the American people toward foreign affairs in the early 1980s are analyzed more fully in Stephen S. Rosenfeld, "Testing the Hard Line," *Foreign Affairs* (Special Issue, 1983): 489-511. See also the following articles in the journal *Foreign Policy:* Leon V. Sigal, "Warming to the Freeze," 48 (Fall 1982): 54-66; L. Bruce van Voorst, "The Critical Masses," 48 (Fall 1982): 82-94; John E. Rielly, "American Opinion: Continuity, Not Reaganism," 50 (Spring 1983): 86-105; and Robert J. Einhorn, "Treaty Compliance," 45 (Winter 1981-1982): 29-48.

21. *New York Times,* January 4, 1980, dispatch by James Reston.

22. James Chace, "Is a Foreign Policy Consensus Possible?" *Foreign Affairs* 57 (Fall 1978): 15-16.

23. U.S. Congress, House Committee on International Relations, *Congress and Foreign Policy: 1976,* 95th Cong., 1st sess., 1977, pp. 188-189. Intense congressional interest in international human rights issues is highlighted in Charles McC. Mathias, "Ethnic Groups and Foreign Affairs," *Foreign Affairs* 59 (Summer 1981): 975-999.

24. Ben J. Wattenberg, *The Real America: A Surprising Examination of the State of the Union* (Garden City, New York: Doubleday and Co., 1974), pp. 211-212.

25. See, for example, the views of former Sen. J. William Fulbright in "The Legislator as Educator," *Foreign Affairs* 57 (Spring 1979): 723-727.

26. "What Carter's Aides Really Think of Congress," *U.S. News & World Report,* August 14, 1978, p. 15.

27. The quotation is from the Supreme Court's decision in *United States v. Curtiss-Wright Export Corp., 299 U.S. 304 (1936).*

28. For a general discussion of the increase in foreign lobbying in America, see "Foreign Grab for Influence in Washington," *U.S. News & World Report,* November 22, 1976, p. 30.

29. See the analysis of lobbying by foreign interests in *U.S. News & World Report,* March 20, 1982, pp. 41-43.

30. For a detailed study of efforts by the executive branch to influence the deliberations of Congress, see Abraham Holtzman, *Legislative Liaison: Executive Leadership in Congress* (Chicago: Rand McNally, 1970).

31. Alton Frye and William D. Rogers, "Linkage Begins at Home," *Foreign Policy* 35 (Summer 1979): 55-56.

32. Lobbying activities by the Reagan administration are described in the *New York Times,* May 16, 1983, dispatch by Francis X. Clines; and *New York Times,* May 27, 1983, dispatch by Steven V. Roberts.

33. See, for example, the views of William P. Bundy in "Who Lost Patagonia? Foreign Policy in the 1980 Campaign," *Foreign Affairs* 58 (Fall 1979): 1-28. More detailed examination of the foreign policy issues contributing to Ronald Reagan's successful bid for the presidency in 1980 is available in Ellis Sandoz and Cecil V. Crabb, Jr., eds., *A Tide of Discontent: The 1980 Elections and Their Meaning* (Washington, D.C.: CQ Press, 1981).

34. *New York Times,* February 17, 1979, dispatch by Hedrick Smith.

35. See the excerpts from majority and minority reports submitted by the Senate Foreign Relations Committee on SALT II, as reprinted in the *New York Times,* November 20, 1979.

36. *New York Times,* October 12, 1979, dispatch by Charles Mohr.

37. *New York Times,* September 21, 1979, dispatch by James Reston. For a more detailed discussion of the implications of the problem of intra-executive conflicts, see Rogers, "Who's in Charge of Foreign Policy?" pp. 44-51.

38. See the *New York Times,* September 21, 1979, article by Theodore C. Sorenson.

39. 1 U.S. Statutes-at-Large 613 (1799).

40. *New York Times,* August 14, 1979, dispatch by Hedrick Smith.

41. *New York Times,* September 21, 1979, dispatch by James Reston.

42. *New York Times,* November 26, 1979, dispatch by John Kifner; and November 27, 1979, dispatch by Bernard Gwertzman.

43. *U.S. News & World Report,* February 19, 1979, pp. 52-54.

44. *New York Times,* March 1, 1979, dispatch by Graham Hovey.

45. See the *Washington Post,* December 14, 1979; and *Congressional Quarterly Weekly Report,* December 15, 1979, p. 2850.

46. For the views of the Nixon-Kissinger White House on the results of congressional action toward the Vietnam War, see Richard Nixon, *The Memoirs of Richard Nixon* (New York: Grosset and Dunlap, 1978), pp. 744, 888-889; and Henry Kissinger, *White House Years* (Boston: Little, Brown and Co., 1979), pp. 1413, 1461.

47. Kissinger, *White House Years,* pp. 400-401.

48. Ibid.

49. George W. Ball, *Diplomacy for a Crowded World: An American Foreign Policy* (Boston: Atlantic/Little, Brown, 1976), p. 204.

50. "What Carter's Aides Really Think of Congress," p. 15.

51. Fulbright, "The Legislator as Educator," pp. 719, 726.

52. See Percy, "The Partisan Gap," p. 12; the views of Sen. Alan K. Simpson in the *New York Times,* March 21, 1983, dispatch by Steven V. Roberts; the views of Sen. John Tower, R-Texas, in "Congress versus the President: the Formulation and Implementation of American Foreign Policy," *Foreign Af-*

fairs 60 (Winter 1981-1982): 229-247; and the views of Sen. Dan Quayle, R-Ind., in the *New York Times,* June 4, 1983, dispatch by Steven V. Roberts.

53. *New York Times,* July 3, 1977, dispatch by Adam Clymer.
54. See "SALT Debate is Complicated by Soviet Troops in Cuba," *Congressional Quarterly Weekly Report,* September 8, 1979, p. 1913; the excerpt from the report by the Senate Foreign Relations Committee on SALT II, in the *New York Times,* November 20, 1979; and *Time,* October 1, 1979, p. 100.
55. See the views of William D. Rogers, in "Who's in Charge of Foreign Policy?" pp. 44, 47, 50. Basically the same criticism is made of Congress's approach to foreign affairs by former Secretary of State Henry Kissinger, who contrasts the fields of law and diplomacy. See Kissinger, *White House Years,* pp. 940-941.
56. Senator Vandenberg's views are quoted in Ben H. Brown, Jr., "Congress and the Department of State," *Annals of the American Academy of Political and Social Science* 289 (September 1953): 107.
57. Hamilton and Dusen, "Making the Separation of Powers Work," p. 39.
58. See Genrikh Trofimenko, "Too Many Negotiators," *New York Times,* July 13, 1979.
59. Ibid.
60. For an excellent interpretation of the philosophical and cultural values of modern American society, see Christopher Lasch, *The Culture of Narcissism: American Life in an Age of Diminishing Expectations* (New York: W. W. Norton, 1978). See also Steven J. Kelman, "Youth and Foreign Policy," *Foreign Affairs* 48 (April 1970): 414-427; and the detailed discussion of the cultural values of the 1970s in *Newsweek,* November 19, 1979.
61. For the views of Assistant Secretary of State for Congressional Relations Douglas J. Bennet, Jr., see "Congress: Its Role in Foreign Policy-Making," *Department of State Bulletin* 78 (June 1978): 35-36; and "Congress in Foreign Policy: Who Needs It?" *Foreign Affairs* 57 (Fall 1978): 40-51.
62. *New York Times,* January 18 and February 2, 1979, dispatches by Bernard Gwertzman.
63. *New York Times,* August 23, 1979, dispatch by Anthony Lewis.
64. The concept of oscillating isolationist and interventionist foreign policy moods by the American people is identified and explained in F. L. Klingberg, "The Historical Alternation of Moods in American Foreign Policy," *World Politics* 4 (January 1952): 239-273.
65. For more detailed discussion of bipartisan collaboration during the Truman administration, see Cecil V. Crabb, Jr., *Bipartisan Foreign Policy: Myth or Reality?* (New York: Harper and Row, 1957); and Arthur H. Vandenberg, Jr., ed., *The Private Papers of Senator Vandenberg* (Boston: Houghton Mifflin Co., 1952).
66. Acheson, *Sketches from Life of Men I Have Known,* pp. 123-146.
67. James L. Sundquist, "Congress and the President: Enemies or Partners?" in Lawrence C. Dodd and Bruce I. Oppenheimer, eds., *Congress Reconsidered* (New York: Praeger Publishers, 1977), p. 222.
68 *U.S. News & World Report,* August 27, 1979, p. 20.
69. Elizabeth Drew, "Why Congress Won't Fight?" *New York Times Magazine,* September 23, 1973, p. 83.
70. The findings of Professors Thomas E. Cronin and Lawrence C. Dodd, are summarized in the *New York Times,* November 18, 1977, dispatch by Tom Wicker.

71. *New York Times,* October 28, 1979, dispatch by Terrence Smith.
72. For detailed analyses of public attitudes toward Congress, "What Congress Really Thinks of Itself," *U.S. News & World Report,* January 14, 1980, pp. 39-42; Malcolm E. Jewell and Samuel C. Patterson, *The Legislative Process in the United States,* 3d ed. (New York: Random House, 1977), pp. 315-317; and Roger H. Davidson, David M. Kovenock, and Michael K. O'Leary, *Congress in Crisis: Politics and Congressional Reform* (Belmont, Calif.: Wadsworth Publishing Co., 1971), pp. 38-66.
73. See the survey data presented in *Time,* October 1, 1979, p. 25; *U.S. News & World Report,* July 16, 1979, p. 21, March 15, 1982, pp. 22-24, and May 23, 1983, p. 48; *New York Times,* December 26, 1982, dispatch by Steven V. Roberts; and the Baton Rouge *Morning Advocate,* August 1, 1982.
74. Ralph B. Levering, *The Public and American Foreign Policy: 1918-1978* (New York: William Morrow and Co., 1978), p. 29.
75. John Bibby and Roger Davidson, *On Capitol Hill: Studies in the Legislative Process* (New York: Holt, Rinehart and Winston, 1967), pp. 111-112. See also McClellan, "The State of the American Congress," pp. 229, 237.
76. *New York Times,* September 21, 1979, dispatch by James Reston.
77. This unnamed senator is quoted in Drew, "Why Congress Won't Fight?" p. 16.
78. For innumerable examples illustrating the decline of the State Department in the foreign policy process during the Nixon administration, see Kissinger, *White House Years.*
79. The influence of pragmatic, trial-and-error criteria in shaping American attitudes is discussed more fully in Wattenberg, *The Real America,* pp. 203-213; and in Ball, *The Discipline of Power,* pp. 343-358.
80. See the views of Assistant Secretary of State for Congressional Relations Brian Atwood in the *New York Times,* December 24, 1979, dispatch by Martin Tolchin.
81. Walter Lippmann, *U.S. Foreign Policy: Shield of the Republic* (Boston: Little, Brown and Co., 1943); and Lippmann, *The Cold War: A Study in U.S. Foreign Policy* (New York: Harper and Row, 1947). More detailed analysis of the respective contributions which executive and legislative officials may usefully make to the foreign policy process are available in Christopher, "Ceasefire between the Branches," 989-1006; and Tower, "Congress versus the President," 229-247.

Suggested Readings

Books

Austin, Anthony. *The President's War: The Story of the Tonkin Gulf Resolution and How the Nation Was Trapped in Vietnam.* Philadelphia: Lippincott, 1971.

Barrett, Laurence I. *Gambling with History: Reagan in the White House.* New York: Doubleday and Co., 1983.

Bathory, Peter D., ed. *Leadership in America: Consensus, Corruption and Charisma.* New York: Longman, 1978.

Becker, Abraham, ed. *Economic Relations with the USSR.* Lexington, Mass.: D. C. Heath, 1983.

Becker, William H. *Economics and World Power: An Assessment of American Diplomacy since 1789.* New York: Columbia University Press, 1984.

Berkowitz, Morton, et al. *The Politics of American Foreign Policy: The Social Context of Decisions.* Englewood Cliffs, N.J.: Prentice-Hall, 1977.

Brenner, Phillip. *The Limits and Possibilities of Congress.* New York: St. Martin's Press, 1983.

Brown, Harold. *Thinking about National Security.* Boulder, Colo.: Westview Press, 1983.

Brown, Peter G., and MacLean, Douglas, eds. *Human Rights and U.S. Foreign Policy: Principles and Applications.* Lexington, Mass.: D. C. Heath, 1979.

Brown, Seyom. *The Crisis of Power: Foreign Policy in the Kissinger Years.* New York: Columbia University Press, 1979.

————. *The Faces of Power: Constancy and Change in United States Foreign Policy from Truman to Reagan.* New York: Columbia University Press, 1983.

Brzezinski, Zbigniew. *Power and Principle.* New York: Farrar, Straus, Giroux, 1983.

Campbell, Colin. *Governments under Stress: Political Executives and Key Bureaucrats in Washington, London, and Ottawa.* Toronto: University of Toronto Press, 1983.

Carter, Jimmy. *Keeping Faith: Memoirs of a President.* New York: Bantam Books, 1982.

Cohen, Stephen D. *The Making of United States International Economic Policy: Principles, Problems and Proposals for Reform.* 2d ed. New York: Praeger Publishers, 1984.

Coker, Christopher. *U.S. Military Power in the 1980s.* Salem, Mass.: Salem House, 1983.

Crabb, Cecil V., Jr. *The Doctrines of American Foreign Policy: Their Meaning, Role, and Future.* Baton Rouge: Louisiana State University Press, 1982.

Dellek, Robert. *The American Style of Foreign Policy.* New York: Alfred A. Knopf, 1983.

Dugger, Ronnie. *On Reagan: The Man and His Presidency.* New York: McGraw-Hill, 1983.

Fallows, James. *National Defense.* New York: Random House, 1982.

Fisher, Louis. *Politics of Shared Power: Congress and the Executive.* Washington, D.C.: CQ Press, 1981.

Forsythe, David P. *Human Rights and World Politics.* Lincoln: University of Nebraska Press, 1983.

Franck, Thomas, and Weisband, Edward. *Foreign Policy by Congress.* New York: Oxford University Press, 1979.

Gati, Toby T. *The U.S., the UN, and the Management of Global Change.* New York: Columbia University Press, 1983.

George, Alexander L. *Managing U.S.-Soviet Rivalry: Problems of Crisis Prevention.* Boulder, Colo.: Westview Press, 1983.

Godson, Roy, ed. *Intelligence Requirements for the 1980s: Clandestine Collection.* New Brunswick, N.J.: Transaction Books, 1982.

Goulden, Joseph C. *Korea: The Untold Story.* New York: Times Books, 1982.

Greenstein, Fred A. *The Hidden-Hand Presidency: Eisenhower as Leader.* New York: Basic Books, 1982.

Haley, P. Edward. *Congress and the Fall of South Vietnam and Cambodia.* East Brunswick, N.J.: Fairleigh Dickinson University Press, 1982.

Hart, John. *The Presidential Branch.* New York: Pergamon Press, 1984.

Havemann, Joel. *Congress and the Budget.* Bloomington: Indiana University Press, 1978.

Heaphey, James J., and Balutis, Alan P. *Legislative Staffing: A Comparative Perspective.* New York: John Wiley and Sons, 1976.

Heclo, Hugh, and Soloman, Lester M., eds. *Illusion of Presidential Government.* Boulder, Colo.: Westview Press, 1981.

Hofstetter, Richard R., ed. *U.S. Immigration Policy.* Durham, N.C.: Duke University Press, 1984.

Holt, Pat M. *The War Powers Resolution: The Role of Congress in U.S. Armed Intervention.* Washington, D.C.: American Enterprise Institute, 1978.

Hughes, Barry B. *The Domestic Context of American Foreign Policy.* San Francisco: W. H. Freeman and Co., 1978.

Jordan, Hamilton. *Crisis: The Last Year of the Carter Presidency.* New York: G. P. Putnam's Sons, 1982.

Joyce, James A. *The New Politics of Human Rights.* New York: St. Martin's Press, 1979.

Kanter, Arnold. *Defense Politics: A Budgetary Perspective.* Chicago: University of Chicago Press, 1979.

Kauppi, Mark V., and Nation, R. Craig, eds. *The Soviet Union and the Middle East in the 1980s.* Lexington, Mass.: D. C. Heath, 1983.

Kissinger, Henry. *White House Years.* Boston: Little, Brown, 1979.

————. *Years of Upheaval.* Boston: Little, Brown, 1982.

Kommers, Donald P., and Loescher, Gilburt D., eds. *Human Rights and American Foreign Policy.* South Bend, Ind.: University of Notre Dame Press, 1979.

Lehman, John F. *The Executive, Congress and Foreign Policy: Studies of the Nixon Administration.* New York: Praeger Publishers, 1976.

Leiken, Robert S., ed. *Central America: Anatomy of a Conflict.* New York: Pergamon Press, 1984.

Leuchtenburg, William E. *In the Shadow of FDR.* Ithaca, N.Y.: Cornell University Press, 1983.

Levering, Ralph B. *The Public and American Foreign Policy, 1918-1978.* New York: William Morrow, 1978.

Lipsen, Charles B., and Lesher, Stephan. *Vested Interest: A Lobbyist's Account of Washington Power and How It Really Works.* New York: Doubleday and Co., 1977.

Mako, William P. *U.S. Ground Forces and the Defense of Central Europe.* Washington, D.C.: Brookings Institution, 1983.

Morris, Roger. *Haig: The General's Progress.* New York: Seaview Books, 1982.

Nelson, Michael. *The Presidency and the Political System.* Washington, D.C.: CQ Press, 1984.

Nuechterlein, Donald E. *National Interests and Presidential Leadership: The Setting of Priorities.* Boulder Colo.: Westview Press, 1978.

O'Heffernan, Patrick, ed. *Defense Sense: The Search for a Rational Military Policy.* Cambridge, Mass.: Ballinger Publishing Co., 1984.

Oisken, Michael, ed. *Trouble in Our Backyard: Central America and the United States in the Eighties.* New York: Pantheon Books, 1984.

Oleszek, Walter J. *Congressional Procedures and the Policy Process.* 2d ed. Washington, D.C.: CQ Press, 1984.

Ornstein, Norman J., and Elder, Shirley. *Interest Groups, Lobbying and Policymaking.* Washington, D.C.: CQ Press, 1978.

Oye, Kenneth; Lieber, Robert J.; and Rothchild, Donald, eds. *Eagle Defiant: United States Foreign Policy in the 1980s.* Boston: Little, Brown, 1983.

Pierre, Andrew J., ed. *Arms Transfers and American Foreign Policy.* New York: New York University Press, 1979.

Pious, Richard M. *The American Presidency.* New York: Basic Books, 1979.

Platt, Alan, and Weiler, Lawrence D. *Congress and Arms Control.* Boulder, Colo.: Westview Press, 1978.

Powers of Congress. 2d ed. Washington, D.C.: Congressional Quarterly, 1982.

Quandt, William B. *Decade of Decision: American Policy toward the Arab-Israeli Conflict, 1967-1976.* Berkeley: University of California Press, 1977.

Ramazani, R. K. *The United States and Iran: Patterns of Influence.* New York: Praeger Publishers, 1982.

Ravenal, Earl C. *Never Again: Learning from America's Foreign Policy Failures.* Philadelphia: Temple University Press, 1978.

Reich, Bernard. *Quest for Peace: United States-Israeli Relations and the Arab-Israeli Conflict.* New Brunswick, N.J.: Transaction Books, 1977.

Rubinstein, Alvin Z., ed. *The Great Game: Rivalry in the Persian Gulf and South Asia.* New York: Praeger Publishers, 1983.

Ryan, Paul B. *The Panama Canal Controversy: U.S. Diplomacy and Defense Interests.* Stanford, Calif.: Hoover Institution Press, 1977.

Said, Abdul A., ed. *Ethnicity and U.S. Foreign Policy.* New York: Praeger Publishers, 1978.

Sarkesian, Sam S., ed. *Defense Policy and the Presidency: Carter's First Years.* Boulder, Colo.: Westview Press, 1979.

Sayigh, Yusif A. *Arab Oil Politics in the 1970s.* Baltimore: The Johns Hopkins University Press, 1983.

Schneider, Jerrold E. *Ideological Coalitions in Congress.* Westport, Conn.: Greenwood Press, 1979.

Smith, Steven S., and Deering, Christopher J. *Committees in Congress.* Washington, D.C.: CQ Press, 1984.

Stern, Paula. *Water's Edge: Domestic Politics and the Making of American Foreign Policy.* Westport, Conn.: Greenwood Press, 1979.

Szulc, Tad. *The Illusion of Peace: Foreign Policy in the Nixon Years.* New York: Viking Press, 1978.

Taylor, William J., and Maaranen, Steven A., eds. *The Future of Conflict in the 1980s.* Lexington, Mass.: D. C. Heath, 1983.

Trade: U.S. Policy since 1945. Washington, D.C.: Congressional Quarterly, 1984.

U.S. Defense Policy. 3rd ed. Washington, D.C.: Congressional Quarterly, 1983.

Vance, Cyrus. *Hard Choices.* New York: Simon and Schuster, 1983.

Vogelgesang, Sandy. *American Dream—Global Nightmare: The Dilemma of U.S. Human Rights Policy.* New York: Norton, 1980.

The Washington Lobby. 4th ed. Washington, D.C.: Congressional Quarterly, 1982.

Wesson, Robert G. *Foreign Policy for a New Age.* Boston: Houghton Mifflin Co., 1977.

Wilcox, Francis O., and Frank, Richard A. *The Constitution and the Conduct of Foreign Policy.* New York: Praeger Publishers, 1976.

Articles

Aspin, L. "The Defense Budget and Foreign Policy: The Role of Congress." *Daedalus* 104 (Summer 1975).

Bertram, Christoph. "Europe and America in 1983." *Foreign Affairs* 62 (Special Issue 1984).

Blechman, Barry M., and Nolan, Janne E. "Reorganizing for More Effective Arms Negotiations." *Foreign Affairs* 61 (Summer 1983).

Brittan, Samuel. "A Very Painful World Adjustment." *Foreign Affairs* 60 (Special Issue 1982).

Bundy, William P. "A Portentous Year." *Foreign Affairs* 62 (Special Issue 1984).

"Caribbean Basin Initiative." Symposium. *Foreign Policy* 47 (Summer 1982).

Christopher, Warren. "Ceasefire between the Branches: A Compact in Foreign Affairs." *Foreign Affairs* 60 (Summer 1982).

Destler, I. M. "Congress as Boss?" *Foreign Policy* 42 (Spring 1981).

Diebold, William. "The United States in the World Economy: A Fifty Year Perspective." *Foreign Affairs* 62 (Fall 1983).

Finger, Seymour M. "Jeane Kirkpatrick at the United Nations." *Foreign Affairs* 62 (Winter 1983-1984).

Kirkpatrick, Jeane J. "Establishing a Viable Human Rights Policy." *World Affairs* 143 (Spring 1981).

Knight, Andrew. "Ronald Reagan's Watershed Year?" *Foreign Affairs* 61 (Special Issue 1982).

Johnson, Loch, and McCormick, James M. "The Making of International Agreements: A Reappraisal of Congressional Involvement." *Journal of Politics* 40 (May 1978).

Livingstone, N. C., and von Nordheim, M. "The United States Congress and the Angola Crisis." *Strategic Review* 5 (Spring 1977).

Lustick, Ian S. "Israeli Politics and American Foreign Policy." *Foreign Affairs* 61 (Winter 1982-1983).

Ornstein, Norman J. "Lobbying for Fun and Policy." *Foreign Policy* 28 (Fall 1977).

Percy, Charles H. "The Partisan Gap." *Foreign Policy* 45 (Winter 1981-1982).

Rhodes, John J. "The Far Side of the Hill." *Foreign Affairs* 61 (Winter 1982-1983).

Riding, Alan. "The Central American Quagmire." *Foreign Affairs* 61 (Special Issue 1982).

Rielly, John E. "American Opinion: Continuity, Not Reaganism." *Foreign Policy* 50 (Spring 1983).

Schlesinger, Arthur, Jr. "Foreign Policy and the American Character." *Foreign Affairs* 62 (Fall 1983).

Sorensen, Theodore C. "The Absent Opposition." *Foreign Policy* 47 (Summer 1982).

Spero, Joan E. "Information: The Policy Void." *Foreign Policy* 48 (Fall 1982).

Tonelson, Alan. "Human Rights: The Bias We Need." *Foreign Policy* 49 (Winter 1982-1983).

Turner, Stansfield, and Thibault, George. "Intelligence: The Right Rules." *Foreign Policy* 48 (Fall 1982).

Ullman, Richard H. "At War with Nicaragua." *Foreign Affairs* 62 (Fall 1983).

van Voorst, L. Bruce. "The Churches and Nuclear Deterrence." *Foreign Affairs* 61 (Spring 1983).

Index

259